MW00892104

A
Mystic's Guide to 2022

By Nicole Marie

BALBOA.PRESS

A DIVISION OF HAY HOUSE

Balboa Press books may be ordered through booksellers or by contacting:

Balboa Press
A Division of Hay House
1663 Liberty Drive
Bloomington, IN 47403
www.balboapress.com
844-682-1282

Canva, Creative Market

ISBN: 978-1-9822-7403-0 (sc)
ISBN: 978-1-9822-7404-7 (e)

Library of Congress Control Number: 2021918469

Printed in the United States of America.

Balboa Press rev. date: 09/14/2021

TABLE OF CONTENTS

SECTION ONE

Welcome to 2022	1
How to Use this Guidebook	2
About Me	5
FIXED VS GROWTH MINDSET	6
LIFE INVENTORY	9
LIMITING BELIEFS	12
MY IDEAL LIFE	14

SECTION TWO

CHAKRAS	19-27
CONSULT THE UNIVERSE	28
2022 ASTROLOGICAL DATES	29
ASTROLOGY GUIDES	30-35
NATAL CHART	36
2022 YEAR AHEAD	38

SECTION THREE

JANUARY	40-83
FEBRUARY	84-123
MARCH	124-167
APRIL	168-211
MAY	212-255
JUNE	256-297
JULY	298-341
AUGUST	342-385
SEPTEMBER	386-427
OCTOBER	428-471
NOVEMBER	472-513
DECEMBER	514-556
2023	561
Glossary	562

This Guidebook
belongs to:

_____

WELCOME TO 2022!

First, I just want to say that it feels SURREAL to be writing this. When I first envisioned this I actually just wanted to create a planner because, FOR THE LOVE OF GOD, I had like 20 planners or journals or some form of item I could write in - anyone feel me? A gratitude planner, a moon planner, an astrology guide, a dream journal, a scripting journal, and some calendar somewhere stuffed under my bed. It was completely impractical, expensive and terrible for the environment, so naturally I said "let's make one ourselves". So, in 2021 I threw the idea around my TikTok community about designing a planner that had it all - I mean WHAT IF? Well, turns out they loved it and suddenly I was getting calls from all over about "When is 2022 going to come out?"

Before we dive into this further, there's something else I want to shamelessly plug. By purchasing this guidebook you've **sponsored a child**, probably not in the way you've thought but you have. A few years back I was in a really dark place, sick, not really sure if I was going to make it. By grace I pulled through and in that experience I learned magic. I learned hope. I learned… possibility. Rewind to one day while I was recovering and my son's nanny brought me some seeds, raw veggies and a juicer. She told me, "The Earth can heal you." She taught me how to plant, how to juice, how to support my body in regenerating itself - everyday I would wobble myself outside to the small garden we made and watch those seeds grow, in a desert mind you. It's been years since that moment and in that time I have grown full harvests of 10 different types of fruit and veggies, sunflower seeds, marigolds, 7 different varieties of teas and herbs, rue, pumpkin… you name it. I have fed my family from a desert garden not more than 1800 cubic feet. I've made remedies that have healed, crafted intentions of abundance, hope, courage and because of your purchase you have brought that same experience to a child.

If you are still confused let me explain further. I have a huge dream. A dream of bringing sustainability to families across America without adding to their budget while simultaneously cutting down on the harsh chemicals that enter their homes. From this dream our sister company, The Leading Leaf was born. Through The Leading Leaf, our nonprofit sector will handle a variety of missions which include our flagship project: Project Iris. Project Iris is centered around our most economically disadvantaged students and communities and is aimed to bring gardens and plant education straight to them. That same hope I was given so many years ago when I was facing my own morality we intend to bring to the faces of children who desperately need to see their own magic come to life. Can you imagine what a gift to a child that is? **Creation.** Something THEY created. So, thank you, thank you for investing in THEM. For more information on our mission, sustainability, or Project Iris you may visit: https://nicolemarieinc.com

Now, as far as this project goes I wanted something that would guide us all to finding our best selves. A place where we could reconnect with our most primal aspects. I wanted to create magic within these pages. I wanted more than a planner. This guidebook will pluck you out of the busy world and into the silent depths of your own whispers. The process can be raw, empowering, independent and truly allows each of us the space to hear our deepest thoughts and influences. I wanted to combine traditional psychology methods, honor eastern spiritual practices and showcase western astrology. The result? **A Mystics Guide to 2022.** My hope is that this reminds each of us to live within ourselves, find our own alignments, trust our intuition, be guided by the cosmos, spend time with personal development and most of all **Own Our Magic.**

HOW TO USE THIS GUIDEBOOK

We've gotten past the point of WHY we created the guidebook so now I want to take a second to walk you through HOW to use it. If you are not a "devil in the details person" this section WILL bore you to DEATH. Feel free to skip ahead as most sections do have light explanations.

The overall flow of this book is designed to go from the bigger picture (Section 1) of how you see yourself to inventorying where you are as we enter 2022. Section 2 is taking the bigger picture and applying it to your individual energy points and Section 3 breaks down your massive energy, massive goals and even obstacles into manageable monthly, weekly and daily MAGIC so you can create the year YOU LOVE.

SECTION ONE

You'll start with the About Me page followed by our Growth Vs Fixed Mindset and then Changing Your Mind. For these pages all you need to know is - please just answer the questions truthfully, no one sees this but you. Honesty is the only policy here.

On Deck is The Self-Assessment, then The Life Inventory and The Wheel of Life. These pages are deeper dives into the dimensions of our life by spreading them into a variety of categories and allowing us to evaluate. Next, Our Limiting Beliefs, is where we start to strip ourselves down even further, what is it that's holding you back? Our belief system instills in us what type of potential we think we have. It's that potential that we then take action on and it's based on those actions that we actually get results. So the truth is - the results we obtain are reflections based on our belief system. If we have limiting beliefs, we are going to have results that in fact back those same limiting beliefs.

I.E. Limiting Belief is: I'm not good enough --->Potential: I'm not a good fit for that job. Action: I don't apply for that job ----> Result: I'm at a dead end job.

There are 5 spaces - you may need more than that - you may need less - only YOU know. The second page of Limiting Beliefs allows you to break down one limiting belief at a time and while we have provided one page, you can do this activity for as many limiting beliefs as you need. Our recommendation is that you sit with each limiting belief and let it settle before moving onto the next one. Some of what you'll find will shake your world, you may unearth childhood traumas, you might realize WHOA this is the shadow work everyone has been telling me to do? Yes, ya'll THIS is self development so you're welcome!

Next is one of my favorites, My Ideal Life, Your Vision Board & Bucket List. There is a prompt that has some questions listed but I wanted to touch on the term for this technique, we call it Scripting. Why? Because when you write your ideal life I want you to feel it, smell it, see it, live it - I want you to script it as if you were writing a movie - THAT HAS ALREADY HAPPENED. Write this in the frame of mind that you are already living your ideal life - did you know your mind does not know the difference between a truth and lie? So whatever you tell yourself repeatedly is what your mind will not only believe but what you will also become. **You create your reality - so let's go create it!**

SECTION TWO

You'll transition into the second section of the guidebook which unpacks how to balance and align our energy centers. A very detailed walk through is provided, don't worry, you are not alone. For free guided meditations for each energy center you can visit our youtube at: www.youtube.com/c/NicoleMarieInc

SECTION THREE

Opens us to Consult the Universe, which as an Astrologer tickles my fancy! We begin with a breakdown on exactly what everything is, why it matters and what to expect for 2022!

We explore your personal Natal Chart, if you need assistance pulling your own chart we recommend using https://horoscopes.astro-seek.com/birth-chart-horoscope-online and enter your information then select Extended Settings under Calculate Chart and change the House System to Whole Sign. Then you'll select "Calculate Chart." and enter your information on the Natal Chart in your guidebook.

If you are more of a visual learner and would like a step by step guide on how to enter your information you can visit our blog post: https://modernmystics.store/blogs/news/how-to-calculate-your-natal-chart-online. For personal interpretations of your natal chart you can book a personal reading with Nicole Marie directly at https://modernmystics.store

We've now entered into a little Tarot or Oracle fun by looking at the energy ahead of us with a 12 month spread and plenty of space to document your findings! Then we'll take the bigger picture in Section 1, Energy in Section 2 and turn it into our plans which are made of Monthly/ Weekly and Daily goals. You'll notice that each month has the same breakdown, a monthly calendar with important US dates that include some space for you to add important notes, a SMART goals sheet, your monthly "Creating Your Reality" check in and habit tracker as well as your monthly Moon Sheet so you can stay aligned with the Moon energy and an optional monthly divination tracker.

Your week ahead sheet focus on taking the above monthly focuses and breaking them down further into a 7-day view and then naturally the daily sheets take that 7 day view and break it down into a single day lens. Your Daily sheet has it all: a spot for gratitude, mood tracker, your personal affirmation, Dream journal, places for meditation minutes and prayer/ritual time, something positive to carry with you, 1 thing you did thtat day to progress and a section to script your reality. I combined all the 20 journals I had and brought you the best of them!

Lastly, as you flip through your daily pages you will notice a Lunation page tucked in between some of them. On the day of the New & Full Moon we have provided Ritual Sheets so you don't have to figure out what you need to do. You can track the moon right here in this guidebook, I know - talk about convenience!

Oh, one more thing, please don't forget. Make Magic. That's what all of this is for. FOR YOU, to create, to become, to BE the magic you were always meant to be.

2022 AT A GLANCE

JANUARY

S	M	T	W	T	F	S
						1
2	3	4	5	6	7	8
9	10	11	12	13	14	15
16	17	18	19	20	21	22
23	24	25	26	27	28	29
30	31					

FEBRUARY

S	M	T	W	T	F	S
		1	2	3	4	5
6	7	8	9	10	11	12
13	14	15	16	17	18	19
20	21	22	23	24	25	26
27	28					

MARCH

S	M	T	W	T	F	S
		1	2	3	4	5
6	7	8	9	10	11	12
13	14	15	16	17	18	19
20	21	22	23	24	25	26
27	28	29	30	31		

APRIL

S	M	T	W	T	F	S
					1	2
3	4	5	6	7	8	9
10	11	12	13	14	15	16
17	18	19	20	21	22	23
24	25	26	27	28	29	30

MAY

S	M	T	W	T	F	S
1	2	3	4	5	6	7
8	9	10	11	12	13	14
15	16	17	18	19	20	21
22	23	24	25	26	27	28
29	30	31				

JUNE

S	M	T	W	T	F	S
			1	2	3	4
5	6	7	8	9	10	11
12	13	14	15	16	17	18
19	20	21	22	23	24	25
26	27	28	29	30		

JULY

S	M	T	W	T	F	S
					1	2
3	4	5	6	7	8	9
10	11	12	13	14	15	16
17	18	19	20	21	22	23
24	25	26	27	28	29	30
31						

AUGUST

S	M	T	W	T	F	S
	1	2	3	4	5	6
7	8	9	10	11	12	13
14	15	16	17	18	19	20
21	22	23	24	25	26	27
28	29	30	31			

SEPTEMBER

S	M	T	W	T	F	S
				1	2	3
4	5	6	7	8	9	10
11	12	13	14	15	16	17
18	19	20	21	22	23	24
25	26	27	28	29	30	

OCTOBER

S	M	T	W	T	F	S
						1
2	3	4	5	6	7	8
9	10	11	12	13	14	15
16	17	18	19	20	21	22
23	24	25	26	27	28	29
30	31					

NOVEMBER

S	M	T	W	T	F	S
		1	2	3	4	5
6	7	8	9	10	11	12
13	14	15	16	17	18	19
20	21	22	23	24	25	26
27	28	29	30			

DECEMBER

S	M	T	W	T	F	S
				1	2	3
4	5	6	7	8	9	10
11	12	13	14	15	16	17
18	19	20	21	22	23	24
25	26	27	28	29	30	31

ABOUT ME

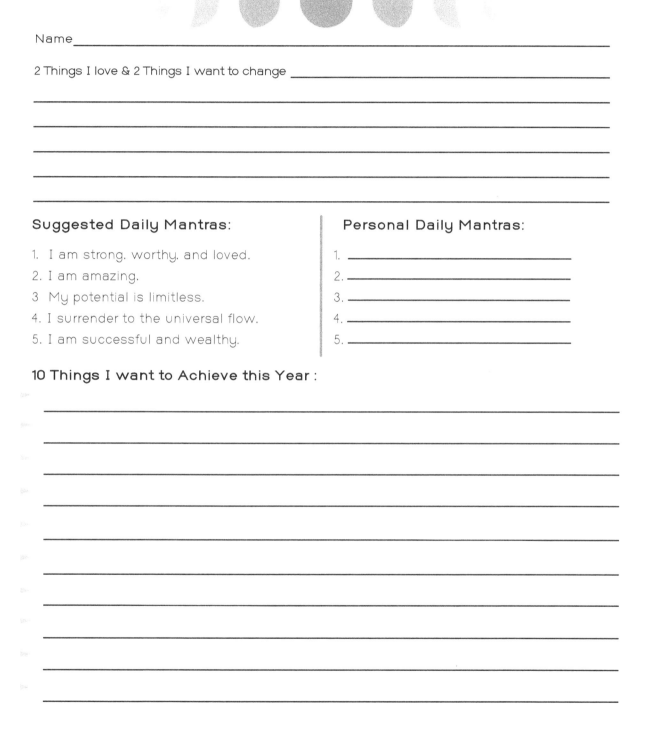

Name_____

2 Things I love & 2 Things I want to change _____

_____

_____

_____

_____

Suggested Daily Mantras:

1. I am strong, worthy, and loved.
2. I am amazing.
3. My potential is limitless.
4. I surrender to the universal flow.
5. I am successful and wealthy.

Personal Daily Mantras:

1. _____
2. _____
3. _____
4. _____
5. _____

10 Things I want to Achieve this Year :

_____

_____

_____

_____

_____

_____

_____

_____

_____

_____

FIXED vs GROWTH MINDSET

Sometimes, making progress with a problem starts with a shift in mindset. According to researchers there are two predominent types of mindsets (fixed and growth). The former means that you believe that any given quality (intelligence or talent for example) is innate and you have what you were given by nature. A growth mindset, by comparison, means that you believe that any given quality, skill or your intelligence itself can improve over time with effort and persistence. Only one of these belief systems truely teaches us what our potential actually is. Below, you will find some examples of how a fixed vs growth mindset may show up in your daily life.

FIXED MINDSET	GROWTH MINDSET
Challenges	**Challenges**
I try to avoid challenges so I don't look stupid.	Challenges are a way for me to get better.
Desires	**Desires**
I'll just stick to what I know.	I'll try new things.
Skills	**Skills**
I'm either good at it or not. If I'm not it's okay.	I can always improve.
Obstacles	**Obstacles**
I'm just not good at it and that's the way it is and always will be.	I'll change my approach until I succeed.
Success of Others	**Success of Others**
It's unfair that they're succeeding and I'm not.	I'm inspired by their success. Maybe I have something to learn from their success.
Criticism	**Criticism**
I feel threatened by the criticism I get.	I can learn from the feedback I receive.

CHANGING YOUR MIND

In this exercise we will identify your own mindset in a range of different categories then write down what would be a more productive mode of thinking instead. It is important to note that productive, here, means anything that will encourage you to take action and actively work on a solution. You will also have an opportunity to identify you own unique limiting beliefs and how you can reframe them for your benefit.

How do I react to challenges or criticism? How I can improve?

How do I react when I don't know what to do next? How can I improve?

How do I express my destires, gratitudes or successes? How can I improve??

Am I taking responsibility for my role in current situations? How so? Do these help me progress forward in my life?

Self-Assessment

Assess your well-being across multiple dimensions of life, including physical, emotional, spiritual, and professional. At the end of the assessment is a box where you can note down the aspects you'd like to improve upon and how you plan to do it.

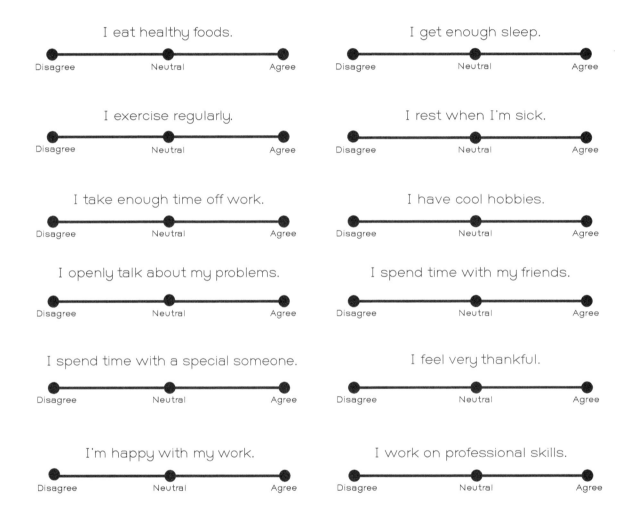

I eat healthy foods.
Disagree — Neutral — Agree

I get enough sleep.
Disagree — Neutral — Agree

I exercise regularly.
Disagree — Neutral — Agree

I rest when I'm sick.
Disagree — Neutral — Agree

I take enough time off work.
Disagree — Neutral — Agree

I have cool hobbies.
Disagree — Neutral — Agree

I openly talk about my problems.
Disagree — Neutral — Agree

I spend time with my friends.
Disagree — Neutral — Agree

I spend time with a special someone.
Disagree — Neutral — Agree

I feel very thankful.
Disagree — Neutral — Agree

I'm happy with my work.
Disagree — Neutral — Agree

I work on professional skills.
Disagree — Neutral — Agree

LIFE INVENTORY

Now it's time to stop and assess your life across a variety of categories. You are going to give scores from 1 to 10 based on how fulfilled you feel in each of these categories - one meaning you're absolutely not satisfied and ten meaning you're abundantly fulfilled. In the boxes provided you'll write some notes about what you are/ are not satisfied with, what is or is not going right etc. The goal of this exercise is to give you a snapshot of where you are at in this moment. By doing this exercise from time to time (once every 6 months for example) you get an overview of the progress you've made.

RELATIONSHIPS

01	02	03	04	05	06	07	08	09	10

FINANCE

01	02	03	04	05	06	07	08	09	10

CAREER

01	02	03	04	05	06	07	08	09	10

HEALTH/FITNESS

01	02	03	04	05	06	07	08	09	10

SPIRITUALITY

01	02	03	04	05	06	07	08	09	10

WHEEL OF LIFE

Now, let's begin to shift into a technique I call Scripting. In this exercise, we are focusing on what we want to bring to life this year so go ahead and give a score from 1 to 10 in each category, one being very little attention is needed in this area and ten meaning that all your focus is in this area. Then, on the next page, you have space to fill out what you're happy with in each area, what needs some work, what you desire and how you think you can improve the situation.

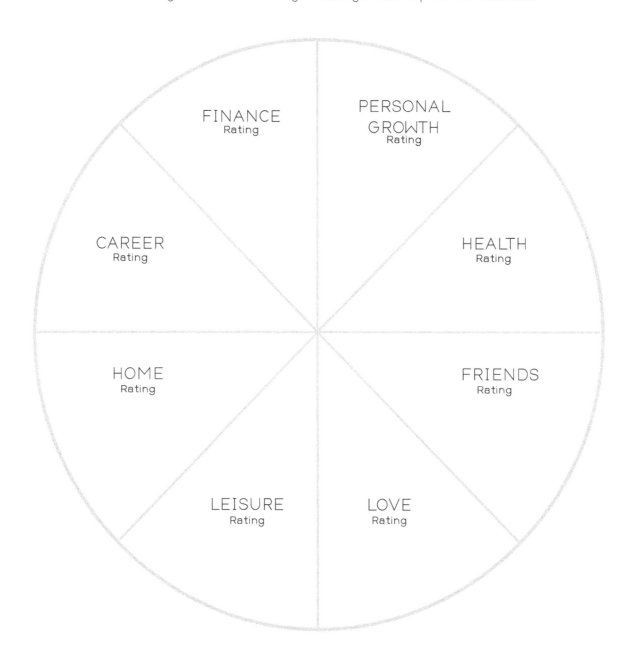

WHEEL OF LIFE

CAREER   FINANCE

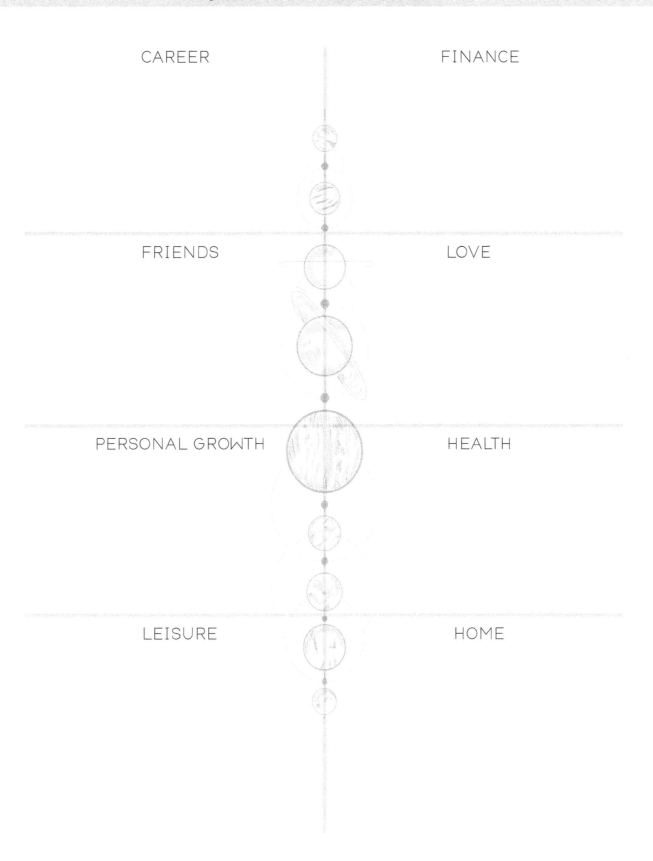

FRIENDS   LOVE

PERSONAL GROWTH   HEALTH

LEISURE   HOME

LIMITING BELIEFS

Now, let's try to identify other limiting beliefs that are preventing your growth and practice reframing them. There is always a better narrative we can speak into existance. For example, when you were young you may have heard, "We will always live paycheck-to-paycheck," while that may have been true a growth mindset approach would be, "My steady paycheck provides for everything I need in this moment."

Current Beliefs	Better Alternative
Example: Money doesn't grow on trees.	Example: I will be rewarded - the more I give, the more I receive.

LIMITING BELIEFS

In this section we will learn how to investigate the limiting beliefs that have held us back. Our realities are a direct reflection of our strongest beliefs and when we get to the root of how these beliefs were formed it allows us to better understand how we can work through them, release ourselves from them and focus on our growth.

What is a belief that is holding you back?
Ex: "I am not good with money."

How old does this belief feel?
Ex: When was the first time you thought this?

Where did this belief come from?
Ex: Did someone say this to you? Did you hear it from others? Did you watch someone with the same characteristics?

How has this belief shaped your life?
Ex: Has it been harmful? What has it led you to do or not do?

MY IDEAL LIFE

In order to accomplish the goals you want to achieve we can work backwards by first describing your ideal life - this is what we will later script into our reality. What would your ideal days consist of? What would you do in the mornings, evenings, and nights? Where would you be and who would you be with? What experiences would you have? What your professional life would be like? Remember, this is just an exercise to give you a vision to work towards - it's not set in stone and can change as you go along.

_____

_____

_____

_____

_____

_____

_____

_____

_____

_____

_____

_____

_____

_____

_____

_____

_____

_____

_____

_____

_____

VISION

This exercise is designed to provide an additional support for your scripting by assisting you with a visual representation of what your ideal life could look like. You can either write, draw, or cut out images and in doing so breathe life into the aspects that truly matter to you.

CAREER	FINANCE
RELATIONSHIPS	LOVE

BOARD

The more personal and unique you make this section the more connected you will feel to it. If we can see it, we can believe it is possible.

HEALTH	PERSONAL GROWTH
SPIRITUALITY	**HOME**

BUCKET LIST

ACHIEVEMENTS

Write down all of the things you want to achieve in your life - physically, financially, relationship wise, in your career, etc.

EXPERIENCES

Write down all of the things you want to experience in your life - physically, financially, relationship wise., etc.

FIND YOUR ZEN

FINDING YOUR ZEN

Welcome to what I'll refer to as **Section 2** of our playbook - I am going to start with an Eastern Practice that originated between 1500 - 500 BC in India called the Chakra system. Now, the Chakra system is widely practiced in the Hindu religion and is actually referred to as Sanskrit cakra but in the West we call it Chakra. So what are they? Why are they important? Why are we including them? Well, Chakars are disks or wheels and they refer to energy centers in our body. The 7 Chakra's that we in the West focus on are covered in this section.

The **Root Chakra or Muladhara** refers to stability, security and our basic needs. It is whatever in the world that keeps us grounded and stable in life. This might include basic needs such as food, water, shelter, safety and well your basic emotional needs of connection and whether or not you live in fear of survival each day. When working through this page keep in mind these qualities. For example, the question that asks "What physical aspects I need to work on…" in this case would be referring to what tangible things in your life may you need to work on so you feel stable, grounded and safe.

The **Sacral Chakra or Svadhisthana** refers to our passion, sexuality, intimacy, relationship with money, creativity and our joy. When we are in alignment our relationships are improved, our intimcy and sexual connection are healthy and we create from a place of joy. When working through this page keep in mind these qualities. For example, the question that asks "Emotional aspects I need to work on…" in this case would be referring to what emotions are out of alignment with respect to the above mentioned items.

The **Solar Plexus Chakra or Manipura** refers to our confidence and self-esteem, how we feel about ourselves and then how we exert ourselves onto the world. If you were to be out of alignment here you might show aggression, lack of purpose, feeling of helplessness or even a dominating personality. When working through this page keep in mind these qualities. For example, the question that asks "Methods that help me connect" in this case would be referring to what actionable methods do you take to align yourself with your confident side, to boost your self-esteem etc.

The **Heart Chakra or Anahata** refers to our ability to love yourself and others, have compassion, empathy and forgiveness. This chakra is often associated with universal love for all humanity and living things. If you are not in alignment you may feel depression, anxiety, shyness and loneliness. If you are in alignment you would be able to process grievances, open yourself up to love and be loved, forgiveness, kindness and compassion.

The **Throat Chakra or Vishuddha** refers to our self expression, ability to speak our truth and is responsible for our means of communication. Things that cause this Chakra to be out of alignment are experiencing too much stress, trauma - physically or mentally, even unhealthy eating/sleep or poor physical health.

The **Third Eye Chakra or Ajna** refers to our perception, awareness and your spiritual communication to whomever or whatever you identify as your creator or source. Unaligned you may experience fear of the unknown, an inability to question or critically think things you have been conditioned or told, process information properly, keep cool under pressure. When you are in alignment you are able to have clear thoughts, spiritual connection, you feel balanced, you can self-reflect honestly and are able to trade the typical black-n-white for the ability to see things in a wider perspective.

The **Crown Chakra or Sahasrara** is our final Chakra and refers to our most spiritual connection with the cosmos. It is our guide for thought, awareness, wisdom, prayer and our gifts or abilities. When we our out of alignment there is a resistance to learning, emotional imbalance, difficulties with self-knowledge, inabilities to seek your own greater expansion, head pains, sensitivity to light and the most severe - mental health concerns including psychosis. When we are in alignment we are able to consciously create, you will be immersed in joy, peace and serenity with a thirst to be more intuitive and perhaps having stepped into your psychic gifts or abilities. You will be self-aware and feel connected.

If you need assistance in figuring out which Chakra's are in alignment we recommend this site: https://www.eclecticenergies.com/chakras/chakratest

ROOT CHAKRA

Physical aspects I need to work on...

_____

_____

_____

_____

_____

AFFIRMATION:

I am connected to Mother Earth, grounded and secure. I am taking responsibility for my life.

Emotional aspects I need to work on...

_____

_____

_____

_____

_____

Methods that help me connect...

I feel most grounded when...

_____

_____

_____

_____

Tools I use are...

▶ _____

▶ _____

▶ _____

▶ _____

▶ _____

Things that represent abundance to me...

● _____

● _____

● _____

● _____

● _____

I FEEL THE MOST SECURE WHEN...

Notes:

_____

_____

_____

_____

_____

_____

CHANGES NOTED OVER TIME:

_____

_____

SACRAL CHAKRA

Physical aspects I need to work on...

_____
_____
_____
_____
_____
_____

AFFIRMATION:

I trust my feelings and give them room to flourish.

Emotional aspects I need to work on...

_____
_____
_____
_____
_____

Methods that help me connect...

_____
_____
_____
_____
_____

I honor my body by...

Tools I use are...

▶ _____
▶ _____
▶ _____
▶ _____
▶ _____

Things that bring me pleasure are...

● _____
● _____
● _____
● _____
● _____

I FEEL THE MOST HAPPINESS WHEN...

_____
_____
_____
_____
_____

Notes:

_____
_____
_____
_____

CHANGES NOTED OVER TIME:

_____
_____

SOLAR PLEXUS CHAKRA

Physical aspects I need to work on...

Emotional aspects I need to work on...

AFFIRMATION:

I choose the best for myself and I am worth twice my weight in gold.

Methods that help me connect...

I feel most confident when...

Tools I use are...

▶ _____
▶ _____
▶ _____
▶ _____
▶ _____

Things that represent self-worth to me...

● _____
● _____
● _____
● _____
● _____

I FEEL THE MOST INNER-STRENGTH WHEN...

Notes:

CHANGES NOTED OVER TIME:

HEART CHAKRA

Physical aspects I need to work on...

AFFIRMATION:

I choose to be united with all beings, visible and invisible.

Emotional aspects I need to work on...

Methods that help me connect...

I feel most at peace when...

Tools I use are...

►
►
►
►
►

Things that represent unity & connection to me...

I FEEL THE MOST LOVE & GRATITUDE WHEN...

Notes:

CHANGES NOTED OVER TIME:

THROAT CHAKRA

Physical aspects I need to work on...

Emotional aspects I need to work on...

:·:·:·:·:·:·:·:·:·:·:·:·:
AFFIRMATION:

I live my truth. I
communicate my truth. I
am my truth.
:·:·:·:·:·:·:·:·:·:·:·:·:

Methods that help me connect...

I feel most creative when...

Tools I use are...
- ▶
- ▶
- ▶
- ▶
- ▶

Things that represent truth & integrity to me...
- ●
- ●
- ●
- ●
- ●

I FEEL FREE TO BE EXPRESSIVE WHEN...

Notes:

CHANGES NOTED OVER TIME:

THIRD EYE CHAKRA

Physical aspects I need to work on...

AFFIRMATION:

I open myself to fully knowing my inner guidance and wisdom.

Emotional aspects I need to work on...

Methods that help me connect...

I feel connected to my intution when...

Tools I use are...

▶ _____
▶ _____
▶ _____
▶ _____
▶ _____

Things that represent wisdom to me...

● _____
● _____
● _____
● _____
● _____

I FEEL MOST RECEPTIVE WHEN...

Notes:

CHANGES NOTED OVER TIME:

CROWN CHAKRA

Physical aspects I need to work on...

_____
_____
_____
_____
_____

AFFIRMATION:

I accept who I am and honor the spirit within me. My spirit is eternal.

Emotional aspects I need to work on...

_____
_____
_____
_____
_____

Methods that help me connect...

I feel most in control when...

_____
_____
_____
_____

Tools I use are...

► _____
► _____
► _____
► _____
► _____

Things that represent spirituality to me...

● _____
● _____
● _____
● _____
● _____

I APPRECIATE...

_____
_____
_____
_____
_____
_____

Notes:

_____
_____
_____
_____
_____

CHANGES NOTED OVER TIME:

_____
_____
_____

CONSULT THE UNIVERSE

I'd like to take this moment to chat a little bit about the astrology ahead of us because well - I'm an Astrologer. The planetary transit and voice of 2022 is Jupiter, which is jamming into its traditional home sign of Pisces which brings some needed harmony after the last two years with a little dip in Aries for some action oriented abundance. We have four Mercury retrogrades this year, Saturn retrograding, Venus retrograding, and Mars, 2 Super Moons and of course- the Eclipses! For detailed information on each transit you can sign up for our newsletter & blog at: https://modernmystics.store/

We start the year off with the continued Venus retrograde in Capricorn that ends Jan 29th finally lifting the fog between our relationships and our money. Mercury retrogrades in Aquarius on Jan 14th so expect communication around the collective as a whole to be unclear, for short distance travel around the country to be hectic or halted and our social lives on edge. In February, Jupiter and Uranus meet up for some much needed feeling, a good type of energy of having some freedom so perhaps some of the restrictions in our lives are scaling back again especially since it's AFTER the Mercury retrograde is over! Early April Neptune finds itself in a conjunction with Jupiter this can really go one of two ways - we can either have some truly amplified mysticism or we can have some heavy deception. We also have our first Solar Eclipse on April 30th in Taurus - if you have prominent fixed sign energy (Taurus, Leo, Scorpio or Aquarius) you'll want to follow our blog closely on this one.

May - July brings the jam packed energy with Pluto as the power back drop and Jupiter as the amplifier aligning on May 3rd. Mercury Retrograde in home sign of Gemini, the Lunar Eclipse in Scorpio May 16th and we can't forget our father planet Saturn beginning it's Retrograde starting June 4th. We round out the end of this season two Super Moons to really pack the punch. September through the rest of the year is ending 2022 with two more Mercury Retrogrades, our planet of action Mars Retrograde nesselted between those and our last eclipses of the season. It's almost like the universe is giving us time to work with each of these energies without a whole lot of overlap - how kind!

This is actually - really chill. Mild compared to what we've been going through, so sit back and relax and let's get to the fun stuff!

2022 ASTROLOGICAL DATES

SUPER NEW MOON

January 2
CAPRICORN

December 23
CAPRICORN

PARTIAL SOLAR ECLIPSE

Apr 30th
TAURUS

Oct 25th
SCORPIO

LUNAR ECLIPSE

May 16th
SCORPIO

Nov 8th
TAURUS

SUPER FULL MOON

June 14th
SAGITTARIUS

July 13th
CAPRICORN

PLUTO RETROGRADE

April 29 - Oct 8
CAPRICORN

RETROGRADES

MERCURY

Jan 14th - Feb 4th
CAPRICORN-AQUARIUS

May 10th - June 3rd
GEMINI-TAURUS

Sept 10th - Oct 2nd
LIBRA-SCORPIO

Dec 29 - Jan 18th
CAPRICORN-CAPRICORN

VENUS

Jan 1st - Jan 29th
CAPRICORN

SATURN

June 4th - Oct 23rd
AQUARIUS

NEPTUNE

June 27 - Dec 3rd
PISCES

JUPITER

July 28 - Nov 23
ARIES

URANUS

Jan 1 - Jan 18
August 24 - Jan 1
TAURUS

MARS

Oct 30th - Jan 1st
GEMINI

ZODIAC SIGNS

ARIES
Mar 21 - Apr 20
THE RAM - I AM

Pioneer, dynamic, energetic, enthusiastic, courageous, impulsive, impetuous, impatient, competitive, reckless.

TAURUS
Apr 21 - May 20
THE BULL - I HAVE

Patient, determined, sensual, stable, reliable, hard worker, peaceful, persistent, possessive, stubborn, slow, inflexible, self-indulgent.

GEMINI
May 21 - Jun 21
THE TWINS - I THINK

Versitile, curious, witty, communicator, restless, lively, fun-loving, multi-tasker, quick-thinker, inconsistent, scattered.

CANCER
Jun 22 - Jul 22
THE CRAB - I FEEL

Sensitive, nurturing, protective, imaginative, intuitive, sympathetic, quick to hurt.

LEO
Jul 23 - Aug 23
THE LION - I CREATE

Leader, loyal, creative, center of attention, expansive, warmhearted, pompous, bossy, intolerant, stubborn.

VIRGO
Aug 24 - Sept 23
THE VIRGIN - I EXAMINE

Organized, neat, efficient, practical, perfectionist, analytical, detail-oriented, self-depricating, shy, overly critical.

LIBRA
Sept 24 - Oct 23
THE SCALES - I RELATE

Diplomatic, harmonious, just, sociable, charming, peaceable, indecisive, changeable, flirtatious.

SCORPIO
Oct 24 - Nov 22
THE SCORPION - I DESIRE

Intense, probing, passionate, forceful, determined, powerful, magnetic, obsessive, resentful, cunning, domineering.

SAGITTARIUS
Nov 23 - Dec 21
THE ARCHER - I UNDERSTAND

Enthusiastic, optimistic, friendly, fortunate, humorous, easy going, spiritual, irresponsible, tactless, careless.

CAPRICORN
Dec 22 - Jan 20
THE GOAT - I USE

Achiever, structured, organized, ambitious, prudent, practical, disciplined, careful, patient, cold, fatalistic, miserly.

AQUARIUS
Jan 20 - Feb 19
THE WATER BEARER - I KNOW

Humanitarian, unique, original, revolutionary, idealistic, friendly, inventive, unpredictable, unemotional, detached.

PISCES
Feb 20 - Mar 20
THE FISH - I BELIEVE

Compassionate, sensitive, visionary, self-sacrificing, charitable, dreamer, martyr, deceptive, escapist, unrealistic.

PLANETS

SUN
LEO - 5TH House

Ego, Basic Personality, Consciousness, Vitality, Stamina

30 days in each sign

MOON
CANCER - 4TH House

Unconsciousness, Emotions, Instincts, Habits, Moods

2.5 days in each sign

MERCURY
GEMINI/VIRGO
3RD/6TH House

Mind, Communication, Intellect, Reason, Language, Intelligence

14/30 days in each sign

VENUS
TAURUS/LIBRA
2ND/7TH House

Attraction, Love, Art, Relationships, Beauty, Harmony

23 days - 2 mos in each sign

MARS
ARIES/SCORPIO - 1ST House

Aggression, Sex, Action, Desire, Competition, Courage, Passion

1.5 months in each sign

JUPITER
PISCES/SAGITTARIUS
9TH House

Growth, Expansion, Optimism, Abundance, Luck, Understanding

Avg 1 year in each sign

SATURN
CAPRICORN/AQUARIUS
10TH House

Structure, Law, Restriction, Obligation, Discipline, Ambition, Responsibility

2.5 years in each sign

URANUS
AQUARIUS - 11TH House

Eccentricity, Unpredictable changes, Rebellion, Reformation

7 years in each sign

NEPTUNE
PISCES - 12TH House

Dreams, Intution, Mysticism, Imagination, Delusions

14 years in each sign

PLUTO
SCORPIO - 8TH House

Transformation, Power, Death, Rebirth, Evolution

14/30 years in each sign

ASTEROIDS

When you look at a natal chart, you will notice that there may be asteroids listed in your natal chart. Even though there are over 17,000 asteroids in the asteroid belt between Mars and Jupiter, most astrologers use 4-5 of them. These are called the Asteroid Goddesses. They are named after feminine figures in Roman Mythology. These asteroids function to expand feminine bodies to more than The Moon and Venus. Asteroids are used to connect particular chart themes and bring clarity to the astrological picture, that may have otherwise been missed.

CHIRON

PALLAS

JUNO

VESTA

CERES

CHIRON
PAIN & HEALING

In our natal charts Chiron points to where we have healing power due to deep spiritual wounds. As the would healer we may face low self-worth and inadequacy to rise above them. We may be great guides or counselors in these areas.

PALLAS
WISDOM

Pallas is the area of our chart where your talents in the arts, deepest wisdom, defense, intuition, and justice appear. This is also where you can master negociation and create win-win situations. The sign Pallas resides in can also offer clues to our way of understanding and expression.

JUNO
MARRIAGE

Juno is enraged by inequality, and shows us where we can create balance, fairness, and right wrongs. This is a placement that indicates a potential trigger, and source of empowerment if the work is done. Juno can show you how to make the most of your connections.

VESTA
INDEPENDENCE & SPIRITUALITY

In our birth charts Vesta shows us what is sacred to us, including how our inner flame translates to spiritual yearning. Vesta also expresses itself in the ways we channel sexual energy, as well as, how sacred sexuality shows up for us.

CERES
NURTURING & MOTHERHOOD

Ceres is centered around agriculture, nourishment, motherhood, and family relationships. This placements brings a love of the simple things in life. Ceres is associated with grief, as well as, this being where you may destroy what's in the path to regain what was lost.

ASPECTS

When you look at a natal chart, you will see an aspect grid below the chart that contains the glyphs of the various aspects. Aspects are also represented by the lines you see in the middle of a chart. The aspects, which describe how various parts of the psyche relate to one another, represent the number of degrees between planet, asteroids, or astrological calculations. The aspects represent the number of degrees between the planets.

CONJUCTION

TRINE

SEXTILE

QUINCUNX

SQUARE

OPPOSITION
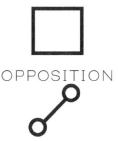

CONJUNCTION 0	SEXTILE 60	SQUARE 90
Two planets or more merge, blend, and unite. This can be positive if the planets work as a team, but negatively it can be a blind spot.	The planets that sextile each other are compatible and easily work together. Planets in a sextile aspect cheer each other on and create opportunities.	A square creates tension between two parts of the psyche, but this eternal war makes each stronger and can over time produce rich rewards.
TRINE 120	QUINCUNX 150	OPPOSITION 180
A trine creates a harmonious, creative, and smooth flow between these parts of your personality.	The planets and points involved in a quincunx don't understand each other, making it difficult to see common ground.	In an opposition, the two planets are polarized and this can create a constant tug-of-war within the psyche.

PLANETARY ANATOMY

Different parts of the body are ruled by different planetary forces. Astrologers have noted relationships and influences of the planets over different glands, organs, and functions of the body.

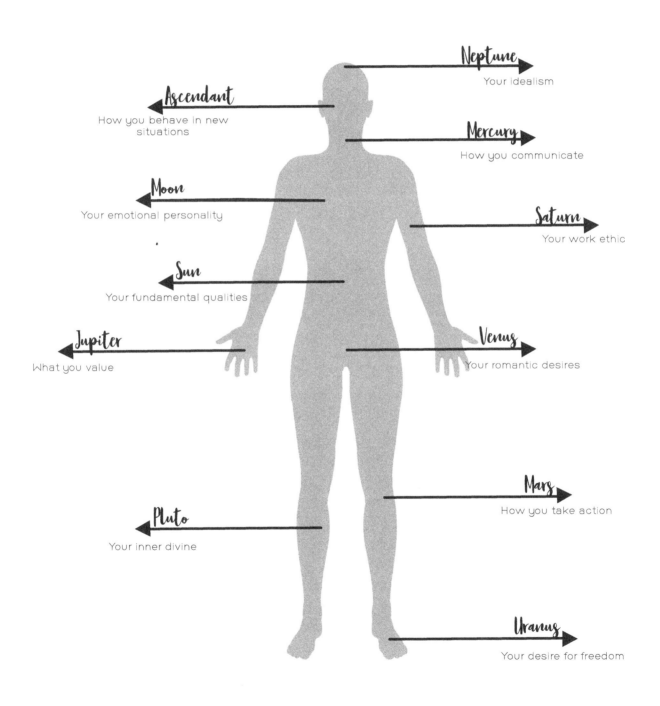

Neptune
Your idealism

Ascendant
How you behave in new situations

Mercury
How you communicate

Moon
Your emotional personality

Saturn
Your work ethic

Sun
Your fundamental qualities

Jupiter
What you value

Venus
Your romantic desires

Mars
How you take action

Pluto
Your inner divine

Uranus
Your desire for freedom

WEEKDAY ASSOCIATIONS

SUNDAY SUN ASSOCIATION Yellow, Gold

Career   Creativity   Expression   Growth   Healing   Intentions   Miracles

Peace • Promotion • Strength • Success

→

MOON ASSOCIATION MONDAY
Blue, Silver, White

Creativity   Dreams   Emotions   Insight   Illusion   Knowledge   Mystery

New Start • Peace • Travel • Wisdom

←

TUESDAY MARS ASSOCIATION Orange, Red

Cleansing   Conflict   Endurance   Obstacles   Protections   Resolution

Strength • Success

→

MERCURY ASSOCIATION WEDNESDAY
Orange, Purple, Green

Art   Change   Creativity   Development   Finance   Luck   Work-Ethic

Business • Practical Matters • Discovery

←

THURSDAY JUPITER ASSOCIATION Blue, Purple, Yellow

Healing   Health   Inner-Work   Music   Obstacles   Protection   Strength

Transportation • Wisdom

→

VENUS ASSOCIATION FRIDAY
Pale Blue, Pink, Red

Alliances   Balance   Fertility   Friendship   Improvement   Love   Passion

Prosperity • Relationships • Romance

←

SATURDAY SATURN ASSOCIATION Black, Burgundy, Purple

Banishing   Cleansing   Grounding   Protection   Psychic Ability   Security

Self-Discipline • Wisdom

NATAL CHART

NAME _____

DOB _____

BIRTH TIME _____

BIRTHPLACE _____

RULING PLANET _____

RULING ELEMENT _____

DOMINANT PLANET _____

DOMINANT ELEMENT _____

NOTES _____

	SIGN	HOUSE	⚬	⚯	△	□	✳	NOTES
☉								
☽								
☿								
♀								
♂								
♃								
♄								
♅								
♆								
♇								
AC								
MC								

NOTES

2022

THE YEAR AHEAD: THIS SECTION IS MEANT TO ALLOW YOU TO USE A FORM OF DIVINATION (TAROT, ORACLE, RUNE, ETC) TO INTERPRET WHAT THE YEAR HAS IN STORE FOR YOU. BEGIN WITH A PULL FOR THE OVERALL ENERGY OF THIS YEAR. CONTINUE BY WRITING EACH MONTH'S INTERPRETATION IN THE CORRESPONDING TEXT BOX. THIS IS OPTIONAL AND CAN BE SKIPPED IF YOU DO NOT UTILIZE A DIVINATION TOOL APPROPRIATE FOR THIS FORMAT.

A YEAR AHEAD

Energy this year:

January:

February:

March:

April:

May:

June:

July:

August:

September:

October:

November:

December:

JANUARY

SUNDAY	MONDAY	TUESDAY	WEDNESDAY
2 NEW MOON IN CAPRICORN	3 QUADRANTIS METEOR SHOWER	4	5
9	10	11	12
16	17 MARTIN LUTHER KING DAY FULL MOON IN CANCER	18 URANUS RETROGRADE ENDS	19
23	24	25	26
30	31		

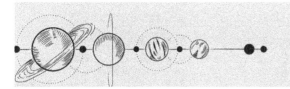

2022

THURSDAY	FRIDAY	SATURDAY	NOTES
		1 VENUS RETROGRADE CON. NEW YEARS DAY	
6	**7**	**8**	
13	**14** MERCURY RETROGRADE BEGINS	**15**	
20	**21**	**22**	
27 AQUARIUS SEASON	**28**	**29** VENUS RETROGRADE ENDS	

41

SMART Goal & Action Plan

This month I will accomplish...

_____
_____
_____
_____
_____
_____
_____

Make your goals easier by making them SMART goals. Know what you want to accomplish and then simply word it to be specific, measureable, attainable, realistic, and time-specific.

Specific → Measurable ↗ Attainable → Realistic ↗ Time-Specific

My SMART Goal

_____
_____
_____
_____
_____

What I need to attract to do this

_____
_____
_____
_____

My Action Plan

_____
_____
_____
_____
_____

What I need to release to do this

_____
_____
_____
_____

CREATING THE REALITY YOU WANT

Scripting
Check-in

How has your scripting been going? Take some time at the beginning of the new month to look over last month's work. Did you use enough detail? Did you honestly believe the changes were possible? Did any of your scripting come true? Use this private space to be honest with yourself. Include changes you want to make to your scripting next month.

_____
_____
_____
_____
_____
_____
_____
_____
_____
_____

Science tells us that it takes roughly 30 days to break or build habits. this wheel will help you keep track of how well you are showing up for your habits. Add up to 7 habits you want to track, whether you want to break old/unhealthy habits or build new/healthier ones.

To make it more interactive use the following key to color-code your habits. by adding the color of your choice. If there is a day you don't have a positive result simply don't color in that day. From month to month evaluate how you are doing with your goals. look for patterns where you've had success or challenges.

☐ Habit 1   ☐ Habit 2   ☐ Habit 3

☐ Habit 4   ☐ Habit 5   ☐ Habit 6

☐ Habit 7

JANUARY - WOLF MOON

CORRESPONDENCES

ENERGETIC:
SAFETY, PROTECTION, STABILITY, LOYALTY, DEPENDABILITY

MAGICAL:
PROTECTION, PERSONAL DEVELOPMENT, MEDITATION, AND FOCUS

ZODIACS:
CAPRICORN, AQUARIUS

TREES:
BIRCH, HAZEL

COLORS:
BLACK, WHITE, SILVER, VIOLET

ELEMENTS:
EARTH, AIR

DEITIES:
INANNA, FREYJA, SKADI,
MORRIGAN, HECATE

CRYSTALS:
HEMATITE, RUBY, SELENITE,
MOONSTONE, OPAL, GARNET,
JET, ONYX, OBSIDIAN

ANIMALS:
WOLVES, FOXES, COYOTES,
BLUE JAY, PHEASANTS

FLOWERS:
CARNATION, CROCUS,
SNOWDROP

HERBS:
MARJORAM, THYME, ANGELICA, HOLY THISTLE,
PATCHOULI, PINE, LAVENDER, MIMOSA,
PEPPERMINT

RITUAL FOCUS:
THE WOLF MOON IS A TIME FOR CONNECTING WITH
YOUR HIGHER, SPIRITUAL SELF. EMBRACE THIS BY
LOOKING INWARD, REST AND SAVE YOUR ENERGY FOR
THE YEAR TO COME.

OTHER COMMON NAMES:
QUIET MOON
SNOW MOON
COLD MOON
CHASTE MOON
DISTING MOON

DIVINATION TRACKER

DATE	PULL	MESSAGE

DAILY

I AM GRATEFUL FOR

_____

_____

_____

MOOD TRACKER

😠 ☹️ 😐 🙂 😄

SELF-CARE

MY AFFIRMATION FOR THE DAY

_____

_____

MY DREAM JOURNAL

_____

_____

_____

_____

_____

_____

_____

_____

SCRIPTING

_____

_____

_____

_____

_____

_____

_____

_____

_____

_____

_____

_____

_____

_____

_____

_____

_____

_____

RITUAL TIME   MINDFUL MINUTES

5
10
15
20
25
30

POSITIVE THOUGHT I AM CARRYING TO SLEEP

_____

_____

1 THING I DID TO MOVE FORWARD

_____

_____

_____

WEEK AHEAD

Sunday

Thursday

Monday

Friday

Tuesday

Saturday

Wednesday

NOTES:

DAILY

I AM GRATEFUL FOR

_____
_____
_____

MOOD TRACKER

SELF-CARE

MY AFFIRMATION FOR THE DAY

_____
_____

MY DREAM JOURNAL

_____
_____
_____
_____
_____
_____
_____
_____
_____
_____
_____
_____
_____

SCRIPTING

_____
_____
_____
_____
_____
_____
_____
_____
_____
_____
_____
_____
_____
_____

RITUAL TIME   MINDFUL MINUTES

5
10
15
20
25
30

POSITIVE THOUGHT I AM CARRYING TO SLEEP

_____
_____

1 THING I DID TO MOVE FORWARD

_____
_____
_____

THIS LUNATION

☐ Full Moon   ☐ New Moon

The sign the moon is in _____ and transits the _____ house.
meaning _____
_____ for me.

Build your Moon ritual: _____
_____
_____
_____
_____
_____
_____
_____
_____

CANDLES	CRYSTALS
HERBS	OTHER

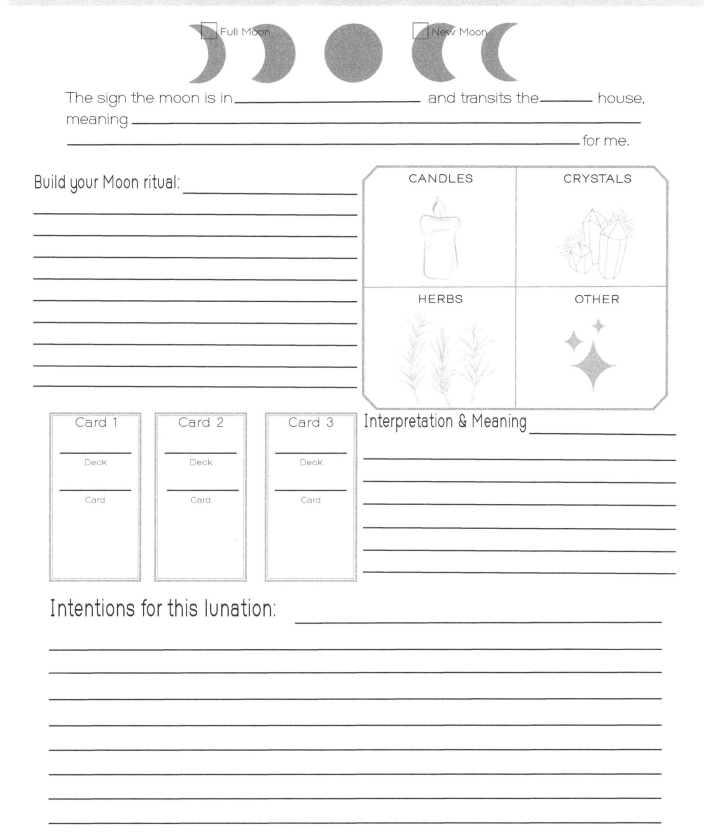

Card 1	Card 2	Card 3
_____	_____	_____
Deck	Deck	Deck
_____	_____	_____
Card	Card	Card

Interpretation & Meaning _____
_____
_____
_____
_____
_____
_____

Intentions for this lunation: _____
_____
_____
_____
_____
_____
_____
_____

DAILY

I AM GRATEFUL FOR

_____
_____
_____

MOOD TRACKER

SELF-CARE

MY AFFIRMATION FOR THE DAY

_____
_____

MY DREAM JOURNAL

_____
_____
_____
_____
_____
_____
_____
_____

_____
_____
_____
_____

SCRIPTING

_____
_____
_____
_____
_____
_____
_____
_____
_____
_____
_____
_____
_____
_____
_____

RITUAL TIME   MINDFUL MINUTES

5
10
15
20
25
30

POSITIVE THOUGHT I AM CARRYING TO SLEEP

_____
_____

1 THING I DID TO MOVE FORWARD

_____
_____

DAILY

I AM GRATEFUL FOR

_____
_____
_____

MOOD TRACKER

SELF-CARE

MY AFFIRMATION FOR THE DAY

_____
_____

MY DREAM JOURNAL

_____
_____
_____
_____
_____
_____
_____
_____

SCRIPTING

_____
_____
_____
_____
_____
_____
_____
_____
_____
_____
_____
_____
_____
_____
_____

_____
_____
_____
_____

RITUAL TIME

MINDFUL MINUTES

5
10
15
20
25
30

POSITIVE THOUGHT I AM CARRYING TO SLEEP

_____
_____

1 THING I DID TO MOVE FORWARD

_____
_____
_____

DAILY

I AM GRATEFUL FOR

_____
_____
_____

MOOD TRACKER

SELF-CARE

MY AFFIRMATION FOR THE DAY

_____
_____

MY DREAM JOURNAL

_____
_____
_____
_____
_____
_____
_____

_____
_____
_____
_____

SCRIPTING

_____
_____
_____
_____
_____
_____
_____
_____
_____
_____
_____
_____
_____

RITUAL TIME

MINDFUL MINUTES

5
10
15
20
25
30

POSITIVE THOUGHT I AM CARRYING TO SLEEP

_____
_____

1 THING I DID TO MOVE FORWARD

_____
_____
_____

DAILY

I AM GRATEFUL FOR

_____
_____
_____

MOOD TRACKER

😠 🙁 😐 🙂 😄

SELF-CARE

MY AFFIRMATION FOR THE DAY

_____
_____

MY DREAM JOURNAL

_____
_____
_____
_____
_____
_____
_____
_____
_____
_____
_____

SCRIPTING

_____
_____
_____
_____
_____
_____
_____
_____
_____
_____
_____
_____
_____
_____

RITUAL TIME

5
10
15
20
25
30

MINDFUL MINUTES

POSITIVE THOUGHT I AM CARRYING TO SLEEP

_____
_____

1 THING I DID TO MOVE FORWARD

_____
_____
_____

DAILY

I AM GRATEFUL FOR

_____
_____
_____

MOOD TRACKER

😠 ☹️ 😐 🙂 😄

SELF-CARE

MY AFFIRMATION FOR THE DAY

_____
_____

MY DREAM JOURNAL

_____
_____
_____
_____
_____
_____
_____
_____
_____
_____
_____

SCRIPTING

_____
_____
_____
_____
_____
_____
_____
_____
_____
_____
_____
_____
_____
_____
_____
_____
_____

RITUAL TIME   MINDFUL MINUTES

5
10
15
20
25
30

POSITIVE THOUGHT I AM CARRYING TO SLEEP

_____
_____

1 THING I DID TO MOVE FORWARD

_____
_____
_____

DAILY

I AM GRATEFUL FOR

_____
_____
_____

MOOD TRACKER

😠 😦 😐 🙂 😀

SELF-CARE

MY AFFIRMATION FOR THE DAY

_____
_____

MY DREAM JOURNAL

_____
_____
_____
_____
_____
_____
_____
_____
_____
_____
_____

SCRIPTING

_____
_____
_____
_____
_____
_____
_____
_____
_____
_____
_____
_____
_____
_____
_____

RITUAL TIME   MINDFUL MINUTES

5
10
15
20
25
30

POSITIVE THOUGHT I AM CARRYING TO SLEEP

_____
_____

1 THING I DID TO MOVE FORWARD

_____
_____
_____

WEEK AHEAD

Sunday

Thursday

Monday

Friday

Tuesday

Saturday

Wednesday

NOTES:

DAILY

I AM GRATEFUL FOR

_____
_____
_____

MOOD TRACKER

SELF-CARE

MY AFFIRMATION FOR THE DAY

_____
_____

MY DREAM JOURNAL

_____
_____
_____
_____
_____
_____
_____

SCRIPTING

_____
_____
_____
_____

RITUAL TIME   MINDFUL MINUTES

5
10
15
20
25
30

POSITIVE THOUGHT I AM CARRYING TO SLEEP

_____
_____

1 THING I DID TO MOVE FORWARD

_____
_____
_____

DAILY

I AM GRATEFUL FOR

_____
_____
_____

MOOD TRACKER

SELF-CARE

MY AFFIRMATION FOR THE DAY

_____
_____

MY DREAM JOURNAL

_____
_____
_____
_____
_____
_____
_____
_____

_____
_____
_____
_____

RITUAL TIME   MINDFUL MINUTES

5
10
15
20
25
30

SCRIPTING

_____
_____
_____
_____
_____
_____
_____
_____
_____
_____
_____
_____
_____

POSITIVE THOUGHT I AM CARRYING TO SLEEP

_____
_____

1 THING I DID TO MOVE FORWARD

_____
_____
_____

DAILY

I AM GRATEFUL FOR

_____
_____
_____

MOOD TRACKER

SELF-CARE

MY AFFIRMATION FOR THE DAY

_____
_____

MY DREAM JOURNAL

_____
_____
_____
_____
_____
_____
_____

SCRIPTING

_____
_____
_____
_____
_____
_____
_____
_____
_____
_____
_____
_____
_____
_____

_____
_____
_____

RITUAL TIME   MINDFUL MINUTES

5
10
15
20
25
30

POSITIVE THOUGHT I AM CARRYING TO SLEEP

_____
_____

1 THING I DID TO MOVE FORWARD

_____
_____
_____

DAILY

I AM GRATEFUL FOR

_____

_____

_____

MOOD TRACKER

SELF-CARE

MY AFFIRMATION FOR THE DAY

_____

_____

MY DREAM JOURNAL

_____

_____

_____

_____

_____

_____

_____

_____

_____

_____

_____

SCRIPTING

RITUAL TIME   MINDFUL MINUTES

5
10
15
20
25
30

POSITIVE THOUGHT I AM CARRYING TO SLEEP

_____

_____

1 THING I DID TO MOVE FORWARD

_____

_____

_____

DAILY

I AM GRATEFUL FOR

_____
_____
_____

MOOD TRACKER

😠 🙁 😐 🙂 😄

SELF-CARE

MY AFFIRMATION FOR THE DAY

_____
_____

MY DREAM JOURNAL

_____
_____
_____
_____
_____
_____
_____
_____
_____
_____
_____

SCRIPTING

RITUAL TIME   MINDFUL MINUTES

5
10
15
20
25
30

POSITIVE THOUGHT I AM CARRYING TO SLEEP

_____
_____

1 THING I DID TO MOVE FORWARD

_____
_____
_____

DAILY

I AM GRATEFUL FOR

_____
_____
_____

MOOD TRACKER

SELF-CARE

MY AFFIRMATION FOR THE DAY

_____
_____

MY DREAM JOURNAL

_____
_____
_____
_____
_____
_____
_____

_____
_____
_____

SCRIPTING

_____
_____
_____
_____
_____
_____
_____
_____
_____
_____
_____
_____
_____

RITUAL TIME

MINDFUL MINUTES

5
10
15
20
25
30

POSITIVE THOUGHT I AM CARRYING TO SLEEP

_____
_____

1 THING I DID TO MOVE FORWARD

_____
_____
_____

DAILY

I AM GRATEFUL FOR

_____
_____
_____

MOOD TRACKER

SELF-CARE

MY AFFIRMATION FOR THE DAY

_____
_____

MY DREAM JOURNAL

_____
_____
_____
_____
_____
_____
_____
_____
_____

SCRIPTING

_____
_____
_____
_____
_____
_____
_____
_____
_____
_____
_____
_____
_____
_____
_____
_____
_____
_____
_____
_____

RITUAL TIME   MINDFUL MINUTES

5
10
15
20
25
30

POSITIVE THOUGHT I AM CARRYING TO SLEEP

_____
_____

1 THING I DID TO MOVE FORWARD

_____
_____
_____

WEEK AHEAD

Sunday

Monday

Tuesday

Wednesday

Thursday

Friday

Saturday

NOTES:

DAILY

I AM GRATEFUL FOR

_____
_____
_____

MOOD TRACKER

SELF-CARE

MY AFFIRMATION FOR THE DAY

_____
_____

MY DREAM JOURNAL

_____
_____
_____
_____
_____
_____
_____

_____
_____
_____
_____

SCRIPTING

_____
_____
_____
_____
_____
_____
_____
_____
_____
_____
_____
_____
_____
_____
_____

RITUAL TIME

MINDFUL MINUTES

5
10
15
20
25
30

POSITIVE THOUGHT I AM CARRYING TO SLEEP

_____
_____

1 THING I DID TO MOVE FORWARD

_____
_____
_____

DAILY

I AM GRATEFUL FOR

_____
_____
_____

MOOD TRACKER

SELF-CARE

MY AFFIRMATION FOR THE DAY

_____
_____

MY DREAM JOURNAL

_____
_____
_____
_____
_____
_____
_____
_____

_____
_____
_____
_____

SCRIPTING

_____
_____
_____
_____
_____
_____
_____
_____
_____
_____
_____
_____
_____
_____
_____

RITUAL TIME   MINDFUL MINUTES

5
10
15
20
25
30

POSITIVE THOUGHT I AM CARRYING TO SLEEP

_____
_____

1 THING I DID TO MOVE FORWARD

_____
_____

THIS LUNATION

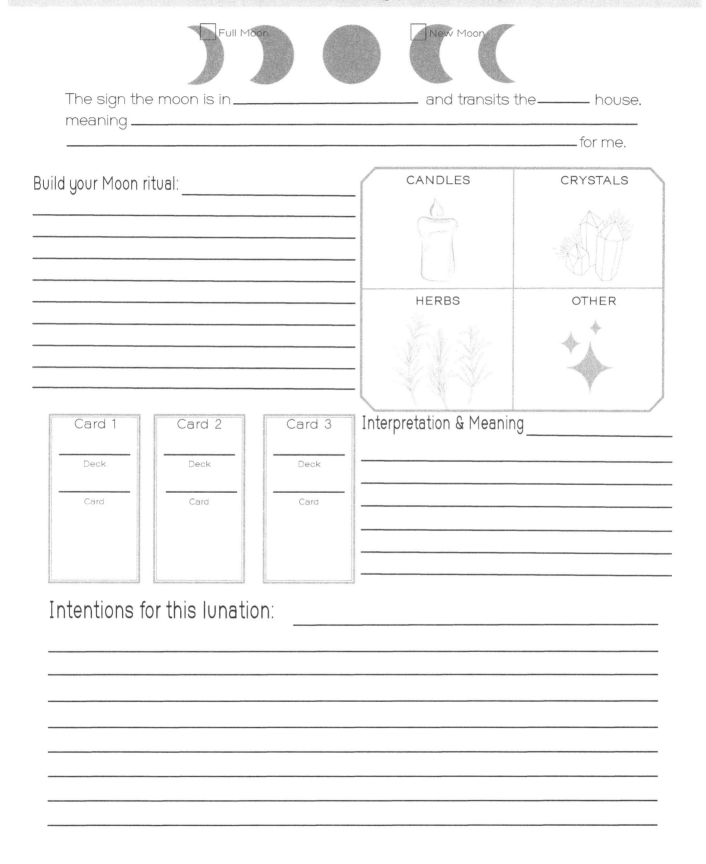

☐ Full Moon   ☐ New Moon

The sign the moon is in _____ and transits the _____ house,
meaning _____
_____ for me.

Build your Moon ritual: _____
_____
_____
_____
_____
_____
_____
_____
_____

CANDLES   CRYSTALS

HERBS   OTHER

Card 1   Card 2   Card 3

_____   _____   _____
Deck   Deck   Deck

_____   _____   _____
Card   Card   Card

Interpretation & Meaning _____
_____
_____
_____
_____
_____
_____
_____

Intentions for this lunation: _____
_____
_____
_____
_____
_____
_____
_____

DAILY

I AM GRATEFUL FOR

_____

_____

_____

MOOD TRACKER

SELF-CARE

MY AFFIRMATION FOR THE DAY

_____

_____

MY DREAM JOURNAL

_____

_____

_____

_____

_____

_____

_____

SCRIPTING

_____

_____

_____

_____

_____

_____

_____

_____

_____

_____

_____

_____

_____

_____

_____

_____

_____

_____

_____

_____

RITUAL TIME   MINDFUL MINUTES

5
10
15
20
25
30

POSITIVE THOUGHT I AM CARRYING TO SLEEP

_____

_____

1 THING I DID TO MOVE FORWARD

_____

_____

DAILY

I AM GRATEFUL FOR

_____
_____
_____

MOOD TRACKER

SELF-CARE

MY AFFIRMATION FOR THE DAY

_____
_____

MY DREAM JOURNAL

_____
_____
_____
_____
_____
_____
_____
_____

SCRIPTING

_____
_____
_____
_____
_____
_____
_____
_____
_____
_____
_____
_____
_____
_____
_____
_____

_____
_____
_____
_____

RITUAL TIME   MINDFUL MINUTES

5
10
15
20
25
30

POSITIVE THOUGHT I AM CARRYING TO SLEEP

_____
_____

1 THING I DID TO MOVE FORWARD

_____
_____
_____

DAILY

I AM GRATEFUL FOR

_____
_____
_____

MOOD TRACKER

😠 ☹️ 😐 🙂 😄

SELF-CARE

MY AFFIRMATION FOR THE DAY

_____
_____

MY DREAM JOURNAL

_____
_____
_____
_____
_____
_____
_____
_____

_____
_____
_____
_____

SCRIPTING

_____
_____
_____
_____
_____
_____
_____
_____
_____
_____
_____
_____
_____

RITUAL TIME   MINDFUL MINUTES

5
10
15
20
25
30

POSITIVE THOUGHT I AM CARRYING TO SLEEP

_____
_____

1 THING I DID TO MOVE FORWARD

_____
_____

DAILY

I AM GRATEFUL FOR

_____
_____
_____

MOOD TRACKER

😠 😦 😐 🙂 😀

SELF-CARE

MY AFFIRMATION FOR THE DAY

_____
_____

MY DREAM JOURNAL

_____
_____
_____
_____
_____
_____
_____
_____

SCRIPTING

_____
_____
_____
_____
_____
_____
_____
_____
_____
_____
_____
_____
_____
_____

_____
_____
_____
_____

RITUAL TIME

MINDFUL MINUTES

5
10
15
20
25
30

POSITIVE THOUGHT I AM CARRYING TO SLEEP

_____
_____

1 THING I DID TO MOVE FORWARD

_____
_____
_____

DAILY

I AM GRATEFUL FOR

_____
_____
_____

MOOD TRACKER

😠 😟 😐 🙂 😄

SELF-CARE

MY AFFIRMATION FOR THE DAY

_____
_____

MY DREAM JOURNAL

_____
_____
_____
_____
_____
_____
_____

_____
_____
_____
_____

SCRIPTING

_____
_____
_____
_____
_____
_____
_____
_____
_____
_____
_____
_____
_____
_____

RITUAL TIME   MINDFUL MINUTES

5
10
15
20
25
30

POSITIVE THOUGHT I AM CARRYING TO SLEEP

_____
_____

1 THING I DID TO MOVE FORWARD

_____
_____
_____

WEEK AHEAD

Sunday

Thursday

Monday

Friday

Tuesday

Saturday

Wednesday

NOTES:

DAILY

I AM GRATEFUL FOR

_____
_____
_____

MOOD TRACKER

😠 😣 😐 🙂 😄

SELF-CARE

MY AFFIRMATION FOR THE DAY

_____
_____

MY DREAM JOURNAL

_____
_____
_____
_____
_____
_____
_____
_____
_____
_____
_____
_____
_____

SCRIPTING

_____
_____
_____
_____
_____
_____
_____
_____
_____
_____
_____
_____
_____
_____
_____

RITUAL TIME   MINDFUL MINUTES

5
10
15
20
25
30

POSITIVE THOUGHT I AM CARRYING TO SLEEP

_____
_____

1 THING I DID TO MOVE FORWARD

_____
_____
_____

DAILY

I AM GRATEFUL FOR

_____
_____
_____

MOOD TRACKER

😠 😟 😐 🙂 😄

SELF-CARE

MY AFFIRMATION FOR THE DAY

_____
_____

MY DREAM JOURNAL

_____
_____
_____
_____
_____
_____
_____
_____

SCRIPTING

_____
_____
_____
_____
_____
_____
_____
_____
_____
_____
_____
_____
_____
_____

_____
_____
_____
_____

RITUAL TIME   MINDFUL MINUTES

5
10
15
20
25
30

POSITIVE THOUGHT I AM CARRYING TO SLEEP

_____
_____

1 THING I DID TO MOVE FORWARD

_____
_____
_____

DAILY

I AM GRATEFUL FOR

_____
_____
_____

MOOD TRACKER

SELF-CARE

MY AFFIRMATION FOR THE DAY

_____
_____

MY DREAM JOURNAL

_____
_____
_____
_____
_____
_____
_____

_____
_____
_____

SCRIPTING

_____
_____
_____
_____
_____
_____
_____
_____
_____
_____
_____
_____
_____
_____

RITUAL TIME   MINDFUL MINUTES

5
10
15
20
25
30

POSITIVE THOUGHT I AM CARRYING TO SLEEP

_____
_____

1 THING I DID TO MOVE FORWARD

_____
_____
_____

DAILY

I AM GRATEFUL FOR

_____
_____
_____

MOOD TRACKER

SELF-CARE

MY AFFIRMATION FOR THE DAY

_____
_____

MY DREAM JOURNAL

_____
_____
_____
_____
_____
_____
_____
_____
_____
_____
_____

SCRIPTING

_____

RITUAL TIME   MINDFUL MINUTES

POSITIVE THOUGHT I AM CARRYING TO SLEEP

_____
_____

1 THING I DID TO MOVE FORWARD

_____
_____
_____

DAILY

I AM GRATEFUL FOR

_____
_____
_____

MOOD TRACKER

😠 😞 😐 🙂 😁

SELF-CARE

MY AFFIRMATION FOR THE DAY

_____
_____

MY DREAM JOURNAL

_____
_____
_____
_____
_____
_____
_____
_____
_____
_____

SCRIPTING

_____
_____
_____
_____
_____
_____
_____
_____
_____
_____
_____
_____
_____
_____
_____
_____

RITUAL TIME   MINDFUL MINUTES

5
10
15
20
25
30

POSITIVE THOUGHT I AM CARRYING TO SLEEP

_____
_____

1 THING I DID TO MOVE FORWARD

_____
_____
_____

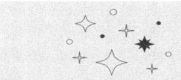

DAILY

I AM GRATEFUL FOR

_____
_____
_____

MOOD TRACKER

😠 🙁 😐 🙂 😄

SELF-CARE

MY AFFIRMATION FOR THE DAY

_____
_____

MY DREAM JOURNAL

_____
_____
_____
_____
_____
_____
_____
_____
_____
_____
_____

SCRIPTING

_____
_____
_____
_____
_____
_____
_____
_____
_____
_____
_____
_____
_____
_____
_____
_____

RITUAL TIME   MINDFUL MINUTES

5
10
15
20
25
30

POSITIVE THOUGHT I AM CARRYING TO SLEEP

_____
_____

1 THING I DID TO MOVE FORWARD

_____
_____
_____

DAILY

I AM GRATEFUL FOR

_____
_____
_____

MOOD TRACKER

😠 😟 😐 🙂 😄

SELF-CARE

MY AFFIRMATION FOR THE DAY

_____
_____

MY DREAM JOURNAL

_____
_____
_____
_____
_____
_____
_____
_____

_____
_____
_____
_____

SCRIPTING

_____
_____
_____
_____
_____
_____
_____
_____
_____
_____
_____
_____
_____
_____

RITUAL TIME   MINDFUL MINUTES

5
10
15
20
25
30

POSITIVE THOUGHT I AM CARRYING TO SLEEP

_____
_____

1 THING I DID TO MOVE FORWARD

_____
_____

WEEK AHEAD

Sunday

Thursday

Monday

Friday

Tuesday

Saturday

Wednesday

NOTES:

DAILY

I AM GRATEFUL FOR

_____
_____
_____

MOOD TRACKER

😠 😞 😐 🙂 😄

SELF-CARE

MY AFFIRMATION FOR THE DAY

_____
_____

MY DREAM JOURNAL

_____
_____
_____
_____
_____
_____
_____
_____

_____
_____
_____
_____

SCRIPTING

_____
_____
_____
_____
_____
_____
_____
_____
_____
_____
_____
_____
_____
_____

RITUAL TIME   MINDFUL MINUTES

5
10
15
20
25
30

POSITIVE THOUGHT I AM CARRYING TO SLEEP

_____
_____

1 THING I DID TO MOVE FORWARD

_____
_____
_____

DAILY

I AM GRATEFUL FOR

_____

_____

_____

MOOD TRACKER

SELF-CARE

MY AFFIRMATION FOR THE DAY

_____

_____

MY DREAM JOURNAL

_____

_____

_____

_____

_____

_____

_____

SCRIPTING

_____

_____

_____

_____

_____

_____

_____

_____

_____

_____

_____

_____

_____

_____

_____

_____

_____

RITUAL TIME

MINDFUL MINUTES

5
10
15
20
25
30

POSITIVE THOUGHT I AM CARRYING TO SLEEP

_____

_____

1 THING I DID TO MOVE FORWARD

_____

_____

_____

FEBRUARY

SUNDAY	MONDAY	TUESDAY	WEDNESDAY
		1	2
		NEW MOON IN AQUARIUS	
6	7	8	9
13	14	15	16
	VALENTINE'S DAY		FULL MOON IN LEO
20	21	22	23
	PRESIDENT'S DAY		
27	28		

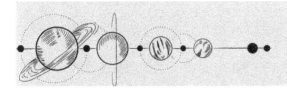

THURSDAY	FRIDAY	SATURDAY	NOTES
	3	4	5
		MERCURY RETROGRADE ENDS	
10	11	12	
17	18	19	
		PISCES SEASON	
24	25	26	

SMART Goal & Action Plan

This month I will accomplish...

_____
_____
_____
_____
_____
_____
_____

Make your goals easier by making them SMART goals. Know what you want to accomplish and then simply word it to be specific, measureable, attainable, realistic, and time-specific.

Specific → Measurable → Attainable → Realistic → Time-Specific

My SMART Goal	My Action Plan
_____	_____
_____	_____
_____	_____
_____	_____
_____	_____
What I need to attract to do this	**What I need to release to do this**
_____	_____
_____	_____
_____	_____
_____	_____
_____	_____

CREATING THE REALITY YOU WANT

Scripting
Check-in

How has your scripting been going? Take some time at the beginning of the new month to look over last month's work. Did you use enough detail? Did you honestly believe the changes were possible? Did any of your scripting come true? Use this private space to be honest with yourself. Include changes you want to make to your scripting next month.

_____

_____

_____

_____

_____

_____

_____

_____

_____

Science tells us that it takes roughly 30 days to break or build habits, this wheel will help you keep track of how well you are showing up for your habits. Add up to 7 habits you want to track, whether you want to break old/unhealthy habits or build new/healthier ones.

To make it more interactive use the following key to color-code your habits, by adding the color of your choice. If there is a day you don't have a positive result simply don't color in that day. From month to month evaluate how you are doing with your goals, look for patterns where you've had success or challenges.

☐ Habit 1   ☐ Habit 2   ☐ Habit 3

☐ Habit 4   ☐ Habit 5   ☐ Habit 6

☐ Habit 7

FEBRUARY - SNOW MOON

ELEMENTS: AIR, WATER
ENERGY: HEALING, MOTIVATION, PLANNING, LOVE

COLORS: PURPLE, BLUE, VIOLET
ZODIACS: AQUARIUS, PISCES
ANIMALS: OTTER, UNICORN
FLOWERS: VIOLET, PRIMROSE

DEITIES: BRIGHID, APHRODITE, JUNO, MARS, PERSEPHONE
CRYSTALS: ROSE QUARTZ, JASPER, AND AMETHYST
HERBS: ROWAN, MYRTLE, SAGE.

RITUAL FOCUS::
This is the perfect time to make plans for the future.
Center your magick around dreams, ambition, career, education, health, etc.
Magical workings this month should focus on ambition, clarity, new beginnings, enlightenment.

OTHER NAMES:
BONE MOON, HUNGER MOON, FAMINE MOON, BUDDING MOON, STORM MOON, ICE MOON

DIVINATION TRACKER

DATE	PULL	MESSAGE

DAILY

I AM GRATEFUL FOR

_____
_____
_____

MOOD TRACKER

😠 🙁 😐 🙂 😄

SELF-CARE

MY AFFIRMATION FOR THE DAY

_____
_____

MY DREAM JOURNAL

_____
_____
_____
_____
_____
_____
_____
_____
_____
_____
_____

SCRIPTING

_____
_____
_____
_____
_____
_____
_____
_____
_____
_____
_____
_____
_____
_____

RITUAL TIME   MINDFUL MINUTES

← 5 →
← 10 →
← 15 →
← 20 →
← 25 →
← 30 →

POSITIVE THOUGHT I AM CARRYING TO SLEEP

_____
_____

1 THING I DID TO MOVE FORWARD

_____
_____
_____

THIS LUNATION

☐ Full Moon   ☐ New Moon

The sign the moon is in _____ and transits the _____ house,
meaning _____
_____ for me.

Build your Moon ritual: _____

_____

_____

_____

_____

_____

_____

_____

CANDLES	CRYSTALS
HERBS	OTHER

Card 1	Card 2	Card 3
_____	_____	_____
Deck	Deck	Deck
_____	_____	_____
Card	Card	Card

Interpretation & Meaning _____

_____

_____

_____

_____

_____

_____

Intentions for this lunation: _____

_____

_____

_____

_____

_____

_____

_____

DAILY

I AM GRATEFUL FOR

_____
_____
_____

MOOD TRACKER

SELF-CARE

MY AFFIRMATION FOR THE DAY

_____
_____

MY DREAM JOURNAL

_____
_____
_____
_____
_____
_____
_____
_____

_____
_____
_____
_____

SCRIPTING

RITUAL TIME   MINDFUL MINUTES

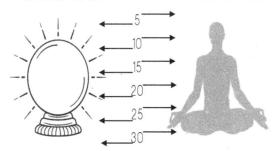

POSITIVE THOUGHT I AM CARRYING TO SLEEP

_____
_____

1 THING I DID TO MOVE FORWARD

_____
_____
_____

DAILY

I AM GRATEFUL FOR

_____
_____
_____

MOOD TRACKER

SELF-CARE

MY AFFIRMATION FOR THE DAY

_____
_____

MY DREAM JOURNAL

_____
_____
_____
_____
_____
_____
_____
_____

SCRIPTING

_____
_____
_____
_____
_____
_____
_____
_____
_____
_____
_____
_____
_____
_____

_____
_____
_____
_____

RITUAL TIME   MINDFUL MINUTES

5
10
15
20
25
30

POSITIVE THOUGHT I AM CARRYING TO SLEEP

_____
_____

1 THING I DID TO MOVE FORWARD

_____
_____
_____

DAILY

I AM GRATEFUL FOR

_____
_____
_____

MOOD TRACKER

SELF-CARE

MY AFFIRMATION FOR THE DAY

_____
_____

MY DREAM JOURNAL

_____
_____
_____
_____
_____
_____
_____
_____

SCRIPTING

_____
_____
_____
_____
_____
_____
_____
_____
_____
_____
_____
_____
_____
_____
_____

_____
_____
_____
_____

RITUAL TIME   MINDFUL MINUTES

5
10
15
20
25
30

POSITIVE THOUGHT I AM CARRYING TO SLEEP

_____
_____

1 THING I DID TO MOVE FORWARD

_____
_____

DAILY

I AM GRATEFUL FOR

_____
_____
_____

MOOD TRACKER

SELF-CARE

MY AFFIRMATION FOR THE DAY

_____
_____

MY DREAM JOURNAL

_____
_____
_____
_____
_____
_____
_____
_____

SCRIPTING

_____
_____
_____
_____
_____
_____
_____
_____
_____
_____
_____
_____
_____
_____
_____

_____
_____
_____
_____

RITUAL TIME   MINDFUL MINUTES

← 5 →
← 10 →
← 15 →
← 20 →
← 25 →
← 30 →

POSITIVE THOUGHT I AM CARRYING TO SLEEP

_____
_____

1 THING I DID TO MOVE FORWARD

_____
_____
_____

WEEK AHEAD

Sunday
_____
_____
_____
_____
_____
_____

Thursday
_____
_____
_____
_____
_____
_____

Monday
_____
_____
_____
_____
_____
_____

Friday
_____
_____
_____
_____
_____
_____

Tuesday
_____
_____
_____
_____
_____
_____

Saturday
_____
_____
_____
_____
_____

NOTES:

Wednesday
_____
_____
_____
_____
_____
_____

DAILY

I AM GRATEFUL FOR

_____
_____
_____

MOOD TRACKER

😠 🙁 😐 🙂 😄

SELF-CARE

MY AFFIRMATION FOR THE DAY

_____
_____

MY DREAM JOURNAL

_____
_____
_____
_____
_____
_____
_____
_____

SCRIPTING

_____
_____
_____
_____
_____
_____
_____
_____
_____
_____
_____
_____
_____
_____
_____

_____
_____
_____
_____

RITUAL TIME

MINDFUL MINUTES

5
10
15
20
25
30

POSITIVE THOUGHT I AM CARRYING TO SLEEP

_____
_____

1 THING I DID TO MOVE FORWARD

_____
_____
_____

DAILY

I AM GRATEFUL FOR

_____
_____
_____

MOOD TRACKER

😠 😞 😐 🙂 😄

SELF-CARE

MY AFFIRMATION FOR THE DAY

_____
_____

MY DREAM JOURNAL

_____
_____
_____
_____
_____
_____
_____
_____

_____

SCRIPTING

_____
_____
_____
_____
_____
_____
_____
_____
_____
_____
_____
_____
_____
_____
_____
_____

_____
_____
_____
_____

RITUAL TIME

→ 5 →
→ 10 →
→ 15 →
→ 20 →
→ 25 →
→ 30 →

MINDFUL MINUTES

POSITIVE THOUGHT I AM CARRYING TO SLEEP

_____
_____

1 THING I DID TO MOVE FORWARD

_____
_____
_____

DAILY

I AM GRATEFUL FOR

_____
_____
_____

MOOD TRACKER

😠 😞 😐 🙂 😄

SELF-CARE

MY AFFIRMATION FOR THE DAY

_____
_____

MY DREAM JOURNAL

_____
_____
_____
_____
_____
_____
_____

SCRIPTING

_____
_____
_____
_____
_____
_____
_____
_____
_____
_____
_____
_____
_____
_____

_____
_____
_____
_____

RITUAL TIME   MINDFUL MINUTES

5
10
15
20
25
30

POSITIVE THOUGHT I AM CARRYING TO SLEEP

_____
_____

1 THING I DID TO MOVE FORWARD

_____
_____
_____

DAILY

I AM GRATEFUL FOR

_____
_____
_____

MOOD TRACKER

SELF-CARE

MY AFFIRMATION FOR THE DAY

_____
_____

MY DREAM JOURNAL

_____
_____
_____
_____
_____
_____
_____
_____

_____
_____
_____
_____

SCRIPTING

RITUAL TIME

MINDFUL MINUTES

5
10
15
20
25
30

POSITIVE THOUGHT I AM CARRYING TO SLEEP

_____
_____

1 THING I DID TO MOVE FORWARD

_____
_____

DAILY

I AM GRATEFUL FOR

_____

_____

_____

MOOD TRACKER

SELF-CARE

MY AFFIRMATION FOR THE DAY

_____

_____

MY DREAM JOURNAL

_____

_____

_____

_____

_____

_____

_____

_____

_____

_____

_____

_____

SCRIPTING

_____

_____

_____

_____

_____

_____

_____

_____

_____

_____

_____

_____

_____

_____

_____

RITUAL TIME   MINDFUL MINUTES

5
10
15
20
25
30

POSITIVE THOUGHT I AM CARRYING TO SLEEP

_____

_____

1 THING I DID TO MOVE FORWARD

_____

_____

_____

DAILY

I AM GRATEFUL FOR

_____
_____
_____

MOOD TRACKER

SELF-CARE

MY AFFIRMATION FOR THE DAY

_____
_____

MY DREAM JOURNAL

_____
_____
_____
_____
_____
_____
_____
_____

_____
_____
_____

SCRIPTING

_____
_____
_____
_____
_____
_____
_____
_____
_____
_____
_____
_____
_____

RITUAL TIME   MINDFUL MINUTES

5
10
15
20
25
30

POSITIVE THOUGHT I AM CARRYING TO SLEEP

_____
_____

1 THING I DID TO MOVE FORWARD

_____
_____
_____

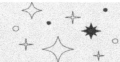

DAILY

I AM GRATEFUL FOR

_____
_____
_____

MOOD TRACKER

😠 😞 😐 🙂 😀

SELF-CARE

MY AFFIRMATION FOR THE DAY

_____
_____

MY DREAM JOURNAL

_____
_____
_____
_____
_____
_____
_____
_____
_____
_____
_____

SCRIPTING

_____
_____
_____
_____
_____
_____
_____
_____
_____
_____
_____
_____
_____
_____

RITUAL TIME

MINDFUL MINUTES

5
10
15
20
25
30

POSITIVE THOUGHT I AM CARRYING TO SLEEP

_____
_____

1 THING I DID TO MOVE FORWARD

_____
_____
_____

WEEK AHEAD

Sunday

Thursday

Monday

Friday

Tuesday

Saturday

Wednesday

NOTES:

DAILY

I AM GRATEFUL FOR

_____
_____
_____

MOOD TRACKER

SELF-CARE

MY AFFIRMATION FOR THE DAY

_____
_____

MY DREAM JOURNAL

_____
_____
_____
_____
_____
_____
_____

SCRIPTING

_____
_____
_____
_____
_____
_____
_____
_____
_____
_____
_____
_____
_____
_____
_____

_____
_____
_____
_____

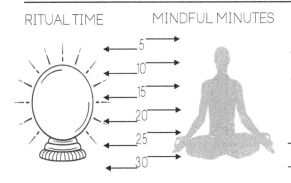

RITUAL TIME   MINDFUL MINUTES

5
10
15
20
25
30

POSITIVE THOUGHT I AM CARRYING TO SLEEP

_____
_____

1 THING I DID TO MOVE FORWARD

_____
_____
_____

DAILY

I AM GRATEFUL FOR

_____
_____
_____

MOOD TRACKER

SELF-CARE

MY AFFIRMATION FOR THE DAY

_____
_____

MY DREAM JOURNAL

_____
_____
_____
_____
_____
_____
_____
_____

SCRIPTING

_____
_____
_____
_____
_____
_____
_____
_____
_____
_____
_____
_____
_____
_____

_____
_____
_____
_____

RITUAL TIME   MINDFUL MINUTES

5
10
15
20
25
30

POSITIVE THOUGHT I AM CARRYING TO SLEEP

_____
_____

1 THING I DID TO MOVE FORWARD

_____
_____
_____

DAILY

I AM GRATEFUL FOR

_____
_____
_____

MOOD TRACKER

SELF-CARE

MY AFFIRMATION FOR THE DAY

_____
_____

MY DREAM JOURNAL

_____
_____
_____
_____
_____
_____
_____
_____
_____
_____
_____
_____

SCRIPTING

_____

RITUAL TIME

MINDFUL MINUTES

5
10
15
20
25
30

POSITIVE THOUGHT I AM CARRYING TO SLEEP

_____
_____

1 THING I DID TO MOVE FORWARD

_____
_____
_____

DAILY

I AM GRATEFUL FOR

_____
_____
_____

MOOD TRACKER

SELF-CARE

MY AFFIRMATION FOR THE DAY

_____
_____

MY DREAM JOURNAL

_____
_____
_____
_____
_____
_____
_____

_____
_____
_____
_____

SCRIPTING

RITUAL TIME   MINDFUL MINUTES

5
10
15
20
25
30

POSITIVE THOUGHT I AM CARRYING TO SLEEP

_____
_____

1 THING I DID TO MOVE FORWARD

_____
_____
_____

THIS LUNATION

☐ Full Moon   ☐ New Moon

The sign the moon is in_____ and transits the_____ house,
meaning _____
_____ for me.

Build your Moon ritual: _____

CANDLES	CRYSTALS
HERBS	OTHER

Card 1	Card 2	Card 3
_____	_____	_____
Deck	Deck	Deck
_____	_____	_____
Card	Card	Card

Interpretation & Meaning _____

Intentions for this lunation: _____

DAILY

I AM GRATEFUL FOR

_____

_____

_____

MOOD TRACKER

😠 😞 😐 🙂 😃

SELF-CARE

MY AFFIRMATION FOR THE DAY

_____

_____

MY DREAM JOURNAL

_____

_____

_____

_____

_____

_____

_____

_____

SCRIPTING

_____

_____

_____

_____

_____

_____

_____

_____

_____

_____

_____

_____

_____

_____

_____

_____

_____

_____

_____

_____

RITUAL TIME

→ 5 →
→ 10 →
→ 15 →
→ 20 →
→ 25 →
→ 30 →

MINDFUL MINUTES

POSITIVE THOUGHT I AM CARRYING TO SLEEP

_____

_____

1 THING I DID TO MOVE FORWARD

_____

_____

_____

DAILY

I AM GRATEFUL FOR

_____
_____
_____

MOOD TRACKER

😠 😟 😐 🙂 😄

SELF-CARE

MY AFFIRMATION FOR THE DAY

_____
_____

MY DREAM JOURNAL

_____
_____
_____
_____
_____
_____
_____
_____

SCRIPTING

_____
_____
_____
_____
_____
_____
_____
_____
_____
_____
_____
_____
_____
_____
_____
_____
_____

_____
_____
_____
_____

RITUAL TIME   MINDFUL MINUTES

5
10
15
20
25
30

POSITIVE THOUGHT I AM CARRYING TO SLEEP

_____
_____

1 THING I DID TO MOVE FORWARD

_____
_____
_____

DAILY

I AM GRATEFUL FOR

_____
_____
_____

MOOD TRACKER

😠 😞 😐 🙂 😃

SELF-CARE

MY AFFIRMATION FOR THE DAY

_____
_____

MY DREAM JOURNAL

_____
_____
_____
_____
_____
_____
_____
_____
_____

SCRIPTING

_____
_____
_____
_____
_____
_____
_____
_____
_____
_____
_____
_____
_____
_____

_____
_____
_____
_____

RITUAL TIME   MINDFUL MINUTES

5
10
15
20
25
30

POSITIVE THOUGHT I AM CARRYING TO SLEEP

_____
_____

1 THING I DID TO MOVE FORWARD

_____
_____
_____

WEEK AHEAD

Sunday

Monday

Tuesday

Wednesday

Thursday

Friday

Saturday

NOTES:

DAILY

I AM GRATEFUL FOR

_____
_____
_____

MOOD TRACKER

😠 🙁 😐 🙂 😃

SELF-CARE

MY AFFIRMATION FOR THE DAY

_____
_____

MY DREAM JOURNAL

_____
_____
_____
_____
_____
_____
_____
_____

_____
_____
_____
_____

SCRIPTING

_____
_____
_____
_____
_____
_____
_____
_____
_____
_____
_____
_____
_____
_____
_____
_____

RITUAL TIME

MINDFUL MINUTES

← 5 →
← 10 →
← 15
← 20
← 25
← 30

POSITIVE THOUGHT I AM CARRYING TO SLEEP

_____
_____

1 THING I DID TO MOVE FORWARD

_____
_____
_____

DAILY

I AM GRATEFUL FOR

_____
_____
_____

MOOD TRACKER

😠 🙁 😐 🙂 😃

SELF-CARE

MY AFFIRMATION FOR THE DAY

_____
_____

MY DREAM JOURNAL

_____
_____
_____
_____
_____
_____
_____

_____
_____
_____
_____

SCRIPTING

_____
_____
_____
_____
_____
_____
_____
_____
_____
_____
_____
_____
_____
_____
_____
_____
_____

RITUAL TIME   MINDFUL MINUTES

5
10
15
20
25
30

POSITIVE THOUGHT I AM CARRYING TO SLEEP

_____
_____

1 THING I DID TO MOVE FORWARD

_____
_____
_____

DAILY

I AM GRATEFUL FOR

_____
_____
_____

MOOD TRACKER

😠 😟 😐 🙂 😃

SELF-CARE

MY AFFIRMATION FOR THE DAY

_____
_____

MY DREAM JOURNAL

_____
_____
_____
_____
_____
_____
_____

_____
_____
_____
_____

SCRIPTING

_____
_____
_____
_____
_____
_____
_____
_____
_____
_____
_____
_____
_____
_____
_____

RITUAL TIME   MINDFUL MINUTES

5
10
15
20
25
30

POSITIVE THOUGHT I AM CARRYING TO SLEEP

_____
_____

1 THING I DID TO MOVE FORWARD

_____
_____
_____

DAILY

I AM GRATEFUL FOR

_____
_____
_____

MOOD TRACKER

SELF-CARE

MY AFFIRMATION FOR THE DAY

_____
_____

MY DREAM JOURNAL

_____
_____
_____
_____
_____
_____
_____
_____

SCRIPTING

_____
_____
_____
_____
_____
_____
_____
_____
_____
_____
_____
_____
_____
_____
_____
_____

_____
_____
_____
_____

RITUAL TIME   MINDFUL MINUTES   POSITIVE THOUGHT I AM CARRYING TO SLEEP

5
10
15
20
25
30

_____
_____

1 THING I DID TO MOVE FORWARD

_____
_____
_____

DAILY

I AM GRATEFUL FOR

_____
_____
_____

MOOD TRACKER

SELF-CARE

MY AFFIRMATION FOR THE DAY

_____
_____

MY DREAM JOURNAL

_____
_____
_____
_____
_____
_____
_____
_____

_____
_____
_____
_____

SCRIPTING

_____
_____
_____
_____
_____
_____
_____
_____
_____
_____
_____
_____
_____
_____
_____

RITUAL TIME   MINDFUL MINUTES

5
10
15
20
25
30

POSITIVE THOUGHT I AM CARRYING TO SLEEP

_____
_____

1 THING I DID TO MOVE FORWARD

_____
_____

DAILY

I AM GRATEFUL FOR

_____

_____

_____

MOOD TRACKER

SELF-CARE

MY AFFIRMATION FOR THE DAY

_____

_____

MY DREAM JOURNAL

_____

_____

_____

_____

_____

_____

_____

_____

_____

_____

_____

_____

SCRIPTING

RITUAL TIME   MINDFUL MINUTES

5
10
15
20
25
30

POSITIVE THOUGHT I AM CARRYING TO SLEEP

_____

_____

1 THING I DID TO MOVE FORWARD

_____

_____

_____

DAILY

I AM GRATEFUL FOR

_____
_____
_____

MOOD TRACKER

SELF-CARE

MY AFFIRMATION FOR THE DAY

_____
_____

MY DREAM JOURNAL

_____
_____
_____
_____
_____
_____
_____
_____

_____
_____
_____
_____

SCRIPTING

_____
_____
_____
_____
_____
_____
_____
_____
_____
_____
_____
_____
_____
_____
_____
_____
_____
_____
_____

RITUAL TIME   MINDFUL MINUTES

5
10
15
20
25
30

POSITIVE THOUGHT I AM CARRYING TO SLEEP

_____
_____

1 THING I DID TO MOVE FORWARD

_____
_____
_____

WEEK AHEAD

Sunday

Monday

Tuesday

Wednesday

Thursday

Friday

Saturday

NOTES:

DAILY

I AM GRATEFUL FOR

_____
_____
_____

MOOD TRACKER

SELF-CARE

MY AFFIRMATION FOR THE DAY

_____
_____

MY DREAM JOURNAL

_____
_____
_____
_____
_____
_____
_____
_____

SCRIPTING

_____
_____
_____
_____
_____
_____
_____
_____
_____
_____
_____
_____
_____
_____
_____

_____
_____
_____
_____

RITUAL TIME

MINDFUL MINUTES

5
10
15
20
25
30

POSITIVE THOUGHT I AM CARRYING TO SLEEP

_____
_____

1 THING I DID TO MOVE FORWARD

_____
_____
_____

DAILY

I AM GRATEFUL FOR

_____
_____
_____

MOOD TRACKER

SELF-CARE

MY AFFIRMATION FOR THE DAY

_____
_____

MY DREAM JOURNAL

_____
_____
_____
_____
_____
_____
_____

SCRIPTING

_____
_____
_____
_____
_____
_____
_____
_____
_____
_____
_____
_____
_____
_____
_____
_____

_____
_____
_____
_____

RITUAL TIME   MINDFUL MINUTES

5
10
15
20
25
30

POSITIVE THOUGHT I AM CARRYING TO SLEEP

_____
_____

1 THING I DID TO MOVE FORWARD

_____
_____
_____

MARCH

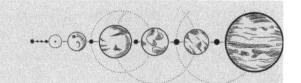

SUNDAY	MONDAY	TUESDAY	WEDNESDAY
		1	2 NEW MOON IN PISCES
6	7	8	9
13 DAYLIGHT SAVINGS	14	15	16
20	21 ARIES SEASON	22	23
27	28	29	30

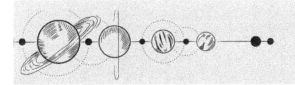

2022

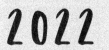

THURSDAY	FRIDAY	SATURDAY	NOTES
3	4	5	
10	11	12	
17	18	19	
	FULL MOON IN VIRGO		
24	25	26	
31			

SMART Goal & Action Plan

This month I will accomplish...

_____
_____
_____
_____
_____
_____
_____

Make your goals easier by making them SMART goals. Know what you want to accomplish and then simply word it to be specific, measureable, attainable, realistic, and time-specific.

Specific	Attainable	Time-Specific
Measurable	Realistic	

My SMART Goal	My Action Plan
_____	_____
_____	_____
_____	_____
_____	_____
What I need to attract to do this	**What I need to release to do this**
_____	_____
_____	_____
_____	_____
_____	_____

CREATING THE REALITY YOU WANT

Scripting Check-in

How has your scripting been going? Take some time at the beginning of the new month to look over last month's work. Did you use enough detail? Did you honestly believe the changes were possible? Did any of your scripting come true? Use this private space to be honest with yourself. Include changes you want to make to your scripting next month.

_____

_____

_____

_____

_____

_____

_____

_____

_____

_____

• •

Science tells us that it takes roughly 30 days to break or build habits, this wheel will help you keep track of how well you are showing up for your habits. Add up to 7 habits you want to track, whether you want to break old/unhealthy habits or build new/healthier ones.

To make it more interactive use the following key to color-code your habits, by adding the color of your choice. If there is a day you don't have a positive result simply don't color in that day. From month to month evaluate how you are doing with your goals, look for patterns where you've had success or challenges.

☐ Habit 1   ☐ Habit 2   ☐ Habit 3

☐ Habit 4   ☐ Habit 5   ☐ Habit 6

☐ Habit 7

MARCH - WORM MOON

ZODIAC: PISCES, ARIES

ELEMENT: WATER, FIRE

ANIMALS: COUGAR, HEDGEHOG, BOAR

COLORS: PALE GREEN, RED, VIOLET

ENERGY: GROWING, PROSPERING, EXPLORATION, GROWTH, BALANCE, NEW BEGINNINGS, PLANTING, RENEWAL

DEITIES: MARS, TYR, ATHENA, MINERVA, MORRIGAN, OSTARA, LIBERA, LIBER, PATER, ISIS, HECATE

HERBS: YELLOW DOCK, WOOD BETONY, IRISH MOSS, JASMINE, SAGE, STAR ANISE

OTHER NAMES: SEED MOON, STORM MOON, DEATH MOON, CRUST MOON, SAP MOON

CRYSTAL: AQUAMARINE, BLOODSTONE, JADE, ROCK CRYSTAL, AMETHYST, PINK FLOURITE

RITUAL: RECONCILIATION, PASSION IN PURSUITS, RENEWAL.

EMBRACE THE MOON:

You can celebrate by tending to your garden. Maybe it's time to plant seeds so you can sow them in time.

Not just the physical tending, you can start thinking of what you would like to grow in your life.

DIVINATION TRACKER

DATE	PULL	MESSAGE

DAILY

I AM GRATEFUL FOR

_____
_____
_____

MOOD TRACKER

SELF-CARE

MY AFFIRMATION FOR THE DAY

_____
_____

MY DREAM JOURNAL

_____
_____
_____
_____
_____
_____
_____

_____
_____
_____
_____

SCRIPTING

_____
_____
_____
_____
_____
_____
_____
_____
_____
_____
_____
_____
_____
_____

RITUAL TIME

MINDFUL MINUTES

5
10
15
20
25
30

POSITIVE THOUGHT I AM CARRYING TO SLEEP

_____
_____

1 THING I DID TO MOVE FORWARD

_____
_____
_____

DAILY

I AM GRATEFUL FOR

_____
_____
_____

MOOD TRACKER

SELF-CARE

MY AFFIRMATION FOR THE DAY

_____
_____

MY DREAM JOURNAL

_____
_____
_____
_____
_____
_____
_____

SCRIPTING

_____
_____
_____
_____
_____
_____
_____
_____
_____
_____
_____
_____
_____
_____
_____
_____
_____

RITUAL TIME   MINDFUL MINUTES

5
10
15
20
25
30

POSITIVE THOUGHT I AM CARRYING TO SLEEP

_____
_____

1 THING I DID TO MOVE FORWARD

_____
_____
_____

THIS LUNATION

☐ Full Moon   ☐ New Moon

The sign the moon is in _____ and transits the _____ house, meaning _____
_____ for me.

Build your Moon ritual: _____

_____

_____

_____

_____

_____

_____

_____

CANDLES	CRYSTALS
HERBS	OTHER

Card 1	Card 2	Card 3
_____	_____	_____
Deck	Deck	Deck
_____	_____	_____
Card	Card	Card

Interpretation & Meaning _____

_____

_____

_____

_____

_____

_____

Intentions for this lunation: _____

_____

_____

_____

_____

_____

_____

DAILY

I AM GRATEFUL FOR

_____

_____

_____

MOOD TRACKER

SELF-CARE

MY AFFIRMATION FOR THE DAY

_____

_____

MY DREAM JOURNAL

_____

_____

_____

_____

_____

_____

_____

SCRIPTING

_____

_____

_____

_____

_____

_____

_____

_____

_____

_____

_____

_____

_____

_____

_____

_____

_____

_____

RITUAL TIME

MINDFUL MINUTES

5
10
15
20
25
30

POSITIVE THOUGHT I AM CARRYING TO SLEEP

_____

_____

1 THING I DID TO MOVE FORWARD

_____

_____

_____

DAILY

I AM GRATEFUL FOR

_____
_____
_____

MOOD TRACKER

SELF-CARE

MY AFFIRMATION FOR THE DAY

_____
_____

MY DREAM JOURNAL

_____
_____
_____
_____
_____
_____
_____
_____

SCRIPTING

_____
_____
_____
_____
_____
_____
_____
_____
_____
_____
_____
_____
_____
_____
_____
_____

_____
_____
_____

RITUAL TIME

MINDFUL MINUTES

5
10
15
20
25
30

POSITIVE THOUGHT I AM CARRYING TO SLEEP

_____
_____

1 THING I DID TO MOVE FORWARD

_____
_____
_____

DAILY

I AM GRATEFUL FOR

_____
_____
_____

MOOD TRACKER

SELF-CARE

MY AFFIRMATION FOR THE DAY

_____
_____

MY DREAM JOURNAL

_____
_____
_____
_____
_____
_____
_____
_____

SCRIPTING

_____
_____
_____
_____
_____
_____
_____
_____
_____
_____
_____
_____
_____
_____
_____

_____
_____
_____
_____

RITUAL TIME   MINDFUL MINUTES

5
10
15
20
25
30

POSITIVE THOUGHT I AM CARRYING TO SLEEP

_____
_____

1 THING I DID TO MOVE FORWARD

_____
_____
_____

WEEK AHEAD

Sunday

_____
_____
_____
_____
_____

Monday

_____
_____
_____
_____
_____

Tuesday

_____
_____
_____
_____
_____

Wednesday

_____
_____
_____
_____
_____

Thursday

_____
_____
_____
_____
_____

Friday

_____
_____
_____
_____
_____

Saturday

_____
_____
_____
_____
_____

NOTES:

DAILY

I AM GRATEFUL FOR

_____
_____
_____

MOOD TRACKER

SELF-CARE

MY AFFIRMATION FOR THE DAY

_____
_____

MY DREAM JOURNAL

_____
_____
_____
_____
_____
_____
_____

_____
_____
_____
_____

SCRIPTING

_____
_____
_____
_____
_____
_____
_____
_____
_____
_____
_____
_____
_____
_____

RITUAL TIME

MINDFUL MINUTES

5
10
15
20
25
30

POSITIVE THOUGHT I AM CARRYING TO SLEEP

_____
_____

1 THING I DID TO MOVE FORWARD

_____
_____
_____

DAILY

I AM GRATEFUL FOR

_____
_____
_____

MOOD TRACKER

SELF-CARE

MY AFFIRMATION FOR THE DAY

_____
_____

MY DREAM JOURNAL

_____
_____
_____
_____
_____
_____
_____
_____
_____
_____
_____

SCRIPTING

_____
_____
_____
_____
_____
_____
_____
_____
_____
_____
_____
_____
_____
_____

RITUAL TIME   MINDFUL MINUTES

5
10
15
20
25
30

POSITIVE THOUGHT I AM CARRYING TO SLEEP

_____
_____

1 THING I DID TO MOVE FORWARD

_____
_____
_____

DAILY

I AM GRATEFUL FOR

_____
_____
_____

MOOD TRACKER

SELF-CARE

MY AFFIRMATION FOR THE DAY

_____
_____

MY DREAM JOURNAL

_____
_____
_____
_____
_____
_____
_____
_____

SCRIPTING

_____
_____
_____
_____
_____
_____
_____
_____
_____
_____
_____
_____
_____
_____
_____
_____

RITUAL TIME   MINDFUL MINUTES

5
10
15
20
25
30

POSITIVE THOUGHT I AM CARRYING TO SLEEP

_____
_____

1 THING I DID TO MOVE FORWARD

_____
_____
_____

DAILY

I AM GRATEFUL FOR

_____

_____

_____

MOOD TRACKER

SELF-CARE

MY AFFIRMATION FOR THE DAY

_____

_____

MY DREAM JOURNAL

_____

_____

_____

_____

_____

_____

_____

_____

SCRIPTING

_____

_____

_____

_____

_____

_____

_____

_____

_____

_____

_____

_____

_____

_____

_____

_____

_____

_____

_____

RITUAL TIME   MINDFUL MINUTES

5

10

15

20

25

30

POSITIVE THOUGHT I AM CARRYING TO SLEEP

_____

_____

1 THING I DID TO MOVE FORWARD

_____

_____

_____

DAILY

I AM GRATEFUL FOR

_____

_____

_____

MOOD TRACKER

SELF-CARE

MY AFFIRMATION FOR THE DAY

_____

_____

MY DREAM JOURNAL

_____

_____

_____

_____

_____

_____

_____

_____

SCRIPTING

_____

_____

_____

_____

_____

_____

_____

_____

_____

_____

_____

_____

_____

_____

_____

_____

_____

_____

_____

_____

_____

_____

RITUAL TIME   MINDFUL MINUTES

5
10
15
20
25
30

POSITIVE THOUGHT I AM CARRYING TO SLEEP

_____

_____

1 THING I DID TO MOVE FORWARD

_____

_____

_____

DAILY

I AM GRATEFUL FOR

_____

_____

_____

MOOD TRACKER

SELF-CARE

MY AFFIRMATION FOR THE DAY

_____

_____

MY DREAM JOURNAL

_____

_____

_____

_____

_____

_____

_____

_____

SCRIPTING

_____

_____

_____

_____

_____

_____

_____

_____

_____

_____

_____

_____

_____

_____

_____

RITUAL TIME   MINDFUL MINUTES

5
10
15
20
25
30

POSITIVE THOUGHT I AM CARRYING TO SLEEP

_____

_____

1 THING I DID TO MOVE FORWARD

_____

_____

_____

DAILY

I AM GRATEFUL FOR

_____
_____
_____

MOOD TRACKER

SELF-CARE

MY AFFIRMATION FOR THE DAY

_____
_____

MY DREAM JOURNAL

_____
_____
_____
_____
_____
_____
_____
_____
_____

SCRIPTING

_____
_____
_____
_____
_____
_____
_____
_____
_____
_____
_____
_____
_____
_____
_____

RITUAL TIME   MINDFUL MINUTES

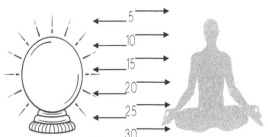

5
10
15
20
25
30

POSITIVE THOUGHT I AM CARRYING TO SLEEP

_____
_____

1 THING I DID TO MOVE FORWARD

_____
_____
_____

WEEK AHEAD

Sunday
_____
_____
_____
_____
_____
_____

Monday
_____
_____
_____
_____
_____
_____

Tuesday
_____
_____
_____
_____
_____
_____

Wednesday
_____
_____
_____
_____
_____
_____

Thursday
_____
_____
_____
_____
_____
_____

Friday
_____
_____
_____
_____
_____
_____

Saturday
_____
_____
_____
_____
_____

NOTES:

DAILY

I AM GRATEFUL FOR

_____
_____
_____

MOOD TRACKER

😣 😞 😐 🙂 😀

SELF-CARE

MY AFFIRMATION FOR THE DAY

_____
_____

MY DREAM JOURNAL

_____
_____
_____
_____
_____
_____
_____
_____

SCRIPTING

_____
_____
_____
_____
_____
_____
_____
_____
_____
_____
_____
_____
_____

_____
_____
_____
_____

RITUAL TIME

5
10
15
20
25
30

MINDFUL MINUTES

POSITIVE THOUGHT I AM CARRYING TO SLEEP

_____
_____

1 THING I DID TO MOVE FORWARD

_____
_____
_____

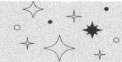

DAILY

I AM GRATEFUL FOR

_____
_____
_____

MOOD TRACKER

😠 😞 😐 🙂 😃

SELF-CARE

MY AFFIRMATION FOR THE DAY

_____
_____

MY DREAM JOURNAL

_____
_____
_____
_____
_____
_____
_____
_____

SCRIPTING

_____
_____
_____
_____
_____
_____
_____
_____
_____
_____
_____
_____
_____
_____
_____
_____

_____
_____
_____
_____

RITUAL TIME   MINDFUL MINUTES

5
10
15
20
25
30

POSITIVE THOUGHT I AM CARRYING TO SLEEP

_____
_____

1 THING I DID TO MOVE FORWARD

_____
_____
_____

DAILY

I AM GRATEFUL FOR

_____
_____
_____

MOOD TRACKER

SELF-CARE

MY AFFIRMATION FOR THE DAY

_____
_____

MY DREAM JOURNAL

_____
_____
_____
_____
_____
_____
_____
_____

SCRIPTING

_____
_____
_____
_____
_____
_____
_____
_____
_____
_____
_____
_____
_____
_____

_____
_____
_____
_____

RITUAL TIME

MINDFUL MINUTES

5
10
15
20
25
30

POSITIVE THOUGHT I AM CARRYING TO SLEEP

_____
_____

1 THING I DID TO MOVE FORWARD

_____
_____
_____

DAILY

I AM GRATEFUL FOR

_____

_____

_____

MOOD TRACKER

SELF-CARE

MY AFFIRMATION FOR THE DAY

_____

_____

MY DREAM JOURNAL

_____

_____

_____

_____

_____

_____

_____

_____

SCRIPTING

_____

_____

_____

_____

_____

_____

_____

_____

_____

_____

_____

_____

_____

_____

_____

_____

RITUAL TIME   MINDFUL MINUTES

5
10
15
20
25
30

POSITIVE THOUGHT I AM CARRYING TO SLEEP

_____

1 THING I DID TO MOVE FORWARD

_____

_____

DAILY

I AM GRATEFUL FOR

_____
_____
_____

MOOD TRACKER

SELF-CARE

MY AFFIRMATION FOR THE DAY

_____
_____

MY DREAM JOURNAL

_____
_____
_____
_____
_____
_____
_____
_____

_____
_____
_____
_____

SCRIPTING

_____
_____
_____
_____
_____
_____
_____
_____
_____
_____
_____
_____
_____
_____
_____

RITUAL TIME   MINDFUL MINUTES

5
10
15
20
25
30

POSITIVE THOUGHT I AM CARRYING TO SLEEP

_____
_____

1 THING I DID TO MOVE FORWARD

_____
_____
_____

DAILY

I AM GRATEFUL FOR

_____
_____
_____

MOOD TRACKER

SELF-CARE

MY AFFIRMATION FOR THE DAY

_____
_____

MY DREAM JOURNAL

_____
_____
_____
_____
_____
_____
_____
_____
_____
_____
_____
_____

SCRIPTING

_____
_____
_____
_____
_____
_____
_____
_____
_____
_____
_____
_____
_____
_____
_____

RITUAL TIME   MINDFUL MINUTES

5
10
15
20
25
30

POSITIVE THOUGHT I AM CARRYING TO SLEEP

_____
_____

1 THING I DID TO MOVE FORWARD

_____
_____
_____

THIS LUNATION

☐ Full Moon   ☐ New Moon

The sign the moon is in _____ and transits the _____ house, meaning _____
_____ for me.

Build your Moon ritual: _____
_____
_____
_____
_____
_____
_____
_____

CANDLES	CRYSTALS
HERBS	OTHER

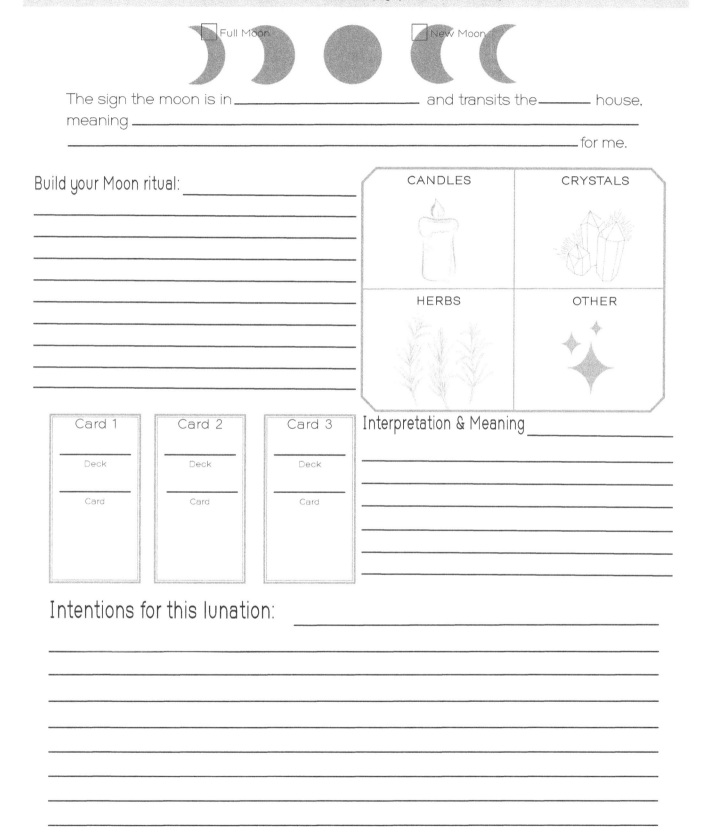

Card 1	Card 2	Card 3
_____	_____	_____
Deck	Deck	Deck
_____	_____	_____
Card	Card	Card

Interpretation & Meaning _____
_____
_____
_____
_____
_____
_____

Intentions for this lunation: _____
_____
_____
_____
_____
_____
_____
_____

DAILY

I AM GRATEFUL FOR

_____

_____

_____

MOOD TRACKER

SELF-CARE

MY AFFIRMATION FOR THE DAY

_____

_____

MY DREAM JOURNAL

_____

_____

_____

_____

_____

_____

_____

SCRIPTING

_____

_____

_____

_____

_____

_____

_____

_____

_____

_____

_____

_____

_____

_____

_____

_____

_____

_____

RITUAL TIME   MINDFUL MINUTES

5
10
15
20
25
30

POSITIVE THOUGHT I AM CARRYING TO SLEEP

_____

_____

1 THING I DID TO MOVE FORWARD

_____

_____

_____

WEEK AHEAD

Sunday

Thursday

Monday

Friday

Tuesday

Saturday

Wednesday

NOTES:

DAILY

I AM GRATEFUL FOR

_____
_____
_____

MOOD TRACKER

SELF-CARE

MY AFFIRMATION FOR THE DAY

_____
_____

MY DREAM JOURNAL

_____
_____
_____
_____
_____
_____
_____
_____

SCRIPTING

_____
_____
_____
_____
_____
_____
_____
_____
_____
_____
_____
_____
_____

_____
_____
_____
_____

RITUAL TIME   MINDFUL MINUTES

5
10
15
20
25
30

POSITIVE THOUGHT I AM CARRYING TO SLEEP

_____
_____

1 THING I DID TO MOVE FORWARD

_____
_____
_____

DAILY

I AM GRATEFUL FOR

_____
_____
_____

MOOD TRACKER

SELF-CARE

MY AFFIRMATION FOR THE DAY

_____
_____

MY DREAM JOURNAL

_____
_____
_____
_____
_____
_____
_____
_____

SCRIPTING

_____
_____
_____
_____
_____
_____
_____
_____
_____
_____
_____
_____
_____
_____
_____

_____
_____
_____
_____

RITUAL TIME   MINDFUL MINUTES

5
10
15
20
25
30

POSITIVE THOUGHT I AM CARRYING TO SLEEP

_____
_____

1 THING I DID TO MOVE FORWARD

_____
_____
_____

DAILY

I AM GRATEFUL FOR

_____
_____
_____

MOOD TRACKER

😠 😟 😐 🙂 😄

SELF-CARE

MY AFFIRMATION FOR THE DAY

_____
_____

MY DREAM JOURNAL

_____
_____
_____
_____
_____
_____
_____

SCRIPTING

_____
_____
_____
_____
_____
_____
_____
_____
_____
_____
_____
_____
_____
_____

_____
_____
_____
_____

RITUAL TIME   MINDFUL MINUTES

5
10
15
20
25
30

POSITIVE THOUGHT I AM CARRYING TO SLEEP

_____
_____

1 THING I DID TO MOVE FORWARD

_____
_____
_____

DAILY

I AM GRATEFUL FOR

_____

_____

_____

MOOD TRACKER

SELF-CARE

MY AFFIRMATION FOR THE DAY

_____

_____

MY DREAM JOURNAL

_____

_____

_____

_____

_____

_____

_____

_____

_____

_____

_____

_____

SCRIPTING

_____

_____

_____

_____

_____

_____

_____

_____

_____

_____

_____

_____

_____

_____

RITUAL TIME   MINDFUL MINUTES

5
10
15
20
25
30

POSITIVE THOUGHT I AM CARRYING TO SLEEP

_____

_____

1 THING I DID TO MOVE FORWARD

_____

_____

_____

DAILY

I AM GRATEFUL FOR

_____
_____
_____

MOOD TRACKER

SELF-CARE

MY AFFIRMATION FOR THE DAY

_____
_____

MY DREAM JOURNAL

_____
_____
_____
_____
_____
_____
_____

SCRIPTING

_____
_____
_____
_____
_____
_____
_____
_____
_____
_____
_____
_____
_____
_____
_____
_____

_____
_____
_____
_____

RITUAL TIME

MINDFUL MINUTES

5
10
15
20
25
30

POSITIVE THOUGHT I AM CARRYING TO SLEEP

_____
_____

1 THING I DID TO MOVE FORWARD

_____
_____
_____

DAILY

I AM GRATEFUL FOR

_____
_____
_____

MOOD TRACKER

SELF-CARE

MY AFFIRMATION FOR THE DAY

_____
_____

MY DREAM JOURNAL

_____
_____
_____
_____
_____
_____
_____

SCRIPTING

_____
_____
_____
_____
_____
_____
_____
_____
_____
_____
_____
_____
_____
_____
_____
_____
_____

_____
_____
_____
_____

RITUAL TIME   MINDFUL MINUTES

5
10
15
20
25
30

POSITIVE THOUGHT I AM CARRYING TO SLEEP

_____
_____

1 THING I DID TO MOVE FORWARD

_____
_____
_____

DAILY

I AM GRATEFUL FOR

_____
_____
_____

MOOD TRACKER

😠 ☹️ 😐 🙂 😄

SELF-CARE

MY AFFIRMATION FOR THE DAY

_____
_____

MY DREAM JOURNAL

_____
_____
_____
_____
_____
_____
_____
_____

_____
_____
_____
_____

SCRIPTING

RITUAL TIME   MINDFUL MINUTES

5
10
15
20
25
30

POSITIVE THOUGHT I AM CARRYING TO SLEEP

_____
_____

1 THING I DID TO MOVE FORWARD

_____
_____

WEEK AHEAD

Sunday
_____
_____
_____
_____
_____

Monday
_____
_____
_____
_____
_____

Tuesday
_____
_____
_____
_____
_____

Wednesday
_____
_____
_____
_____
_____

Thursday
_____
_____
_____
_____
_____

Friday
_____
_____
_____
_____
_____

Saturday
_____
_____
_____
_____
_____

NOTES:

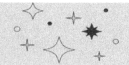

DAILY

I AM GRATEFUL FOR

_____

_____

_____

MOOD TRACKER

SELF-CARE

MY AFFIRMATION FOR THE DAY

_____

_____

MY DREAM JOURNAL

_____

_____

_____

_____

_____

_____

_____

_____

_____

_____

_____

SCRIPTING

_____

_____

_____

_____

_____

_____

_____

_____

_____

_____

_____

_____

_____

_____

_____

_____

_____

RITUAL TIME   MINDFUL MINUTES

5
10
15
20
25
30

POSITIVE THOUGHT I AM CARRYING TO SLEEP

_____

_____

1 THING I DID TO MOVE FORWARD

_____

_____

_____

DAILY

I AM GRATEFUL FOR

_____
_____
_____

MOOD TRACKER

😠 😞 😐 🙂 😄

SELF-CARE

MY AFFIRMATION FOR THE DAY

_____
_____

MY DREAM JOURNAL

_____
_____
_____
_____
_____
_____
_____

_____
_____
_____
_____

SCRIPTING

_____
_____
_____
_____
_____
_____
_____
_____
_____
_____
_____
_____
_____
_____
_____

RITUAL TIME

MINDFUL MINUTES

5
10
15
20
25
30

POSITIVE THOUGHT I AM CARRYING TO SLEEP

_____
_____

1 THING I DID TO MOVE FORWARD

_____
_____
_____

DAILY

I AM GRATEFUL FOR

_____

_____

_____

MOOD TRACKER

SELF-CARE

MY AFFIRMATION FOR THE DAY

_____

_____

MY DREAM JOURNAL

_____

_____

_____

_____

_____

_____

_____

SCRIPTING

_____

_____

_____

_____

_____

_____

_____

_____

_____

_____

_____

_____

_____

_____

_____

_____

_____

_____

RITUAL TIME

MINDFUL MINUTES

5
10
15
20
25
30

POSITIVE THOUGHT I AM CARRYING TO SLEEP

_____

_____

1 THING I DID TO MOVE FORWARD

_____

_____

_____

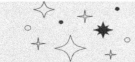

DAILY

I AM GRATEFUL FOR

_____
_____
_____

MOOD TRACKER

😠 😞 😐 🙂 😄

SELF-CARE

MY AFFIRMATION FOR THE DAY

_____
_____

MY DREAM JOURNAL

_____
_____
_____
_____
_____
_____
_____
_____

_____
_____
_____

SCRIPTING

_____
_____
_____
_____
_____
_____
_____
_____
_____
_____
_____
_____
_____

RITUAL TIME   MINDFUL MINUTES

← 5 →
← 10 →
← 15 →
← 20 →
← 25 →
← 30 →

POSITIVE THOUGHT I AM CARRYING TO SLEEP

_____
_____

1 THING I DID TO MOVE FORWARD

_____
_____
_____

DAILY

I AM GRATEFUL FOR

_____
_____
_____

MOOD TRACKER

SELF-CARE

MY AFFIRMATION FOR THE DAY

_____
_____

MY DREAM JOURNAL

_____
_____
_____
_____
_____
_____
_____

SCRIPTING

_____
_____
_____
_____
_____
_____
_____
_____
_____
_____
_____
_____
_____
_____

_____
_____
_____
_____

RITUAL TIME   MINDFUL MINUTES

5
10
15
20
25
30

POSITIVE THOUGHT I AM CARRYING TO SLEEP

_____
_____

1 THING I DID TO MOVE FORWARD

_____
_____
_____

NOTES

APRIL

SUNDAY	MONDAY	TUESDAY	WEDNESDAY
3	4	5	6
10	11	12	13
17	18	19	20
EASTER			
24	25	26	27

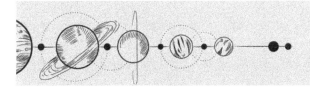

2022

THURSDAY	FRIDAY	SATURDAY	NOTES
	1 NEW MOON IN ARIES	2	
7	8	9	
14	15 GOOD FRIDAY	16 FULL MOON IN LIBRA	
21 TAURUS SEASON	22 EARTH DAY LYRIDS METEOR SHOWER	23	
28	29 PLUTO RETROGRADE BEGINS IN CAPRICORN	30 NEW MOON IN TAURUS PARTIAL SOLAR ECLIPSE	

SMART Goal & Action Plan

This month I will accomplish...

_____
_____
_____
_____
_____
_____
_____

Make your goals easier by making them SMART goals. Know what you want to accomplish and then simply word it to be specific, measureable, attainable, realistic, and time-specific.

Specific → Measurable → Attainable → Realistic → Time-Specific

My SMART Goal

_____
_____
_____
_____
_____

What I need to attract to do this

_____
_____
_____
_____

My Action Plan

_____
_____
_____
_____
_____

What I need to release to do this

_____
_____
_____
_____

CREATING THE REALITY YOU WANT

Scripting Check-in

How has your scripting been going? Take some time at the beginning of the new month to look over last month's work. Did you use enough detail? Did you honestly believe the changes were possible? Did any of your scripting come true? Use this private space to be honest with yourself. Include changes you want to make to your scripting next month.

_____

_____

_____

_____

_____

_____

_____

_____

_____

Science tells us that it takes roughly 30 days to break or build habits, this wheel will help you keep track of how well you are showing up for your habits. Add up to 7 habits you want to track, whether you want to break old/unhealthy habits or build new/healthier ones.

To make it more interactive use the following key to color-code your habits, by adding the color of your choice. If there is a day you don't have a positive result simply don't color in that day. From month to month evaluate how you are doing with your goals. look for patterns where you've had success or challenges.

☐ Habit 1   ☐ Habit 2   ☐ Habit 3

☐ Habit 4   ☐ Habit 5   ☐ Habit 6

☐ Habit 7

APRIL - PINK MOON

OTHER NAMES

HARE MOON, WIND MOON, GROWING MOON, SPROUTING GRASS MOON, EGG MOON

DEITIES

APHRODITE, VENUS, HATHOR, ISHTAR, KALI, RHIANNON, CERES, BAST

CRYSTALS

DIAMOND, QUARTZ, WHITE SAPPHIRE, EMERALD, CRYSTALLINE KYANITE

HERBS

BASIL, COMFREY, CHIVES, DRAGONS BLOOD, ALLSPICE, FENNEL, FRANKINCENSE

ENERGY OF THE MOON

FERTILITY, CREATIVITY, OPENINGS, OPPORTUNITIES, PROSPERITY

MAGICAL POTENTIALS

TRANSFORMATION, BANISHING BAD HABITS, GAINING CONFIDENCE

COLORS

- PALE YELLOW
- PINK
- VIOLET
- PALE GREEN
- GOLD

FLOWERS

- DAISY
- SWEET PEA

ZODIAC

ARIES   TAURUS

ELEMENTS

FIRE   EARTH

DIVINATION TRACKER

DATE	PULL	MESSAGE

DAILY

I AM GRATEFUL FOR

_____
_____
_____

MOOD TRACKER

SELF-CARE

MY AFFIRMATION FOR THE DAY

_____
_____

MY DREAM JOURNAL

_____
_____
_____
_____
_____
_____
_____
_____

_____
_____
_____
_____

SCRIPTING

_____
_____
_____
_____
_____
_____
_____
_____
_____
_____
_____
_____
_____
_____
_____

RITUAL TIME   MINDFUL MINUTES

← 5 →
← 10
← 15
← 20
← 25
← 30

POSITIVE THOUGHT I AM CARRYING TO SLEEP

_____
_____

1 THING I DID TO MOVE FORWARD

_____
_____
_____

THIS LUNATION

☐ Full Moon   ☐ New Moon

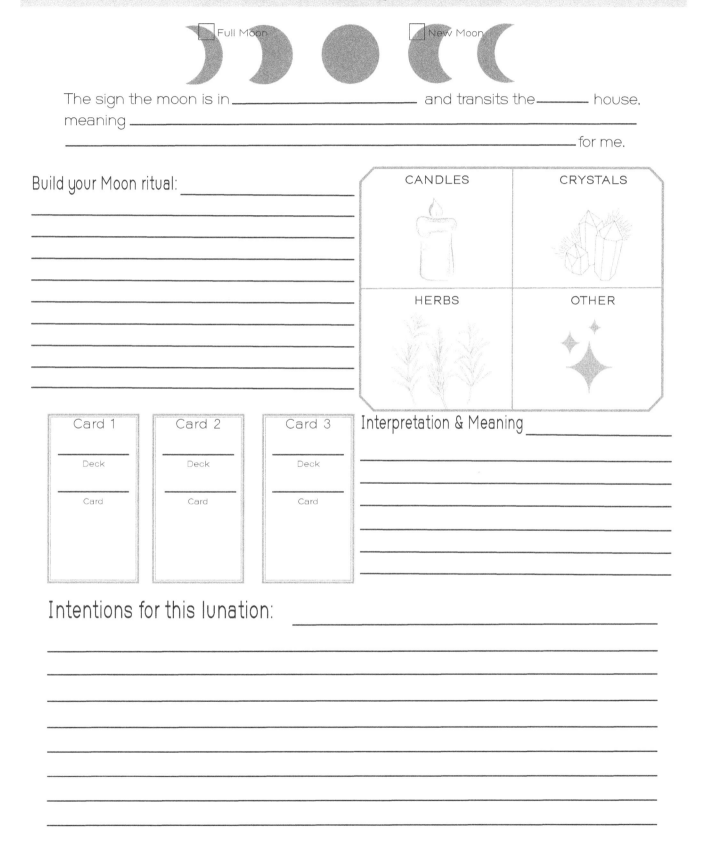

The sign the moon is in _____ and transits the _____ house,
meaning _____
_____ for me.

Build your Moon ritual: _____
_____
_____
_____
_____
_____
_____
_____

CANDLES	CRYSTALS
HERBS	OTHER

Card 1	Card 2	Card 3
_____ Deck	_____ Deck	_____ Deck
_____ Card	_____ Card	_____ Card

Interpretation & Meaning _____
_____
_____
_____
_____
_____
_____

Intentions for this lunation: _____
_____
_____
_____
_____
_____
_____
_____

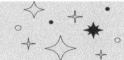

DAILY

I AM GRATEFUL FOR

_____
_____
_____

MOOD TRACKER

SELF-CARE

MY AFFIRMATION FOR THE DAY

_____
_____

MY DREAM JOURNAL

_____
_____
_____
_____
_____
_____
_____
_____

SCRIPTING

_____
_____
_____
_____
_____
_____
_____
_____
_____
_____
_____
_____
_____
_____
_____

_____
_____
_____
_____

RITUAL TIME   MINDFUL MINUTES

5
10
15
20
25
30

POSITIVE THOUGHT I AM CARRYING TO SLEEP

_____
_____

1 THING I DID TO MOVE FORWARD

_____
_____
_____

WEEK AHEAD

Sunday
_____
_____
_____
_____
_____

Monday
_____
_____
_____
_____
_____

Tuesday
_____
_____
_____
_____
_____

Wednesday
_____
_____
_____
_____
_____

Thursday
_____
_____
_____
_____
_____

Friday
_____
_____
_____
_____
_____

Saturday
_____
_____
_____
_____
_____

NOTES:

DAILY

I AM GRATEFUL FOR

_____
_____
_____

MOOD TRACKER

SELF-CARE

MY AFFIRMATION FOR THE DAY

_____
_____

MY DREAM JOURNAL

_____
_____
_____
_____
_____
_____
_____
_____

SCRIPTING

_____
_____
_____
_____
_____
_____
_____
_____
_____
_____
_____
_____
_____

_____
_____
_____

RITUAL TIME   MINDFUL MINUTES

5
10
15
20
25
30

POSITIVE THOUGHT I AM CARRYING TO SLEEP

_____
_____

1 THING I DID TO MOVE FORWARD

_____
_____

DAILY

I AM GRATEFUL FOR

_____
_____
_____

MOOD TRACKER

SELF-CARE

MY AFFIRMATION FOR THE DAY

_____
_____

MY DREAM JOURNAL

_____
_____
_____
_____
_____
_____
_____
_____

SCRIPTING

_____
_____
_____
_____
_____
_____
_____
_____
_____
_____
_____
_____
_____
_____
_____
_____

_____
_____
_____
_____

RITUAL TIME   MINDFUL MINUTES

5
10
15
20
25
30

POSITIVE THOUGHT I AM CARRYING TO SLEEP

_____
_____

1 THING I DID TO MOVE FORWARD

_____
_____
_____

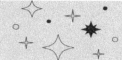

DAILY

I AM GRATEFUL FOR

_____

_____

_____

MOOD TRACKER

SELF-CARE

MY AFFIRMATION FOR THE DAY

_____

_____

MY DREAM JOURNAL

_____

_____

_____

_____

_____

_____

_____

_____

SCRIPTING

_____

_____

_____

_____

_____

_____

_____

_____

_____

_____

_____

_____

_____

_____

_____

_____

_____

_____

_____

_____

_____

_____

RITUAL TIME   MINDFUL MINUTES

5
10
15
20
25
30

POSITIVE THOUGHT I AM CARRYING TO SLEEP

_____

1 THING I DID TO MOVE FORWARD

_____

_____

DAILY

I AM GRATEFUL FOR

_____
_____

MOOD TRACKER

SELF-CARE

MY AFFIRMATION FOR THE DAY

_____
_____

MY DREAM JOURNAL

_____
_____
_____
_____
_____
_____
_____

_____
_____
_____
_____

SCRIPTING

RITUAL TIME   MINDFUL MINUTES

5
10
15
20
25
30

POSITIVE THOUGHT I AM CARRYING TO SLEEP

_____
_____

1 THING I DID TO MOVE FORWARD

_____
_____
_____

DAILY

I AM GRATEFUL FOR

_____
_____
_____

MOOD TRACKER

😠 😞 😐 🙂 😃

SELF-CARE

MY AFFIRMATION FOR THE DAY

_____
_____

MY DREAM JOURNAL

_____
_____
_____
_____
_____
_____
_____
_____

SCRIPTING

_____
_____
_____
_____
_____
_____
_____
_____
_____
_____
_____
_____
_____
_____

_____
_____
_____
_____

RITUAL TIME

MINDFUL MINUTES

5
10
15
20
25
30

POSITIVE THOUGHT I AM CARRYING TO SLEEP

_____
_____

1 THING I DID TO MOVE FORWARD

_____
_____
_____

DAILY

I AM GRATEFUL FOR

_____

_____

_____

MOOD TRACKER

SELF-CARE

MY AFFIRMATION FOR THE DAY

_____

_____

MY DREAM JOURNAL

_____

_____

_____

_____

_____

_____

_____

SCRIPTING

_____

_____

_____

_____

_____

_____

_____

_____

_____

_____

_____

_____

_____

_____

_____

_____

_____

RITUAL TIME   MINDFUL MINUTES

5

10

15

20

25

30

POSITIVE THOUGHT I AM CARRYING TO SLEEP

_____

_____

1 THING I DID TO MOVE FORWARD

_____

_____

_____

DAILY

I AM GRATEFUL FOR

_____

_____

_____

MOOD TRACKER

SELF-CARE

MY AFFIRMATION FOR THE DAY

_____

_____

MY DREAM JOURNAL

_____

_____

_____

_____

_____

_____

_____

_____

_____

_____

SCRIPTING

_____

_____

_____

_____

_____

_____

_____

_____

_____

_____

_____

_____

_____

_____

RITUAL TIME   MINDFUL MINUTES

5
10
15
20
25
30

POSITIVE THOUGHT I AM CARRYING TO SLEEP

_____

_____

1 THING I DID TO MOVE FORWARD

_____

_____

_____

WEEK AHEAD

Sunday
_____
_____
_____
_____
_____

Monday
_____
_____
_____
_____
_____

Tuesday
_____
_____
_____
_____
_____

Wednesday
_____
_____
_____
_____
_____

Thursday
_____
_____
_____
_____
_____

Friday
_____
_____
_____
_____
_____

Saturday
_____
_____
_____
_____
_____

NOTES:

DAILY

I AM GRATEFUL FOR

_____
_____
_____

MOOD TRACKER

SELF-CARE

MY AFFIRMATION FOR THE DAY

_____
_____

MY DREAM JOURNAL

_____
_____
_____
_____
_____
_____
_____

SCRIPTING

_____
_____
_____
_____
_____
_____
_____
_____
_____
_____
_____
_____
_____
_____

_____
_____
_____
_____

RITUAL TIME   MINDFUL MINUTES

5
10
15
20
25
30

POSITIVE THOUGHT I AM CARRYING TO SLEEP

_____
_____

1 THING I DID TO MOVE FORWARD

_____
_____
_____

DAILY

I AM GRATEFUL FOR

_____
_____
_____

MOOD TRACKER

SELF-CARE

MY AFFIRMATION FOR THE DAY

_____
_____

MY DREAM JOURNAL

_____
_____
_____
_____
_____
_____
_____
_____

SCRIPTING

_____
_____
_____
_____
_____
_____
_____
_____
_____
_____
_____
_____
_____
_____
_____
_____
_____
_____

_____
_____
_____
_____

RITUAL TIME   MINDFUL MINUTES

5
10
15
20
25
30

POSITIVE THOUGHT I AM CARRYING TO SLEEP

_____
_____

1 THING I DID TO MOVE FORWARD

_____
_____
_____

DAILY

I AM GRATEFUL FOR

_____

_____

_____

MOOD TRACKER

SELF-CARE

MY AFFIRMATION FOR THE DAY

_____

_____

MY DREAM JOURNAL

_____

_____

_____

_____

_____

_____

_____

_____

SCRIPTING

_____

_____

_____

_____

_____

_____

_____

_____

_____

_____

_____

_____

_____

_____

_____

_____

_____

_____

_____

_____

_____

RITUAL TIME   MINDFUL MINUTES

5
10
15
20
25
30

POSITIVE THOUGHT I AM CARRYING TO SLEEP

_____

_____

1 THING I DID TO MOVE FORWARD

_____

_____

_____

DAILY

I AM GRATEFUL FOR

_____
_____
_____

MOOD TRACKER

SELF-CARE

MY AFFIRMATION FOR THE DAY

_____
_____

MY DREAM JOURNAL

_____
_____
_____
_____
_____
_____
_____
_____

SCRIPTING

_____
_____
_____
_____
_____
_____
_____
_____
_____
_____
_____
_____
_____
_____
_____

_____
_____
_____

RITUAL TIME

MINDFUL MINUTES

5
10
15
20
25
30

POSITIVE THOUGHT I AM CARRYING TO SLEEP

_____
_____

1 THING I DID TO MOVE FORWARD

_____
_____
_____

DAILY

I AM GRATEFUL FOR

_____

_____

_____

MOOD TRACKER

SELF-CARE

MY AFFIRMATION FOR THE DAY

_____

_____

MY DREAM JOURNAL

_____

_____

_____

_____

_____

_____

_____

_____

_____

_____

SCRIPTING

_____

_____

_____

_____

_____

_____

_____

_____

_____

_____

_____

_____

RITUAL TIME   MINDFUL MINUTES

5
10
15
20
25
30

POSITIVE THOUGHT I AM CARRYING TO SLEEP

_____

_____

1 THING I DID TO MOVE FORWARD

_____

_____

_____

DAILY

I AM GRATEFUL FOR

_____
_____
_____

MOOD TRACKER

SELF-CARE

MY AFFIRMATION FOR THE DAY

_____
_____

MY DREAM JOURNAL

_____
_____
_____
_____
_____
_____
_____

SCRIPTING

_____
_____
_____
_____
_____
_____
_____
_____
_____
_____
_____
_____
_____

_____
_____
_____
_____

RITUAL TIME

MINDFUL MINUTES

5
10
15
20
25
30

POSITIVE THOUGHT I AM CARRYING TO SLEEP

_____
_____

1 THING I DID TO MOVE FORWARD

_____
_____
_____

DAILY

I AM GRATEFUL FOR

_____
_____
_____

MOOD TRACKER

😠 😦 😐 🙂 😃

SELF-CARE

MY AFFIRMATION FOR THE DAY

_____
_____

MY DREAM JOURNAL

_____
_____
_____
_____
_____
_____
_____
_____

_____
_____
_____
_____

SCRIPTING

_____
_____
_____
_____
_____
_____
_____
_____
_____
_____
_____
_____
_____
_____

RITUAL TIME

MINDFUL MINUTES

5
10
15
20
25
30

POSITIVE THOUGHT I AM CARRYING TO SLEEP

_____
_____

1 THING I DID TO MOVE FORWARD

_____
_____
_____

THIS LUNATION

☐ Full Moon   ☐ New Moon

The sign the moon is in _____ and transits the _____ house,
meaning _____
_____ for me.

Build your Moon ritual: _____
_____
_____
_____
_____
_____
_____
_____
_____
_____

CANDLES	CRYSTALS
HERBS	OTHER

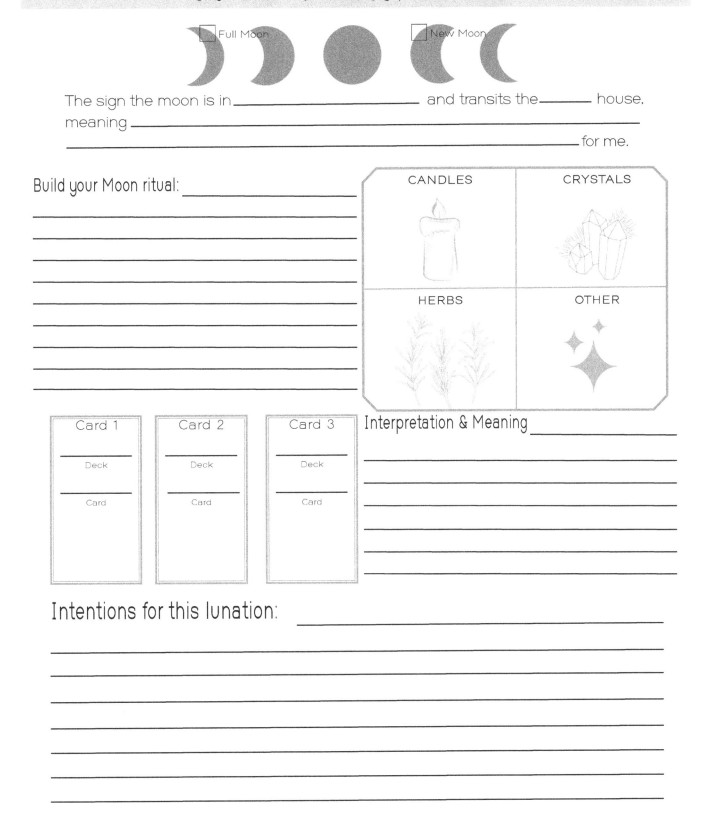

Card 1	Card 2	Card 3
_____	_____	_____
Deck	Deck	Deck
_____	_____	_____
Card	Card	Card

Interpretation & Meaning _____
_____
_____
_____
_____
_____
_____

Intentions for this lunation: _____
_____
_____
_____
_____
_____
_____
_____

WEEK AHEAD

Sunday
_____
_____
_____
_____
_____
_____

Monday
_____
_____
_____
_____
_____
_____

Tuesday
_____
_____
_____
_____
_____
_____

Wednesday
_____
_____
_____
_____
_____
_____

Thursday
_____
_____
_____
_____
_____
_____

Friday
_____
_____
_____
_____
_____
_____

Saturday
_____
_____
_____
_____
_____
_____

NOTES:

DAILY

I AM GRATEFUL FOR

_____
_____
_____

MOOD TRACKER

😠 😞 😐 🙂 😄

SELF-CARE

MY AFFIRMATION FOR THE DAY

_____
_____

MY DREAM JOURNAL

_____
_____
_____
_____
_____
_____
_____
_____

SCRIPTING

_____
_____
_____
_____
_____
_____
_____
_____
_____
_____
_____
_____
_____
_____

_____
_____
_____
_____

RITUAL TIME

MINDFUL MINUTES

5
10
15
20
25
30

POSITIVE THOUGHT I AM CARRYING TO SLEEP

_____
_____

1 THING I DID TO MOVE FORWARD

_____
_____
_____

DAILY

I AM GRATEFUL FOR

_____
_____
_____

MOOD TRACKER

😠 😞 😐 🙂 😃

SELF-CARE

MY AFFIRMATION FOR THE DAY

_____
_____

MY DREAM JOURNAL

_____
_____
_____
_____
_____
_____
_____
_____
_____

SCRIPTING

_____
_____
_____
_____
_____
_____
_____
_____
_____
_____
_____
_____
_____
_____

_____
_____
_____
_____

RITUAL TIME   MINDFUL MINUTES

5
10
15
20
25
30

POSITIVE THOUGHT I AM CARRYING TO SLEEP

_____
_____

1 THING I DID TO MOVE FORWARD

_____
_____
_____

DAILY

I AM GRATEFUL FOR

_____

_____

_____

MOOD TRACKER

SELF-CARE

MY AFFIRMATION FOR THE DAY

_____

_____

MY DREAM JOURNAL

_____

_____

_____

_____

_____

_____

_____

SCRIPTING

_____

_____

_____

_____

_____

_____

_____

_____

_____

_____

_____

_____

_____

_____

_____

_____

_____

RITUAL TIME   MINDFUL MINUTES

5
10
15
20
25
30

POSITIVE THOUGHT I AM CARRYING TO SLEEP

_____

_____

1 THING I DID TO MOVE FORWARD

_____

_____

_____

DAILY

I AM GRATEFUL FOR

_____
_____
_____

MOOD TRACKER

SELF-CARE

MY AFFIRMATION FOR THE DAY

_____
_____

MY DREAM JOURNAL

_____
_____
_____
_____
_____
_____
_____
_____
_____
_____
_____
_____

SCRIPTING

_____
_____
_____
_____
_____
_____
_____
_____
_____
_____
_____
_____
_____
_____
_____
_____

RITUAL TIME   MINDFUL MINUTES

5
10
15
20
25
30

POSITIVE THOUGHT I AM CARRYING TO SLEEP

_____
_____

1 THING I DID TO MOVE FORWARD

_____
_____

DAILY

I AM GRATEFUL FOR

_____
_____
_____

MOOD TRACKER

😠 😕 😐 🙂 😄

SELF-CARE

MY AFFIRMATION FOR THE DAY

_____
_____

MY DREAM JOURNAL

_____
_____
_____
_____
_____
_____
_____
_____

SCRIPTING

_____
_____
_____
_____
_____
_____
_____
_____
_____
_____
_____
_____
_____
_____
_____
_____
_____
_____
_____

RITUAL TIME   MINDFUL MINUTES

5
10
15
20
25
30

POSITIVE THOUGHT I AM CARRYING TO SLEEP

_____
_____

1 THING I DID TO MOVE FORWARD

_____
_____
_____

DAILY

I AM GRATEFUL FOR

_____
_____
_____

MOOD TRACKER

SELF-CARE

MY AFFIRMATION FOR THE DAY

_____
_____

MY DREAM JOURNAL

_____
_____
_____
_____
_____
_____
_____
_____

SCRIPTING

_____
_____
_____
_____
_____
_____
_____
_____
_____
_____
_____
_____
_____
_____
_____

_____
_____
_____
_____

RITUAL TIME   MINDFUL MINUTES

5
10
15
20
25
30

POSITIVE THOUGHT I AM CARRYING TO SLEEP

_____
_____

1 THING I DID TO MOVE FORWARD

_____
_____
_____

DAILY

I AM GRATEFUL FOR

_____

_____

_____

MOOD TRACKER

SELF-CARE

MY AFFIRMATION FOR THE DAY

_____

_____

MY DREAM JOURNAL

_____

_____

_____

_____

_____

_____

_____

SCRIPTING

_____

_____

_____

_____

_____

_____

_____

_____

_____

_____

_____

_____

_____

_____

_____

_____

_____

_____

RITUAL TIME   MINDFUL MINUTES

5
10
15
20
25
30

POSITIVE THOUGHT I AM CARRYING TO SLEEP

_____

_____

1 THING I DID TO MOVE FORWARD

_____

_____

_____

WEEK AHEAD

Sunday

_____
_____
_____
_____
_____
_____

Monday

_____
_____
_____
_____
_____
_____

Tuesday

_____
_____
_____
_____
_____
_____

Wednesday

_____
_____
_____
_____
_____
_____

Thursday

_____
_____
_____
_____
_____
_____

Friday

_____
_____
_____
_____
_____
_____

Saturday

_____
_____
_____
_____
_____
_____

NOTES:

DAILY

I AM GRATEFUL FOR

_____
_____
_____

MOOD TRACKER

SELF-CARE

MY AFFIRMATION FOR THE DAY

_____
_____

MY DREAM JOURNAL

_____
_____
_____
_____
_____
_____
_____
_____
_____
_____
_____
_____

SCRIPTING

RITUAL TIME   MINDFUL MINUTES

5
10
15
20
25
30

POSITIVE THOUGHT I AM CARRYING TO SLEEP

_____
_____

1 THING I DID TO MOVE FORWARD

_____
_____
_____

DAILY

I AM GRATEFUL FOR

_____
_____
_____

MOOD TRACKER

SELF-CARE

MY AFFIRMATION FOR THE DAY

_____
_____

MY DREAM JOURNAL

_____
_____
_____
_____
_____
_____
_____
_____
_____
_____
_____

SCRIPTING

_____
_____
_____
_____
_____
_____
_____
_____
_____
_____
_____
_____
_____
_____

RITUAL TIME   MINDFUL MINUTES

5
10
15
20
25
30

POSITIVE THOUGHT I AM CARRYING TO SLEEP

_____
_____

1 THING I DID TO MOVE FORWARD

_____
_____
_____

DAILY

I AM GRATEFUL FOR

_____
_____
_____

MOOD TRACKER

SELF-CARE

MY AFFIRMATION FOR THE DAY

_____
_____

MY DREAM JOURNAL

_____
_____
_____
_____
_____
_____
_____
_____

SCRIPTING

_____
_____
_____
_____
_____
_____
_____
_____
_____
_____
_____
_____

_____
_____
_____
_____

RITUAL TIME   MINDFUL MINUTES

5
10
15
20
25
30

POSITIVE THOUGHT I AM CARRYING TO SLEEP

_____
_____

1 THING I DID TO MOVE FORWARD

_____
_____
_____

DAILY

I AM GRATEFUL FOR

_____
_____

MOOD TRACKER

SELF-CARE

MY AFFIRMATION FOR THE DAY

_____
_____

MY DREAM JOURNAL

_____
_____
_____
_____
_____
_____
_____
_____

SCRIPTING

_____
_____
_____
_____
_____
_____
_____
_____
_____
_____
_____
_____
_____

_____
_____
_____
_____

RITUAL TIME   MINDFUL MINUTES

5
10
15
20
25
30

POSITIVE THOUGHT I AM CARRYING TO SLEEP

_____
_____

1 THING I DID TO MOVE FORWARD

_____
_____
_____

DAILY

I AM GRATEFUL FOR

_____
_____
_____

MOOD TRACKER

SELF-CARE

MY AFFIRMATION FOR THE DAY

_____
_____

MY DREAM JOURNAL

_____
_____
_____
_____
_____
_____
_____
_____

SCRIPTING

_____
_____
_____
_____
_____
_____
_____
_____
_____
_____
_____
_____
_____
_____
_____
_____
_____

_____
_____
_____
_____

RITUAL TIME   MINDFUL MINUTES

5
10
15
20
25
30

POSITIVE THOUGHT I AM CARRYING TO SLEEP

_____
_____

1 THING I DID TO MOVE FORWARD

_____
_____
_____

DAILY

I AM GRATEFUL FOR

_____

_____

_____

MOOD TRACKER

😠 😞 😐 🙂 😀

SELF-CARE

MY AFFIRMATION FOR THE DAY

_____

_____

MY DREAM JOURNAL

_____

_____

_____

_____

_____

_____

_____

_____

_____

_____

_____

_____

SCRIPTING

_____

_____

_____

_____

_____

_____

_____

_____

_____

_____

_____

_____

_____

_____

_____

_____

RITUAL TIME   MINDFUL MINUTES

5
10
15
20
25
30

POSITIVE THOUGHT I AM CARRYING TO SLEEP

_____

_____

1 THING I DID TO MOVE FORWARD

_____

_____

_____

DAILY

I AM GRATEFUL FOR

_____
_____
_____

MOOD TRACKER

😠 ☹️ 😐 🙂 😀

SELF-CARE

MY AFFIRMATION FOR THE DAY

_____
_____

MY DREAM JOURNAL

_____
_____
_____
_____
_____
_____
_____
_____
_____
_____

SCRIPTING

_____
_____
_____
_____
_____
_____
_____
_____
_____
_____
_____
_____
_____
_____

RITUAL TIME   MINDFUL MINUTES

5
10
15
20
25
30

POSITIVE THOUGHT I AM CARRYING TO SLEEP

_____
_____

1 THING I DID TO MOVE FORWARD

_____
_____
_____

THIS LUNATION

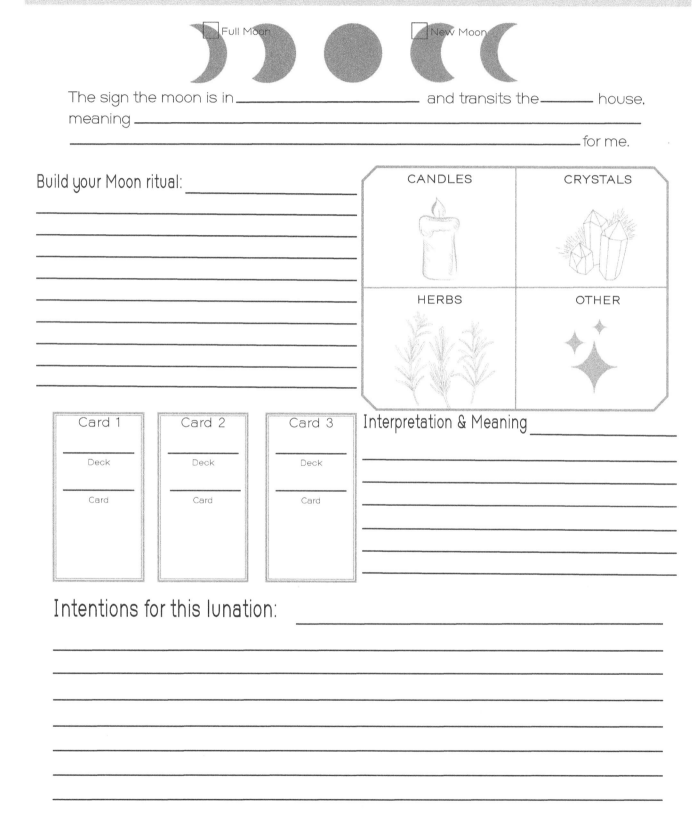

☐ Full Moon   ☐ New Moon

The sign the moon is in ＿＿＿＿＿＿＿＿＿ and transits the ＿＿＿ house,
meaning ＿＿＿＿＿＿＿＿＿＿＿＿＿＿＿＿＿＿＿＿＿＿＿＿＿＿＿
＿＿＿＿＿＿＿＿＿＿＿＿＿＿＿＿＿＿＿＿＿＿＿ for me.

Build your Moon ritual: ＿＿＿＿＿＿＿＿＿
＿＿＿＿＿＿＿＿＿＿＿＿＿＿＿＿＿＿＿＿＿
＿＿＿＿＿＿＿＿＿＿＿＿＿＿＿＿＿＿＿＿＿
＿＿＿＿＿＿＿＿＿＿＿＿＿＿＿＿＿＿＿＿＿
＿＿＿＿＿＿＿＿＿＿＿＿＿＿＿＿＿＿＿＿＿
＿＿＿＿＿＿＿＿＿＿＿＿＿＿＿＿＿＿＿＿＿
＿＿＿＿＿＿＿＿＿＿＿＿＿＿＿＿＿＿＿＿＿
＿＿＿＿＿＿＿＿＿＿＿＿＿＿＿＿＿＿＿＿＿

CANDLES	CRYSTALS
HERBS	OTHER

Card 1

＿＿＿＿＿
Deck

＿＿＿＿＿
Card

Card 2

＿＿＿＿＿
Deck

＿＿＿＿＿
Card

Card 3

＿＿＿＿＿
Deck

＿＿＿＿＿
Card

Interpretation & Meaning ＿＿＿＿＿＿
＿＿＿＿＿＿＿＿＿＿＿＿＿＿＿＿＿＿＿＿＿
＿＿＿＿＿＿＿＿＿＿＿＿＿＿＿＿＿＿＿＿＿
＿＿＿＿＿＿＿＿＿＿＿＿＿＿＿＿＿＿＿＿＿
＿＿＿＿＿＿＿＿＿＿＿＿＿＿＿＿＿＿＿＿＿
＿＿＿＿＿＿＿＿＿＿＿＿＿＿＿＿＿＿＿＿＿
＿＿＿＿＿＿＿＿＿＿＿＿＿＿＿＿＿＿＿＿＿
＿＿＿＿＿＿＿＿＿＿＿＿＿＿＿＿＿＿＿＿＿

Intentions for this lunation: ＿＿＿＿＿＿
＿＿＿＿＿＿＿＿＿＿＿＿＿＿＿＿＿＿＿＿＿＿＿＿＿＿＿＿＿＿＿
＿＿＿＿＿＿＿＿＿＿＿＿＿＿＿＿＿＿＿＿＿＿＿＿＿＿＿＿＿＿＿
＿＿＿＿＿＿＿＿＿＿＿＿＿＿＿＿＿＿＿＿＿＿＿＿＿＿＿＿＿＿＿
＿＿＿＿＿＿＿＿＿＿＿＿＿＿＿＿＿＿＿＿＿＿＿＿＿＿＿＿＿＿＿
＿＿＿＿＿＿＿＿＿＿＿＿＿＿＿＿＿＿＿＿＿＿＿＿＿＿＿＿＿＿＿
＿＿＿＿＿＿＿＿＿＿＿＿＿＿＿＿＿＿＿＿＿＿＿＿＿＿＿＿＿＿＿
＿＿＿＿＿＿＿＿＿＿＿＿＿＿＿＿＿＿＿＿＿＿＿＿＿＿＿＿＿＿＿

NOTES

MAY

SUNDAY	MONDAY	TUESDAY	WEDNESDAY
1	2	3	4
8 MOTHER'S DAY	9	10 MERCURY RETROGRADE BEGINS	11
15	16 FULL MOON IN SCORPIO LUNAR ECLIPSE	17	18
22	23	24	25
29	30 MEMORIAL DAY NEW MOON IN GEMINI	31	

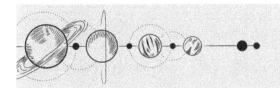

2022

THURSDAY	FRIDAY	SATURDAY	NOTES
5	6	7	
	ETA AQUARIDS	METEOR SHOWER	
12	13	14	
19	20	21	
		GEMINI SEASON	
26	27	28	

SMART Goal & Action Plan

This month I will accomplish...

_____
_____
_____
_____
_____
_____
_____

Make your goals easier by making them SMART goals. Know what you want to accomplish and then simply word it to be specific, measureable, attainable, realistic, and time-specific.

Specific → Measurable → Attainable → Realistic → Time-Specific

My SMART Goal

_____
_____
_____
_____

What I need to attract to do this

_____
_____
_____
_____

My Action Plan

_____
_____
_____
_____

What I need to release to do this

_____
_____
_____
_____

CREATING THE REALITY YOU WANT

Scripting
Check-in

How has your scripting been going? Take some time at the beginning of the new month to look over last month's work. Did you use enough detail? Did you honestly believe the changes were possible? Did any of your scripting come true? Use this private space to be honest with yourself. Include changes you want to make to your scripting next month.

_____

_____

_____

_____

_____

_____

_____

_____

_____

• •

Science tells us that it takes roughly 30 days to break or build habits. this wheel will help you keep track of how well you are showing up for your habits. Add up to 7 habits you want to track. whether you want to break old/unhealthy habits or build new/healthier ones.

To make it more interactive use the following key to color-code your habits. by adding the color of your choice. If there is a day you don't have a positive result simply don't color in that day. From month to month evaluate how you are doing with your goals. look for patterns where you've had success or challenges.

☐ Habit 1   ☐ Habit 2   ☐ Habit 3

☐ Habit 4   ☐ Habit 5   ☐ Habit 6

☐ Habit 7

MAY

FLOWER MOON

ZODIAC SIGNS

TAURUS
&
GEMINI

ELEMENTS

EARTH   AIR

CRYSTALS
- EMERALD
- SAPPHIRE
- AGATE
- CHRYSOPRASE
- BERYL
- CHRYSOTILE
- SEPTARIAN

HERBS
- MINT
- ROSE
- MUGWORT
- THYME
- YARROW
- APPLE BLOSSOM
- MAGNOLIA

DEITIES
- MAIA
- BAST
- VENUS
- APHRODITE
- DIANA
- ARTEMIS

COLORS: PINK, GREEN, BROWN   **FLOWERS**: LILY OF THE VALLEY, HAWTHORN

ENERGIES OF THE MONTH

DEVELOPMENT, GROWTH, MATURITY, INTUITION

POTENTIAL OF THE MONTH

DUALITY, EXPANDING HORIZONS, SEX MAGIC.

DIVINATION TRACKER

DATE	PULL	MESSAGE

WEEK AHEAD

Sunday
_____
_____
_____
_____
_____
_____

Monday
_____
_____
_____
_____
_____
_____

Tuesday
_____
_____
_____
_____
_____
_____

Wednesday
_____
_____
_____
_____
_____
_____

Thursday
_____
_____
_____
_____
_____
_____

Friday
_____
_____
_____
_____
_____
_____

Saturday
_____
_____
_____
_____
_____
_____

NOTES:

DAILY

I AM GRATEFUL FOR

_____
_____
_____

MOOD TRACKER

SELF-CARE

MY AFFIRMATION FOR THE DAY

_____
_____

MY DREAM JOURNAL

_____
_____
_____
_____
_____
_____
_____
_____

SCRIPTING

_____
_____
_____
_____
_____
_____
_____
_____
_____
_____
_____
_____
_____

_____
_____
_____
_____

RITUAL TIME   MINDFUL MINUTES

5
10
15
20
25
30

POSITIVE THOUGHT I AM CARRYING TO SLEEP

_____
_____

1 THING I DID TO MOVE FORWARD

_____
_____
_____

DAILY

I AM GRATEFUL FOR

_____
_____
_____

MOOD TRACKER

SELF-CARE

MY AFFIRMATION FOR THE DAY

_____
_____

MY DREAM JOURNAL

_____
_____
_____
_____
_____
_____
_____
_____
_____

SCRIPTING

_____
_____
_____
_____
_____
_____
_____
_____
_____
_____
_____
_____
_____
_____
_____

_____
_____
_____
_____

RITUAL TIME

MINDFUL MINUTES

5
10
15
20
25
30

POSITIVE THOUGHT I AM CARRYING TO SLEEP

_____
_____

1 THING I DID TO MOVE FORWARD

_____
_____
_____

DAILY

I AM GRATEFUL FOR

_____

_____

_____

MOOD TRACKER

SELF-CARE

MY AFFIRMATION FOR THE DAY

_____

_____

MY DREAM JOURNAL

_____

_____

_____

_____

_____

_____

_____

_____

_____

_____

_____

_____

SCRIPTING

RITUAL TIME   MINDFUL MINUTES

5
10
15
20
25
30

POSITIVE THOUGHT I AM CARRYING TO SLEEP

_____

_____

1 THING I DID TO MOVE FORWARD

_____

_____

_____

DAILY

I AM GRATEFUL FOR

_____

_____

_____

MOOD TRACKER

SELF-CARE

MY AFFIRMATION FOR THE DAY

_____

_____

MY DREAM JOURNAL

_____

_____

_____

_____

_____

_____

_____

_____

_____

_____

_____

SCRIPTING

_____

_____

_____

_____

_____

_____

_____

_____

_____

_____

_____

_____

_____

_____

_____

RITUAL TIME   MINDFUL MINUTES

← 5 →
← 10
← 15
← 20
← 25
← 30

POSITIVE THOUGHT I AM CARRYING TO SLEEP

_____

1 THING I DID TO MOVE FORWARD

_____

_____

DAILY

I AM GRATEFUL FOR

_____
_____
_____

MOOD TRACKER

SELF-CARE

MY AFFIRMATION FOR THE DAY

_____
_____

MY DREAM JOURNAL

_____
_____
_____
_____
_____
_____
_____
_____
_____
_____
_____
_____

SCRIPTING

RITUAL TIME   MINDFUL MINUTES

5
10
15
20
25
30

POSITIVE THOUGHT I AM CARRYING TO SLEEP

_____
_____

1 THING I DID TO MOVE FORWARD

_____
_____
_____

DAILY

I AM GRATEFUL FOR

_____
_____
_____

MOOD TRACKER

😠 😟 😐 🙂 😄

SELF-CARE

MY AFFIRMATION FOR THE DAY

_____
_____

MY DREAM JOURNAL

_____
_____
_____
_____
_____
_____
_____
_____

SCRIPTING

_____
_____
_____
_____
_____
_____
_____
_____
_____
_____
_____
_____
_____
_____
_____
_____
_____
_____
_____

RITUAL TIME   MINDFUL MINUTES

5
10
15
20
25
30

POSITIVE THOUGHT I AM CARRYING TO SLEEP

_____
_____

1 THING I DID TO MOVE FORWARD

_____
_____
_____

DAILY

I AM GRATEFUL FOR

_____
_____
_____

MOOD TRACKER

SELF-CARE

MY AFFIRMATION FOR THE DAY

_____
_____

MY DREAM JOURNAL

_____
_____
_____
_____
_____
_____
_____
_____

SCRIPTING

_____
_____
_____
_____
_____
_____
_____
_____
_____
_____
_____
_____
_____
_____
_____

_____
_____
_____
_____

RITUAL TIME

MINDFUL MINUTES

5
10
15
20
25
30

POSITIVE THOUGHT I AM CARRYING TO SLEEP

_____
_____

1 THING I DID TO MOVE FORWARD

_____
_____
_____

WEEK AHEAD

Sunday

Monday

Tuesday

Wednesday

Thursday

Friday

Saturday

NOTES:

DAILY

I AM GRATEFUL FOR

_____

_____

_____

MOOD TRACKER

SELF-CARE

MY AFFIRMATION FOR THE DAY

_____

_____

MY DREAM JOURNAL

_____

_____

_____

_____

_____

_____

_____

_____

_____

_____

_____

SCRIPTING

_____

_____

_____

_____

_____

_____

_____

_____

_____

_____

_____

_____

_____

_____

_____

_____

_____

RITUAL TIME   MINDFUL MINUTES

5
10
15
20
25
30

POSITIVE THOUGHT I AM CARRYING TO SLEEP

_____

_____

1 THING I DID TO MOVE FORWARD

_____

_____

_____

DAILY

I AM GRATEFUL FOR

_____
_____
_____

MOOD TRACKER

SELF-CARE

MY AFFIRMATION FOR THE DAY

_____
_____

MY DREAM JOURNAL

_____
_____
_____
_____
_____
_____
_____

_____
_____
_____
_____

SCRIPTING

_____
_____
_____
_____
_____
_____
_____
_____
_____
_____
_____
_____
_____
_____

RITUAL TIME   MINDFUL MINUTES

5
10
15
20
25
30

POSITIVE THOUGHT I AM CARRYING TO SLEEP

_____
_____

1 THING I DID TO MOVE FORWARD

_____
_____
_____

DAILY

I AM GRATEFUL FOR

_____
_____
_____

MOOD TRACKER

SELF-CARE

MY AFFIRMATION FOR THE DAY

_____
_____

MY DREAM JOURNAL

_____
_____
_____
_____
_____
_____
_____
_____
_____

SCRIPTING

RITUAL TIME

MINDFUL MINUTES

5
10
15
20
25
30

POSITIVE THOUGHT I AM CARRYING TO SLEEP

_____
_____

1 THING I DID TO MOVE FORWARD

_____
_____
_____

DAILY

I AM GRATEFUL FOR

_____
_____
_____

MOOD TRACKER

SELF-CARE

MY AFFIRMATION FOR THE DAY

_____
_____

MY DREAM JOURNAL

_____
_____
_____
_____
_____
_____
_____
_____

SCRIPTING

_____
_____
_____
_____
_____
_____
_____
_____
_____
_____
_____
_____
_____
_____

RITUAL TIME   MINDFUL MINUTES

5
10
15
20
25
30

POSITIVE THOUGHT I AM CARRYING TO SLEEP

_____
_____

1 THING I DID TO MOVE FORWARD

_____
_____

DAILY

I AM GRATEFUL FOR

_____
_____
_____

MOOD TRACKER

SELF-CARE

MY AFFIRMATION FOR THE DAY

_____
_____

MY DREAM JOURNAL

_____
_____
_____
_____
_____
_____
_____

_____
_____
_____
_____

SCRIPTING

_____
_____
_____
_____
_____
_____
_____
_____
_____
_____
_____
_____
_____
_____
_____

RITUAL TIME   MINDFUL MINUTES

5
10
15
20
25
30

POSITIVE THOUGHT I AM CARRYING TO SLEEP

_____
_____

1 THING I DID TO MOVE FORWARD

_____
_____
_____

DAILY

I AM GRATEFUL FOR

_____
_____
_____

MOOD TRACKER

SELF-CARE

MY AFFIRMATION FOR THE DAY

_____
_____

MY DREAM JOURNAL

_____
_____
_____
_____
_____
_____
_____
_____

_____
_____
_____
_____

SCRIPTING

_____
_____
_____
_____
_____
_____
_____
_____
_____
_____
_____

RITUAL TIME   MINDFUL MINUTES

5
10
15
20
25
30

POSITIVE THOUGHT I AM CARRYING TO SLEEP

_____
_____

1 THING I DID TO MOVE FORWARD

_____
_____
_____

DAILY

I AM GRATEFUL FOR

_____
_____
_____

MOOD TRACKER

😠 😦 😐 🙂 😃

SELF-CARE

MY AFFIRMATION FOR THE DAY

_____
_____

MY DREAM JOURNAL

_____
_____
_____
_____
_____
_____
_____
_____

SCRIPTING

_____
_____
_____
_____
_____
_____
_____
_____
_____
_____
_____
_____
_____

_____
_____
_____
_____

RITUAL TIME   MINDFUL MINUTES

5
10
15
20
25
30

POSITIVE THOUGHT I AM CARRYING TO SLEEP

_____
_____

1 THING I DID TO MOVE FORWARD

_____
_____
_____

WEEK AHEAD

Sunday
_____
_____
_____
_____
_____
_____

Monday
_____
_____
_____
_____
_____
_____

Tuesday
_____
_____
_____
_____
_____
_____

Wednesday
_____
_____
_____
_____
_____
_____

Thursday
_____
_____
_____
_____
_____

Friday
_____
_____
_____
_____
_____
_____

Saturday
_____
_____
_____
_____
_____

NOTES:

DAILY

I AM GRATEFUL FOR

_____
_____
_____

MOOD TRACKER

😠 😦 😐 🙂 😀

SELF-CARE

MY AFFIRMATION FOR THE DAY

_____
_____

MY DREAM JOURNAL

_____
_____
_____
_____
_____
_____
_____
_____
_____
_____
_____
_____

SCRIPTING

_____
_____
_____
_____
_____
_____
_____
_____
_____
_____
_____
_____
_____
_____
_____

RITUAL TIME   MINDFUL MINUTES

5
10
15
20
25
30

POSITIVE THOUGHT I AM CARRYING TO SLEEP

_____
_____

1 THING I DID TO MOVE FORWARD

_____
_____
_____

DAILY

I AM GRATEFUL FOR

_____
_____
_____

MOOD TRACKER

SELF-CARE

MY AFFIRMATION FOR THE DAY

_____
_____

MY DREAM JOURNAL

_____
_____
_____
_____
_____
_____
_____

SCRIPTING

_____
_____
_____
_____
_____
_____
_____
_____
_____
_____
_____
_____
_____

_____
_____
_____
_____

RITUAL TIME

MINDFUL MINUTES

5
10
15
20
25
30

POSITIVE THOUGHT I AM CARRYING TO SLEEP

_____
_____

1 THING I DID TO MOVE FORWARD

_____
_____
_____

THIS LUNATION

☐ Full Moon   ☐ New Moon

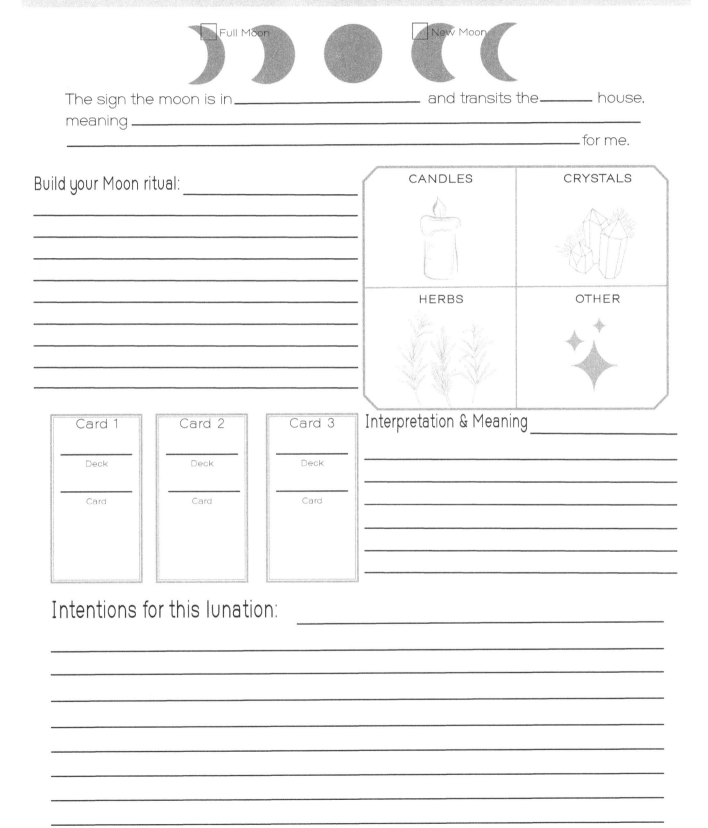

The sign the moon is in _____ and transits the _____ house,
meaning _____
_____ for me.

Build your Moon ritual: _____

CANDLES	CRYSTALS
HERBS	OTHER

Card 1	Card 2	Card 3
_____ Deck	_____ Deck	_____ Deck
Card	Card	Card

Interpretation & Meaning _____

Intentions for this lunation: _____

DAILY

I AM GRATEFUL FOR

_____

_____

_____

MOOD TRACKER

SELF-CARE

MY AFFIRMATION FOR THE DAY

_____

MY DREAM JOURNAL

_____

_____

_____

_____

_____

_____

_____

_____

_____

_____

SCRIPTING

_____

_____

_____

_____

_____

_____

_____

_____

_____

_____

_____

_____

_____

RITUAL TIME   MINDFUL MINUTES

5
10
15
20
25
30

POSITIVE THOUGHT I AM CARRYING TO SLEEP

_____

_____

1 THING I DID TO MOVE FORWARD

_____

_____

_____

DAILY

I AM GRATEFUL FOR

_____
_____
_____

MOOD TRACKER

SELF-CARE

MY AFFIRMATION FOR THE DAY

_____
_____

MY DREAM JOURNAL

_____
_____
_____
_____
_____
_____
_____

SCRIPTING

_____
_____
_____
_____
_____
_____
_____
_____
_____
_____
_____
_____
_____
_____
_____

_____
_____
_____
_____

RITUAL TIME   MINDFUL MINUTES

5
10
15
20
25
30

POSITIVE THOUGHT I AM CARRYING TO SLEEP

_____
_____

1 THING I DID TO MOVE FORWARD

_____
_____
_____

DAILY

I AM GRATEFUL FOR

_____
_____
_____

MOOD TRACKER

😠 🙁 😐 🙂 😃

SELF-CARE

MY AFFIRMATION FOR THE DAY

_____
_____

MY DREAM JOURNAL

_____
_____
_____
_____
_____
_____
_____
_____

_____
_____
_____
_____

SCRIPTING

_____
_____
_____
_____
_____
_____
_____
_____
_____
_____
_____
_____
_____
_____
_____

RITUAL TIME

MINDFUL MINUTES

← 5 →
← 10 →
← 15 →
← 20 →
← 25 →
← 30 →

POSITIVE THOUGHT I AM CARRYING TO SLEEP

_____
_____

1 THING I DID TO MOVE FORWARD

_____
_____
_____

DAILY

I AM GRATEFUL FOR

_____
_____
_____

MOOD TRACKER

SELF-CARE

MY AFFIRMATION FOR THE DAY

_____
_____

MY DREAM JOURNAL

_____
_____
_____
_____
_____
_____
_____
_____

SCRIPTING

_____
_____
_____
_____
_____
_____
_____
_____
_____
_____
_____
_____
_____
_____
_____
_____
_____

_____
_____
_____
_____

RITUAL TIME

MINDFUL MINUTES

5
10
15
20
25
30

POSITIVE THOUGHT I AM CARRYING TO SLEEP

_____
_____

1 THING I DID TO MOVE FORWARD

_____
_____
_____

DAILY

I AM GRATEFUL FOR

_____

_____

_____

MOOD TRACKER

SELF-CARE

MY AFFIRMATION FOR THE DAY

_____

_____

MY DREAM JOURNAL

_____

_____

_____

_____

_____

_____

_____

_____

_____

SCRIPTING

_____

_____

_____

_____

_____

_____

_____

_____

_____

_____

_____

_____

_____

_____

RITUAL TIME   MINDFUL MINUTES

5
10
15
20
25
30

POSITIVE THOUGHT I AM CARRYING TO SLEEP

_____

_____

1 THING I DID TO MOVE FORWARD

_____

_____

_____

WEEK AHEAD

Sunday

Thursday

Monday

Friday

Tuesday

Saturday

Wednesday

NOTES:

DAILY

I AM GRATEFUL FOR

_____
_____
_____

MOOD TRACKER

😠 ☹️ 😐 🙂 😃

SELF-CARE

MY AFFIRMATION FOR THE DAY

_____
_____

MY DREAM JOURNAL

_____
_____
_____
_____
_____
_____
_____
_____

_____
_____
_____
_____

SCRIPTING

_____
_____
_____
_____
_____
_____
_____
_____
_____
_____
_____
_____
_____
_____

RITUAL TIME   MINDFUL MINUTES

5
10
15
20
25
30

POSITIVE THOUGHT I AM CARRYING TO SLEEP

_____
_____

1 THING I DID TO MOVE FORWARD

_____
_____
_____

DAILY

I AM GRATEFUL FOR

_____
_____
_____

MOOD TRACKER

SELF-CARE

MY AFFIRMATION FOR THE DAY

_____
_____

MY DREAM JOURNAL

_____
_____
_____
_____
_____
_____
_____
_____
_____
_____
_____
_____

SCRIPTING

_____
_____
_____
_____
_____
_____
_____
_____
_____
_____
_____
_____
_____
_____
_____

RITUAL TIME   MINDFUL MINUTES

5
10
15
20
25
30

POSITIVE THOUGHT I AM CARRYING TO SLEEP

_____
_____

1 THING I DID TO MOVE FORWARD

_____
_____
_____

DAILY

I AM GRATEFUL FOR

_____
_____
_____

MOOD TRACKER

😠 ☹️ 😐 🙂 😄

SELF-CARE

MY AFFIRMATION FOR THE DAY

_____
_____

MY DREAM JOURNAL

_____
_____
_____
_____
_____
_____
_____
_____
_____
_____
_____

SCRIPTING

_____
_____
_____
_____
_____
_____
_____
_____
_____
_____
_____
_____
_____
_____
_____

RITUAL TIME   MINDFUL MINUTES

5
10
15
20
25
30

POSITIVE THOUGHT I AM CARRYING TO SLEEP

_____
_____

1 THING I DID TO MOVE FORWARD

_____
_____
_____

DAILY

I AM GRATEFUL FOR

_____
_____
_____

MOOD TRACKER

😠 ☹️ 😐 🙂 😀

SELF-CARE

MY AFFIRMATION FOR THE DAY

_____
_____

MY DREAM JOURNAL

_____
_____
_____
_____
_____
_____
_____
_____

_____
_____
_____
_____

SCRIPTING

_____
_____
_____
_____
_____
_____
_____
_____
_____
_____
_____
_____
_____
_____
_____
_____
_____
_____

RITUAL TIME

MINDFUL MINUTES

5
10
15
20
25
30

POSITIVE THOUGHT I AM CARRYING TO SLEEP

_____
_____

1 THING I DID TO MOVE FORWARD

_____
_____
_____

DAILY

I AM GRATEFUL FOR

_____

_____

_____

MOOD TRACKER

SELF-CARE

MY AFFIRMATION FOR THE DAY

_____

_____

MY DREAM JOURNAL

_____

_____

_____

_____

_____

_____

_____

SCRIPTING

_____

_____

_____

_____

_____

_____

_____

_____

_____

_____

_____

_____

_____

_____

_____

_____

_____

_____

_____

RITUAL TIME   MINDFUL MINUTES

5
10
15
20
25
30

POSITIVE THOUGHT I AM CARRYING TO SLEEP

_____

_____

1 THING I DID TO MOVE FORWARD

_____

_____

_____

DAILY

I AM GRATEFUL FOR

_____
_____
_____

MOOD TRACKER

😠 😞 😐 🙂 😃

SELF-CARE

MY AFFIRMATION FOR THE DAY

_____
_____

MY DREAM JOURNAL

_____
_____
_____
_____
_____
_____
_____

SCRIPTING

_____
_____
_____
_____
_____
_____
_____
_____
_____
_____
_____
_____
_____
_____
_____

_____
_____
_____
_____

RITUAL TIME

MINDFUL MINUTES

5
10
15
20
25
30

POSITIVE THOUGHT I AM CARRYING TO SLEEP

_____
_____

1 THING I DID TO MOVE FORWARD

_____
_____
_____

DAILY

I AM GRATEFUL FOR

_____

_____

_____

MOOD TRACKER

😠 😞 😐 🙂 😄

SELF-CARE

MY AFFIRMATION FOR THE DAY

_____

_____

MY DREAM JOURNAL

_____

_____

_____

_____

_____

_____

_____

_____

_____

_____

_____

_____

SCRIPTING

_____

_____

_____

_____

_____

_____

_____

_____

_____

_____

_____

_____

_____

_____

_____

_____

RITUAL TIME MINDFUL MINUTES

5
10
15
20
25
30

POSITIVE THOUGHT I AM CARRYING TO SLEEP

_____

_____

1 THING I DID TO MOVE FORWARD

_____

_____

_____

WEEK AHEAD

Sunday

Thursday

Monday

Friday

Tuesday

Saturday

NOTES:

Wednesday

DAILY

I AM GRATEFUL FOR

_____

_____

_____

MOOD TRACKER

SELF-CARE

MY AFFIRMATION FOR THE DAY

_____

_____

MY DREAM JOURNAL

_____

_____

_____

_____

_____

_____

_____

_____

SCRIPTING

_____

_____

_____

_____

_____

_____

_____

_____

_____

_____

_____

_____

_____

_____

_____

_____

_____

_____

RITUAL TIME   MINDFUL MINUTES

5
10
15
20
25
30

POSITIVE THOUGHT I AM CARRYING TO SLEEP

_____

_____

1 THING I DID TO MOVE FORWARD

_____

_____

_____

DAILY

I AM GRATEFUL FOR

_____

_____

_____

MOOD TRACKER

SELF-CARE

MY AFFIRMATION FOR THE DAY

_____

_____

MY DREAM JOURNAL

_____

_____

_____

_____

_____

_____

_____

_____

SCRIPTING

_____

_____

_____

_____

_____

_____

_____

_____

_____

_____

_____

_____

_____

_____

_____

_____

_____

_____

_____

_____

_____

_____

_____

_____

_____

_____

RITUAL TIME

MINDFUL MINUTES

5
10
15
20
25
30

POSITIVE THOUGHT I AM CARRYING TO SLEEP

_____

_____

1 THING I DID TO MOVE FORWARD

_____

_____

_____

THIS LUNATION

☐ Full Moon   ☐ New Moon

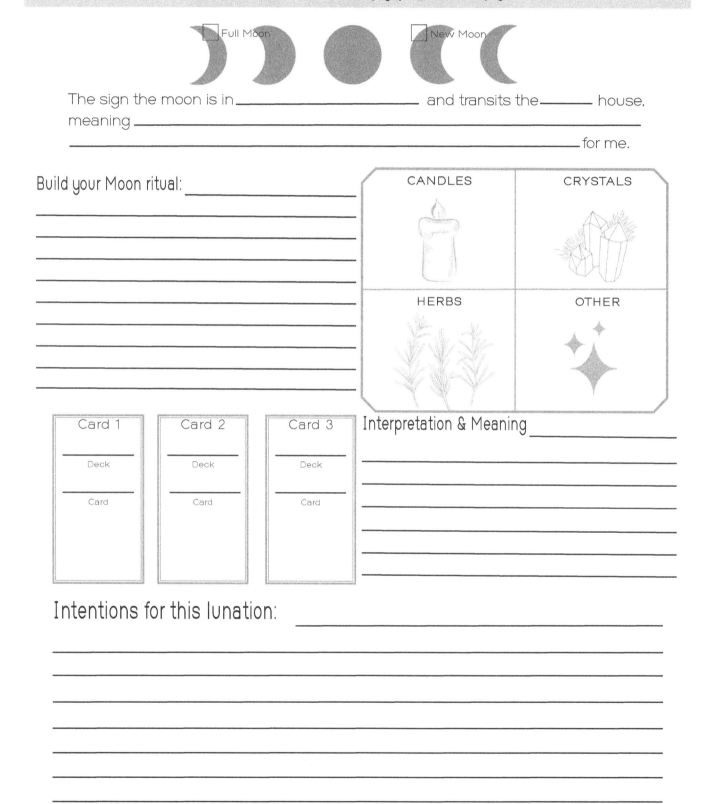

The sign the moon is in _____ and transits the _____ house, meaning _____

_____ for me.

Build your Moon ritual: _____

_____

_____

_____

_____

_____

_____

_____

CANDLES	CRYSTALS
HERBS	OTHER

Card 1	Card 2	Card 3
_____	_____	_____
Deck	Deck	Deck
_____	_____	_____
Card	Card	Card

Interpretation & Meaning _____

_____

_____

_____

_____

_____

Intentions for this lunation:

_____

_____

_____

_____

_____

_____

_____

_____

DAILY

I AM GRATEFUL FOR

_____
_____
_____

MOOD TRACKER

SELF-CARE

MY AFFIRMATION FOR THE DAY

_____
_____

MY DREAM JOURNAL

_____
_____
_____
_____
_____
_____
_____
_____

SCRIPTING

_____
_____
_____
_____
_____
_____
_____
_____
_____
_____
_____
_____
_____
_____

_____
_____
_____
_____

RITUAL TIME   MINDFUL MINUTES

5
10
15
20
25
30

POSITIVE THOUGHT I AM CARRYING TO SLEEP

_____
_____

1 THING I DID TO MOVE FORWARD

_____
_____
_____

JUNE

SUNDAY	MONDAY	TUESDAY	WEDNESDAY
			1
5	6	7	8
12	13	14 FULL MOON IN SAGITARRIUS SUPER MOON	15
19 FATHER'S DAY	20	21	22 CANCER SEASON
26	27 NEPTUNE RETROGRADE STARTS	28 NEW MOON IN CANCER	29

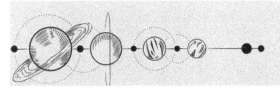

2022

THURSDAY	FRIDAY	SATURDAY	NOTES
	2	3	4	
		MERCURY RETROGRADE ENDS	SATURN RETROGRADE STARTS	
9	10	11	
16	17	18	
23	24	25	
30			

SMART Goal & Action Plan

This month I will accomplish...

_____
_____
_____
_____
_____
_____
_____

Make your goals easier by making them SMART goals. Know what you want to accomplish and then simply word it to be specific, measureable, attainable, realistic, and time-specific.

Specific → Measurable → Attainable → Realistic → Time-Specific

My SMART Goal

_____
_____
_____
_____

What I need to attract to do this

_____
_____
_____
_____

My Action Plan

_____
_____
_____
_____

What I need to release to do this

_____
_____
_____
_____

CREATING THE REALITY YOU WANT

Scripting
Check-in

How has your scripting been going? Take some time at the beginning of the new month to look over last month's work. Did you use enough detail? Did you honestly believe the changes were possible? Did any of your scripting come true? Use this private space to be honest with yourself. Include changes you want to make to your scripting next month.

_____

_____

_____

_____

_____

_____

_____

_____

_____

Science tells us that it takes roughly 30 days to break or build habits, this wheel will help you keep track of how well you are showing up for your habits. Add up to 7 habits you want to track, whether you want to break old/unhealthy habits or build new/healthier ones.

To make it more interactive use the following key to color-code your habits, by adding the color of your choice. If there is a day you don't have a positive result simply don't color in that day. From month to month evaluate how you are doing with your goals, look for patterns where you've had success or challenges.

☐ Habit 1   ☐ Habit 2   ☐ Habit 3

☐ Habit 4   ☐ Habit 5   ☐ Habit 6

☐ Habit 7

JUNE
STRAWBERRY MOON

ZODIAC

 GEMINI CANCER

DEITIES

JUNO
HERA
ISIS
NEITH
CERRIDWEN
GREEN MAN

ELEMENT

 AIR WATER

HERBS

- MEADOWSWEET
- VERVAIN
- TANSY
- ALMOND
- DILL
- LILY
- CLOVER
- LEMONGRASS

CRYSTALS

- PEARL
- MOONSTONE
- ALEXANDRITE
- CITRINE
- BLUE LACE AGATE
- HERKIMER DIAMOND

ENERGY

- COMMITMENT
- LOVE
- GOOD HEALTH
- ENERGY INCREASE
- EVOLUTION

COLORS:

YELLOW
GREEN
ORANGE

MAGIC

- COMMUNICATION
- TRANSFORMATION
- CLARIFICATION
- FAIRY MAGIC
- EMPOWERMENT

DIVINATION TRACKER

DATE	PULL	MESSAGE

DAILY

I AM GRATEFUL FOR

_____
_____
_____

MOOD TRACKER

SELF-CARE

MY AFFIRMATION FOR THE DAY

_____
_____

MY DREAM JOURNAL

_____
_____
_____
_____
_____
_____
_____
_____

SCRIPTING

_____
_____
_____
_____
_____
_____
_____
_____
_____
_____
_____
_____
_____
_____

_____
_____
_____

RITUAL TIME   MINDFUL MINUTES

5
10
15
20
25
30

POSITIVE THOUGHT I AM CARRYING TO SLEEP

_____
_____

1 THING I DID TO MOVE FORWARD

_____
_____
_____

DAILY

I AM GRATEFUL FOR

_____
_____
_____

MOOD TRACKER

SELF-CARE

MY AFFIRMATION FOR THE DAY

_____
_____

MY DREAM JOURNAL

_____
_____
_____
_____
_____
_____
_____
_____
_____

SCRIPTING

_____
_____
_____
_____
_____
_____
_____
_____
_____
_____
_____
_____
_____
_____
_____

_____
_____
_____

RITUAL TIME   MINDFUL MINUTES

5
10
15
20
25
30

POSITIVE THOUGHT I AM CARRYING TO SLEEP

_____
_____

1 THING I DID TO MOVE FORWARD

_____
_____
_____

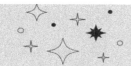

DAILY

I AM GRATEFUL FOR

_____
_____
_____

MOOD TRACKER

SELF-CARE

MY AFFIRMATION FOR THE DAY

_____
_____

MY DREAM JOURNAL

_____
_____
_____
_____
_____
_____
_____

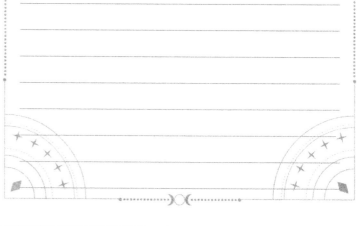

SCRIPTING

_____
_____
_____
_____
_____
_____
_____
_____
_____
_____
_____
_____
_____
_____
_____
_____

RITUAL TIME   MINDFUL MINUTES

5
10
15
20
25
30

POSITIVE THOUGHT I AM CARRYING TO SLEEP

_____
_____

1 THING I DID TO MOVE FORWARD

_____
_____
_____

DAILY

I AM GRATEFUL FOR

_____
_____
_____

MOOD TRACKER

😠 😟 😐 🙂 😀

SELF-CARE

MY AFFIRMATION FOR THE DAY

_____
_____

MY DREAM JOURNAL

_____
_____
_____
_____
_____
_____
_____
_____

SCRIPTING

_____
_____
_____
_____
_____
_____
_____
_____
_____
_____
_____
_____
_____
_____

_____
_____
_____
_____

RITUAL TIME

MINDFUL MINUTES

5
10
15
20
25
30

POSITIVE THOUGHT I AM CARRYING TO SLEEP

_____
_____

1 THING I DID TO MOVE FORWARD

_____
_____
_____

WEEK AHEAD

Sunday

Thursday

Monday

Friday

Tuesday

Saturday

Wednesday

NOTES:

DAILY

I AM GRATEFUL FOR

_____

_____

_____

MOOD TRACKER

SELF-CARE

MY AFFIRMATION FOR THE DAY

_____

_____

MY DREAM JOURNAL

_____

_____

_____

_____

_____

_____

_____

_____

_____

_____

_____

SCRIPTING

_____

_____

_____

_____

_____

_____

_____

_____

_____

_____

_____

_____

_____

RITUAL TIME   MINDFUL MINUTES

5
10
15
20
25
30

POSITIVE THOUGHT I AM CARRYING TO SLEEP

_____

_____

1 THING I DID TO MOVE FORWARD

_____

_____

_____

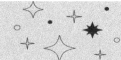

DAILY

I AM GRATEFUL FOR

_____

_____

_____

MOOD TRACKER

SELF-CARE

MY AFFIRMATION FOR THE DAY

_____

_____

MY DREAM JOURNAL

_____

_____

_____

_____

_____

_____

_____

SCRIPTING

_____

_____

_____

_____

_____

_____

_____

_____

_____

_____

_____

_____

_____

_____

_____

_____

RITUAL TIME   MINDFUL MINUTES

5
10
15
20
25
30

POSITIVE THOUGHT I AM CARRYING TO SLEEP

_____

_____

1 THING I DID TO MOVE FORWARD

_____

_____

DAILY

I AM GRATEFUL FOR

_____
_____
_____

MOOD TRACKER

SELF-CARE

MY AFFIRMATION FOR THE DAY

_____
_____

MY DREAM JOURNAL

_____
_____
_____
_____
_____
_____
_____
_____

_____
_____
_____

SCRIPTING

RITUAL TIME   MINDFUL MINUTES

5
10
15
20
25
30

POSITIVE THOUGHT I AM CARRYING TO SLEEP

_____
_____

1 THING I DID TO MOVE FORWARD

_____
_____
_____

DAILY

I AM GRATEFUL FOR

_____
_____
_____

MOOD TRACKER

😠 😦 😐 🙂 😃

SELF-CARE

MY AFFIRMATION FOR THE DAY

_____
_____

MY DREAM JOURNAL

_____
_____
_____
_____
_____
_____
_____
_____
_____
_____
_____
_____

SCRIPTING

_____
_____
_____
_____
_____
_____
_____
_____
_____
_____
_____
_____
_____
_____

RITUAL TIME

MINDFUL MINUTES

5
10
15
20
25
30

POSITIVE THOUGHT I AM CARRYING TO SLEEP

_____
_____

1 THING I DID TO MOVE FORWARD

_____
_____

DAILY

I AM GRATEFUL FOR

_____
_____
_____

MOOD TRACKER

SELF-CARE

MY AFFIRMATION FOR THE DAY

_____
_____

MY DREAM JOURNAL

_____
_____
_____
_____
_____
_____
_____

_____
_____
_____
_____

SCRIPTING

_____
_____
_____
_____
_____
_____
_____
_____
_____
_____
_____
_____
_____
_____

RITUAL TIME   MINDFUL MINUTES

5
10
15
20
25
30

POSITIVE THOUGHT I AM CARRYING TO SLEEP

_____
_____

1 THING I DID TO MOVE FORWARD

_____
_____
_____

DAILY

I AM GRATEFUL FOR

_____
_____
_____

MOOD TRACKER

SELF-CARE

MY AFFIRMATION FOR THE DAY

_____
_____

MY DREAM JOURNAL

_____
_____
_____
_____
_____
_____
_____
_____
_____

SCRIPTING

_____
_____
_____
_____
_____
_____
_____
_____
_____
_____
_____
_____
_____
_____
_____
_____

_____
_____
_____
_____

RITUAL TIME   MINDFUL MINUTES

5
10
15
20
25
30

POSITIVE THOUGHT I AM CARRYING TO SLEEP

_____
_____

1 THING I DID TO MOVE FORWARD

_____
_____
_____

DAILY

I AM GRATEFUL FOR

_____
_____
_____

MOOD TRACKER

SELF-CARE

MY AFFIRMATION FOR THE DAY

_____
_____

MY DREAM JOURNAL

_____
_____
_____
_____
_____
_____
_____
_____

SCRIPTING

_____
_____
_____
_____
_____
_____
_____
_____
_____
_____
_____
_____
_____
_____

_____
_____
_____

RITUAL TIME   MINDFUL MINUTES

5
10
15
20
25
30

POSITIVE THOUGHT I AM CARRYING TO SLEEP

_____
_____

1 THING I DID TO MOVE FORWARD

_____
_____
_____

WEEK AHEAD

Sunday
_____
_____
_____
_____
_____
_____

Monday
_____
_____
_____
_____
_____
_____

Tuesday
_____
_____
_____
_____
_____
_____

Wednesday
_____
_____
_____
_____
_____
_____

Thursday
_____
_____
_____
_____
_____
_____

Friday
_____
_____
_____
_____
_____
_____

Saturday
_____
_____
_____
_____
_____
_____

NOTES:

DAILY

I AM GRATEFUL FOR

_____
_____
_____

MOOD TRACKER

SELF-CARE

MY AFFIRMATION FOR THE DAY

_____
_____

MY DREAM JOURNAL

_____
_____
_____
_____
_____
_____
_____

_____
_____
_____
_____

SCRIPTING

_____
_____
_____
_____
_____
_____
_____
_____
_____
_____
_____
_____
_____
_____
_____
_____
_____

RITUAL TIME

MINDFUL MINUTES

5
10
15
20
25
30

POSITIVE THOUGHT I AM CARRYING TO SLEEP

_____
_____

1 THING I DID TO MOVE FORWARD

_____
_____
_____

DAILY

I AM GRATEFUL FOR

_____
_____
_____

MOOD TRACKER

😠 😞 😐 🙂 😄

SELF-CARE

MY AFFIRMATION FOR THE DAY

_____
_____

MY DREAM JOURNAL

_____
_____
_____
_____
_____
_____
_____
_____

SCRIPTING

_____
_____
_____
_____
_____
_____
_____
_____
_____
_____
_____
_____
_____

_____
_____
_____
_____

RITUAL TIME

← 5 →
← 10 →
← 15 →
← 20 →
← 25 →
← 30 →

MINDFUL MINUTES

POSITIVE THOUGHT I AM CARRYING TO SLEEP

_____
_____

1 THING I DID TO MOVE FORWARD

_____
_____
_____

DAILY

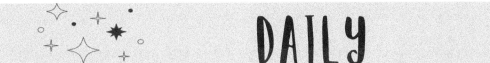

I AM GRATEFUL FOR

_____
_____
_____

MOOD TRACKER

😠 😞 😐 🙂 😄

SELF-CARE

MY AFFIRMATION FOR THE DAY

_____
_____

MY DREAM JOURNAL

_____
_____
_____
_____
_____
_____
_____
_____

SCRIPTING

_____
_____
_____
_____
_____
_____
_____
_____
_____
_____
_____
_____
_____
_____
_____
_____

_____
_____
_____
_____

RITUAL TIME   MINDFUL MINUTES

5
10
15
20
25
30

POSITIVE THOUGHT I AM CARRYING TO SLEEP

_____
_____

1 THING I DID TO MOVE FORWARD

_____
_____

THIS LUNATION

☐ Full Moon   ☐ New Moon

The sign the moon is in _____ and transits the _____ house, meaning _____
_____ for me.

Build your Moon ritual: _____
_____
_____
_____
_____
_____
_____
_____
_____
_____

CANDLES	CRYSTALS
HERBS	OTHER

Card 1	Card 2	Card 3
_____ Deck _____ Card	_____ Deck _____ Card	_____ Deck _____ Card

Interpretation & Meaning _____
_____
_____
_____
_____
_____
_____

Intentions for this lunation: _____
_____
_____
_____
_____
_____
_____
_____

DAILY

I AM GRATEFUL FOR

_____

_____

_____

MOOD TRACKER

SELF-CARE

MY AFFIRMATION FOR THE DAY

_____

_____

MY DREAM JOURNAL

_____

_____

_____

_____

_____

_____

_____

_____

_____

_____

_____

_____

SCRIPTING

_____

_____

_____

_____

_____

_____

_____

_____

_____

_____

_____

_____

_____

_____

_____

_____

RITUAL TIME   MINDFUL MINUTES

5

10

15

20

25

30

POSITIVE THOUGHT I AM CARRYING TO SLEEP

_____

_____

1 THING I DID TO MOVE FORWARD

_____

_____

_____

DAILY

I AM GRATEFUL FOR

_____
_____
_____

MOOD TRACKER

😠 😞 😐 🙂 😀

SELF-CARE

MY AFFIRMATION FOR THE DAY

_____
_____

MY DREAM JOURNAL

_____
_____
_____
_____
_____
_____
_____

SCRIPTING

_____
_____
_____
_____
_____
_____
_____
_____
_____
_____
_____
_____
_____
_____
_____
_____

_____
_____
_____
_____

RITUAL TIME   MINDFUL MINUTES

5
10
15
20
25
30

POSITIVE THOUGHT I AM CARRYING TO SLEEP

_____
_____

1 THING I DID TO MOVE FORWARD

_____
_____
_____

DAILY

I AM GRATEFUL FOR

_____
_____
_____

MOOD TRACKER

SELF-CARE

MY AFFIRMATION FOR THE DAY

_____
_____

MY DREAM JOURNAL

_____
_____
_____
_____
_____
_____
_____

_____
_____
_____
_____

SCRIPTING

_____
_____
_____
_____
_____
_____
_____
_____
_____
_____
_____
_____
_____
_____

RITUAL TIME   MINDFUL MINUTES

5
10
15
20
25
30

POSITIVE THOUGHT I AM CARRYING TO SLEEP

_____
_____

1 THING I DID TO MOVE FORWARD

_____
_____
_____

DAILY

I AM GRATEFUL FOR

_____
_____
_____

MOOD TRACKER

😠 🙁 😐 🙂 😄

SELF-CARE

MY AFFIRMATION FOR THE DAY

_____
_____

MY DREAM JOURNAL

_____
_____
_____
_____
_____
_____
_____
_____
_____
_____
_____

SCRIPTING

_____
_____
_____
_____
_____
_____
_____
_____
_____
_____
_____
_____
_____
_____
_____

RITUAL TIME   MINDFUL MINUTES

5
10
15
20
25
30

POSITIVE THOUGHT I AM CARRYING TO SLEEP

_____
_____

1 THING I DID TO MOVE FORWARD

_____
_____
_____

WEEK AHEAD

Sunday

Monday

Tuesday

Wednesday

Thursday

Friday

Saturday

NOTES:

DAILY

I AM GRATEFUL FOR

_____
_____
_____

MOOD TRACKER

😠 😞 😐 🙂 😃

SELF-CARE

MY AFFIRMATION FOR THE DAY

_____
_____

MY DREAM JOURNAL

_____
_____
_____
_____
_____
_____
_____
_____

_____
_____
_____
_____

SCRIPTING

_____
_____
_____
_____
_____
_____
_____
_____
_____
_____
_____
_____
_____
_____
_____

RITUAL TIME

MINDFUL MINUTES

5
10
15
20
25
30

POSITIVE THOUGHT I AM CARRYING TO SLEEP

_____
_____

1 THING I DID TO MOVE FORWARD

_____
_____
_____

DAILY

I AM GRATEFUL FOR

_____

_____

_____

MOOD TRACKER

😠 😞 😐 🙂 😄

SELF-CARE

MY AFFIRMATION FOR THE DAY

_____

_____

MY DREAM JOURNAL

_____

_____

_____

_____

_____

_____

_____

SCRIPTING

_____

_____

_____

_____

_____

_____

_____

_____

_____

_____

_____

_____

_____

_____

_____

_____

_____

_____

_____

RITUAL TIME

MINDFUL MINUTES

5
10
15
20
25
30

POSITIVE THOUGHT I AM CARRYING TO SLEEP

_____

_____

1 THING I DID TO MOVE FORWARD

_____

_____

_____

DAILY

I AM GRATEFUL FOR

_____
_____
_____

MOOD TRACKER

SELF-CARE

MY AFFIRMATION FOR THE DAY

_____
_____

MY DREAM JOURNAL

_____
_____
_____
_____
_____
_____
_____
_____
_____

SCRIPTING

_____
_____
_____
_____
_____
_____
_____
_____
_____
_____
_____
_____
_____
_____
_____
_____
_____

_____
_____
_____
_____

RITUAL TIME   MINDFUL MINUTES

5
10
15
20
25
30

POSITIVE THOUGHT I AM CARRYING TO SLEEP

_____
_____

1 THING I DID TO MOVE FORWARD

_____
_____
_____

DAILY

I AM GRATEFUL FOR

_____
_____
_____

MOOD TRACKER

SELF-CARE

MY AFFIRMATION FOR THE DAY

_____
_____

MY DREAM JOURNAL

_____
_____
_____
_____
_____
_____
_____
_____
_____
_____
_____
_____

SCRIPTING

_____
_____
_____
_____
_____
_____
_____
_____
_____
_____
_____
_____
_____
_____
_____
_____
_____
_____

RITUAL TIME   MINDFUL MINUTES

5
10
15
20
25
30

POSITIVE THOUGHT I AM CARRYING TO SLEEP

_____
_____

1 THING I DID TO MOVE FORWARD

_____
_____
_____

DAILY

I AM GRATEFUL FOR

_____
_____
_____

MOOD TRACKER

😠 😟 😐 🙂 😄

SELF-CARE

MY AFFIRMATION FOR THE DAY

_____
_____

MY DREAM JOURNAL

_____
_____
_____
_____
_____
_____
_____

_____
_____
_____

SCRIPTING

_____
_____
_____
_____
_____
_____
_____
_____
_____
_____
_____
_____
_____
_____
_____
_____

RITUAL TIME   MINDFUL MINUTES

5
10
15
20
25
30

POSITIVE THOUGHT I AM CARRYING TO SLEEP

_____
_____

1 THING I DID TO MOVE FORWARD

_____
_____
_____

DAILY

I AM GRATEFUL FOR

_____
_____
_____

MOOD TRACKER

😠 😟 😐 🙂 😄

SELF-CARE

MY AFFIRMATION FOR THE DAY

_____
_____

MY DREAM JOURNAL

_____
_____
_____
_____
_____
_____
_____

SCRIPTING

_____
_____
_____
_____
_____
_____
_____
_____
_____
_____
_____
_____
_____
_____
_____
_____

_____
_____
_____
_____

RITUAL TIME   MINDFUL MINUTES

5
10
15
20
25
30

POSITIVE THOUGHT I AM CARRYING TO SLEEP

_____
_____

1 THING I DID TO MOVE FORWARD

_____
_____
_____

DAILY

I AM GRATEFUL FOR

_____
_____
_____

MOOD TRACKER

SELF-CARE

MY AFFIRMATION FOR THE DAY

_____
_____

MY DREAM JOURNAL

_____
_____
_____
_____
_____
_____
_____
_____

SCRIPTING

_____
_____
_____
_____
_____
_____
_____
_____
_____
_____
_____
_____
_____
_____
_____
_____
_____

_____
_____
_____
_____

RITUAL TIME   MINDFUL MINUTES

5
10
15
20
25
30

POSITIVE THOUGHT I AM CARRYING TO SLEEP

_____
_____

1 THING I DID TO MOVE FORWARD

_____
_____
_____

WEEK AHEAD

Sunday

Monday

Tuesday

Wednesday

Thursday

Friday

Saturday

NOTES:

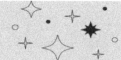

DAILY

I AM GRATEFUL FOR

_____
_____
_____

MOOD TRACKER

😠 🙁 😐 🙂 😄

SELF-CARE

MY AFFIRMATION FOR THE DAY

_____
_____

MY DREAM JOURNAL

_____
_____
_____
_____
_____
_____
_____

SCRIPTING

_____
_____
_____
_____
_____
_____
_____
_____
_____
_____
_____
_____
_____
_____
_____

_____
_____
_____
_____

RITUAL TIME

MINDFUL MINUTES

5
10
15
20
25
30

POSITIVE THOUGHT I AM CARRYING TO SLEEP

_____
_____

1 THING I DID TO MOVE FORWARD

_____
_____
_____

DAILY

I AM GRATEFUL FOR

_____
_____
_____

MOOD TRACKER

SELF-CARE

MY AFFIRMATION FOR THE DAY

_____
_____

MY DREAM JOURNAL

_____
_____
_____
_____
_____
_____
_____
_____

_____
_____
_____
_____

SCRIPTING

_____
_____
_____
_____
_____
_____
_____
_____
_____
_____
_____
_____
_____
_____
_____
_____
_____

RITUAL TIME   MINDFUL MINUTES

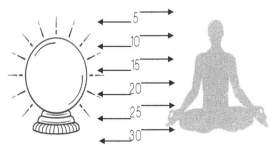

5
10
15
20
25
30

POSITIVE THOUGHT I AM CARRYING TO SLEEP

_____
_____

1 THING I DID TO MOVE FORWARD

_____
_____
_____

DAILY

I AM GRATEFUL FOR

_____
_____
_____

MOOD TRACKER

SELF-CARE

MY AFFIRMATION FOR THE DAY

_____
_____

MY DREAM JOURNAL

_____
_____
_____
_____
_____
_____
_____
_____
_____
_____

SCRIPTING

_____
_____
_____
_____
_____
_____
_____
_____
_____
_____
_____
_____
_____
_____

RITUAL TIME   MINDFUL MINUTES

5
10
15
20
25
30

POSITIVE THOUGHT I AM CARRYING TO SLEEP

_____
_____

1 THING I DID TO MOVE FORWARD

_____
_____

THIS LUNATION

☐ Full Moon   ☐ New Moon

The sign the moon is in _____ and transits the _____ house,
meaning _____
_____ for me.

Build your Moon ritual: _____

_____
_____
_____
_____
_____
_____
_____

CANDLES	CRYSTALS
HERBS	OTHER

Card 1	Card 2	Card 3
_____	_____	_____
Deck	Deck	Deck
_____	_____	_____
Card	Card	Card

Interpretation & Meaning _____

_____
_____
_____
_____
_____
_____

Intentions for this lunation: _____

_____
_____
_____
_____
_____
_____
_____

DAILY

I AM GRATEFUL FOR

_____
_____
_____

MOOD TRACKER

😠 😞 😐 🙂 😄

SELF-CARE

MY AFFIRMATION FOR THE DAY

_____
_____

MY DREAM JOURNAL

_____
_____
_____
_____
_____
_____
_____
_____

_____
_____
_____
_____

SCRIPTING

_____
_____
_____
_____
_____
_____
_____
_____
_____
_____
_____
_____
_____
_____
_____

RITUAL TIME   MINDFUL MINUTES

5
10
15
20
25
30

POSITIVE THOUGHT I AM CARRYING TO SLEEP

_____
_____

1 THING I DID TO MOVE FORWARD

_____
_____
_____

DAILY

I AM GRATEFUL FOR

_____
_____
_____

MOOD TRACKER

😠 😞 😐 🙂 😀

SELF-CARE

MY AFFIRMATION FOR THE DAY

_____
_____

MY DREAM JOURNAL

_____
_____
_____
_____
_____
_____
_____
_____

SCRIPTING

_____
_____
_____
_____
_____
_____
_____
_____
_____
_____
_____
_____
_____
_____
_____
_____

_____
_____
_____
_____

RITUAL TIME

MINDFUL MINUTES

5
10
15
20
25
30

POSITIVE THOUGHT I AM CARRYING TO SLEEP

_____
_____

1 THING I DID TO MOVE FORWARD

_____
_____
_____

JULY

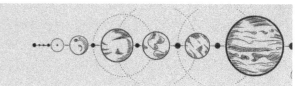

SUNDAY	MONDAY	TUESDAY	WEDNESDAY
3	4 INDEPENDENCE DAY	5	6
10	11	12	13 FULL MOON IN CAPRICORN
17	18	19	20
24	25	26	27
31			

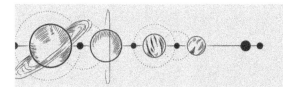

2022

THURSDAY	FRIDAY	SATURDAY	NOTES
	1	2	
7	8	9	
14	15	16	
21	22	23 LEO SEASON	
28 JUPITER RETROGRADE STARTS NEW MOON IN LEO DELTA AQUARIDS	29 METEOR SHOWER	30	

SMART Goal & Action Plan

This month I will accomplish...

_____
_____
_____
_____
_____
_____
_____

Make your goals easier by making them SMART goals. Know what you want to accomplish and then simply word it to be specific, measureable, attainable, realistic, and time-specific.

Specific → Measurable → Attainable → Realistic → Time-Specific

My SMART Goal

_____
_____
_____
_____

What I need to attract to do this

_____
_____
_____
_____

My Action Plan

_____
_____
_____
_____

What I need to release to do this

_____
_____
_____
_____

CREATING THE REALITY YOU WANT

Scripting
Check-in

How has your scripting been going? Take some time at the beginning of the new month to look over last month's work. Did you use enough detail? Did you honestly believe the changes were possible? Did any of your scripting come true? Use this private space to be honest with yourself. Include changes you want to make to your scripting next month.

_____

_____

_____

_____

_____

_____

_____

_____

_____

Science tells us that it takes roughly 30 days to break or build habits. this wheel will help you keep track of how well you are showing up for your habits. Add up to 7 habits you want to track. whether you want to break old/unhealthy habits or build new/healthier ones.

To make it more interactive use the following key to color-code your habits. by adding the color of your choice. If there is a day you don't have a positive result simply don't color in that day. From month to month evaluate how you are doing with your goals. look for patterns where you've had success or challenges.

[ ] Habit 1   [ ] Habit 2   [ ] Habit 3

[ ] Habit 4   [ ] Habit 5   [ ] Habit 6

[ ] Habit 7

BUCK MOON

OTHER NAMES
THUNDER MOON, HAY MOON,
BLESSING MOON, HERB MOON

HERBS
HONEYSUCKLE, LEMON BALM,
HYSSOP, AGRIMONY, GARDENIA,
MYRRH

DEITIES
HEL, ATHENA, VENUS, JUNO,
KHEPHRI

MAGIC
LEADERSHIP, LONG-TERM GOALS,
DIVINATION, DREAMSCAPING

CRYSTALS
RUBY, CARNELIAN, GREEN CAL-
CITE, PEACOCK ORE

FLOWERS
LARKSPUR, WATER LILY, DEL-
PHINIUM

ENERGY
SELF-REGULATION, DIVINATION

COLORS
BLUE, GRAY, SILVER

WATER   CANCER   LEO   FIRE

JULY

DIVINATION TRACKER

DATE	PULL	MESSAGE

DAILY

I AM GRATEFUL FOR

_____
_____
_____

MOOD TRACKER

SELF-CARE

MY AFFIRMATION FOR THE DAY

_____
_____

MY DREAM JOURNAL

_____
_____
_____
_____
_____
_____
_____
_____
_____

SCRIPTING

_____
_____
_____
_____
_____
_____
_____
_____
_____
_____
_____
_____
_____
_____
_____
_____
_____

_____
_____
_____

RITUAL TIME   MINDFUL MINUTES

5
10
15
20
25
30

POSITIVE THOUGHT I AM CARRYING TO SLEEP

_____
_____

1 THING I DID TO MOVE FORWARD

_____
_____
_____

DAILY

I AM GRATEFUL FOR

_____
_____
_____

MOOD TRACKER

😠 😞 😐 🙂 😃

SELF-CARE

MY AFFIRMATION FOR THE DAY

_____
_____

MY DREAM JOURNAL

_____
_____
_____
_____
_____
_____
_____
_____
_____
_____
_____
_____

SCRIPTING

_____
_____
_____
_____
_____
_____
_____
_____
_____
_____
_____
_____
_____
_____
_____
_____

RITUAL TIME

MINDFUL MINUTES

5
10
15
20
25
30

POSITIVE THOUGHT I AM CARRYING TO SLEEP

_____
_____

1 THING I DID TO MOVE FORWARD

_____
_____
_____

WEEK AHEAD

Sunday
_____
_____
_____
_____
_____
_____

Monday
_____
_____
_____
_____
_____
_____

Tuesday
_____
_____
_____
_____
_____
_____

Wednesday
_____
_____
_____
_____
_____
_____

Thursday
_____
_____
_____
_____
_____

Friday
_____
_____
_____
_____
_____

Saturday
_____
_____
_____
_____
_____

NOTES:

DAILY

I AM GRATEFUL FOR

_____
_____
_____

MOOD TRACKER

SELF-CARE

MY AFFIRMATION FOR THE DAY

_____
_____

MY DREAM JOURNAL

_____
_____
_____
_____
_____
_____
_____

_____
_____
_____
_____

SCRIPTING

RITUAL TIME   MINDFUL MINUTES

5
10
15
20
25
30

POSITIVE THOUGHT I AM CARRYING TO SLEEP

_____

1 THING I DID TO MOVE FORWARD

_____
_____

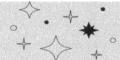

DAILY

I AM GRATEFUL FOR

_____
_____
_____

MOOD TRACKER

😠 😟 😐 🙂 😄

SELF-CARE

MY AFFIRMATION FOR THE DAY

_____
_____

MY DREAM JOURNAL

_____
_____
_____
_____
_____
_____
_____
_____

SCRIPTING

_____
_____
_____
_____
_____
_____
_____
_____
_____
_____
_____
_____
_____
_____
_____
_____
_____

_____
_____
_____
_____

RITUAL TIME   MINDFUL MINUTES

5
10
15
20
25
30

POSITIVE THOUGHT I AM CARRYING TO SLEEP

_____
_____

1 THING I DID TO MOVE FORWARD

_____
_____
_____

DAILY

I AM GRATEFUL FOR

_____
_____

_____

MOOD TRACKER

😠 😞 😐 🙂 😃

SELF-CARE

MY AFFIRMATION FOR THE DAY

_____

_____

MY DREAM JOURNAL

_____
_____
_____
_____
_____
_____
_____
_____

_____
_____
_____
_____

SCRIPTING

_____
_____
_____
_____
_____
_____
_____
_____
_____
_____
_____
_____
_____
_____

RITUAL TIME   MINDFUL MINUTES

5
10
15
20
25
30

POSITIVE THOUGHT I AM CARRYING TO SLEEP

_____
_____

1 THING I DID TO MOVE FORWARD

_____
_____
_____

DAILY

I AM GRATEFUL FOR

_____
_____
_____

MOOD TRACKER

😠 ☹️ 😐 🙂 😃

SELF-CARE

MY AFFIRMATION FOR THE DAY

_____
_____

MY DREAM JOURNAL

_____
_____
_____
_____
_____
_____
_____
_____

SCRIPTING

_____
_____
_____
_____
_____
_____
_____
_____
_____
_____
_____
_____

_____
_____
_____
_____

RITUAL TIME   MINDFUL MINUTES

5
10
15
20
25
30

POSITIVE THOUGHT I AM CARRYING TO SLEEP

_____
_____

1 THING I DID TO MOVE FORWARD

_____
_____

DAILY

I AM GRATEFUL FOR

_____
_____
_____

MOOD TRACKER

SELF-CARE

MY AFFIRMATION FOR THE DAY

_____
_____

MY DREAM JOURNAL

_____
_____
_____
_____
_____
_____
_____
_____

SCRIPTING

_____
_____
_____
_____
_____
_____
_____
_____
_____
_____
_____
_____
_____
_____

_____
_____
_____
_____

RITUAL TIME   MINDFUL MINUTES

5
10
15
20
25
30

POSITIVE THOUGHT I AM CARRYING TO SLEEP

_____
_____

1 THING I DID TO MOVE FORWARD

_____
_____
_____

DAILY

I AM GRATEFUL FOR

_____

_____

_____

MOOD TRACKER

😠 ☹️ 😐 🙂 😄

SELF-CARE

MY AFFIRMATION FOR THE DAY

_____

_____

MY DREAM JOURNAL

_____

_____

_____

_____

_____

_____

_____

_____

SCRIPTING

_____

_____

_____

_____

_____

_____

_____

_____

_____

_____

_____

_____

_____

_____

_____

_____

_____

_____

_____

_____

RITUAL TIME   MINDFUL MINUTES

5
10
15
20
25
30

POSITIVE THOUGHT I AM CARRYING TO SLEEP

_____

_____

1 THING I DID TO MOVE FORWARD

_____

_____

DAILY

I AM GRATEFUL FOR

_____
_____
_____

MOOD TRACKER

SELF-CARE

MY AFFIRMATION FOR THE DAY

_____
_____

MY DREAM JOURNAL

_____
_____
_____
_____
_____
_____
_____
_____

SCRIPTING

_____
_____
_____
_____
_____
_____
_____
_____
_____
_____
_____
_____
_____
_____

_____
_____
_____

RITUAL TIME   MINDFUL MINUTES

5
10
15
20
25
30

POSITIVE THOUGHT I AM CARRYING TO SLEEP

_____
_____

1 THING I DID TO MOVE FORWARD

_____
_____
_____

WEEK AHEAD

Sunday

Thursday

Monday

Friday

Tuesday

Saturday

Wednesday

NOTES:

DAILY

I AM GRATEFUL FOR

_____
_____
_____

MOOD TRACKER

SELF-CARE

MY AFFIRMATION FOR THE DAY

_____
_____

MY DREAM JOURNAL

_____
_____
_____
_____
_____
_____
_____
_____

_____
_____
_____
_____

SCRIPTING

_____
_____
_____
_____
_____
_____
_____
_____
_____
_____
_____
_____
_____
_____
_____
_____

RITUAL TIME   MINDFUL MINUTES

5
10
15
20
25
30

POSITIVE THOUGHT I AM CARRYING TO SLEEP

_____
_____

1 THING I DID TO MOVE FORWARD

_____
_____
_____

DAILY

I AM GRATEFUL FOR

_____
_____
_____

MOOD TRACKER

😠 😦 😐 🙂 😃

SELF-CARE

MY AFFIRMATION FOR THE DAY

_____
_____

MY DREAM JOURNAL

_____
_____
_____
_____
_____
_____
_____
_____

_____
_____
_____
_____

SCRIPTING

_____
_____
_____
_____
_____
_____
_____
_____
_____
_____
_____
_____
_____
_____
_____

RITUAL TIME   MINDFUL MINUTES

5
10
15
20
25
30

POSITIVE THOUGHT I AM CARRYING TO SLEEP

_____
_____

1 THING I DID TO MOVE FORWARD

_____
_____
_____

DAILY

I AM GRATEFUL FOR

_____
_____
_____

MOOD TRACKER

SELF-CARE

MY AFFIRMATION FOR THE DAY

_____
_____

MY DREAM JOURNAL

_____
_____
_____
_____
_____
_____
_____
_____
_____
_____
_____
_____

SCRIPTING

_____
_____
_____
_____
_____
_____
_____
_____
_____
_____
_____
_____
_____
_____
_____

RITUAL TIME

MINDFUL MINUTES

5
10
15
20
25
30

POSITIVE THOUGHT I AM CARRYING TO SLEEP

_____
_____

1 THING I DID TO MOVE FORWARD

_____
_____
_____

DAILY

I AM GRATEFUL FOR

_____
_____
_____

MOOD TRACKER

😠 🙁 😐 🙂 😄

SELF-CARE

MY AFFIRMATION FOR THE DAY

_____
_____

MY DREAM JOURNAL

_____
_____
_____
_____
_____
_____
_____
_____
_____
_____

SCRIPTING

_____
_____
_____
_____
_____
_____
_____
_____
_____
_____
_____
_____
_____
_____
_____
_____

RITUAL TIME

MINDFUL MINUTES

5
10
15
20
25
30

POSITIVE THOUGHT I AM CARRYING TO SLEEP

_____
_____

1 THING I DID TO MOVE FORWARD

_____
_____
_____

THIS LUNATION

☐ Full Moon   ☐ New Moon

The sign the moon is in _____ and transits the _____ house,
meaning _____
_____ for me.

Build your Moon ritual: _____

_____
_____
_____
_____
_____
_____
_____

CANDLES	CRYSTALS
HERBS	OTHER

Card 1	Card 2	Card 3
_____	_____	_____
Deck	Deck	Deck
_____	_____	_____
Card	Card	Card

Interpretation & Meaning _____
_____
_____
_____
_____
_____
_____

Intentions for this lunation: _____

_____
_____
_____
_____
_____
_____
_____

DAILY

I AM GRATEFUL FOR

_____
_____
_____

MOOD TRACKER

SELF-CARE

MY AFFIRMATION FOR THE DAY

_____
_____

MY DREAM JOURNAL

_____
_____
_____
_____
_____
_____
_____
_____

SCRIPTING

_____
_____
_____
_____
_____
_____
_____
_____
_____
_____
_____
_____
_____
_____
_____
_____

_____
_____
_____
_____

RITUAL TIME   MINDFUL MINUTES

5
10
15
20
25
30

POSITIVE THOUGHT I AM CARRYING TO SLEEP

_____
_____

1 THING I DID TO MOVE FORWARD

_____
_____
_____

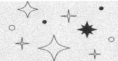

DAILY

I AM GRATEFUL FOR

_____
_____
_____

MOOD TRACKER

SELF-CARE

MY AFFIRMATION FOR THE DAY

_____
_____

MY DREAM JOURNAL

_____
_____
_____
_____
_____
_____
_____

SCRIPTING

_____
_____
_____
_____
_____
_____
_____
_____
_____
_____
_____
_____
_____

_____
_____
_____
_____

RITUAL TIME   MINDFUL MINUTES

5
10
15
20
25
30

POSITIVE THOUGHT I AM CARRYING TO SLEEP

_____
_____

1 THING I DID TO MOVE FORWARD

_____
_____
_____

DAILY

I AM GRATEFUL FOR

_____
_____
_____

MOOD TRACKER

SELF-CARE

MY AFFIRMATION FOR THE DAY

_____
_____

MY DREAM JOURNAL

_____
_____
_____
_____
_____
_____
_____
_____

SCRIPTING

_____
_____
_____
_____
_____
_____
_____
_____
_____
_____
_____
_____
_____
_____
_____
_____

_____
_____
_____
_____

RITUAL TIME   MINDFUL MINUTES

5
10
15
20
25
30

POSITIVE THOUGHT I AM CARRYING TO SLEEP

_____
_____

1 THING I DID TO MOVE FORWARD

_____
_____
_____

WEEK AHEAD

Sunday
_____
_____
_____
_____
_____
_____

Monday
_____
_____
_____
_____
_____
_____

Tuesday
_____
_____
_____
_____
_____
_____

Wednesday
_____
_____
_____
_____
_____
_____

Thursday
_____
_____
_____
_____
_____
_____

Friday
_____
_____
_____
_____
_____
_____

Saturday
_____
_____
_____
_____
_____
_____

NOTES:

DAILY

I AM GRATEFUL FOR

_____
_____
_____

MOOD TRACKER

SELF-CARE

MY AFFIRMATION FOR THE DAY

_____
_____

MY DREAM JOURNAL

_____
_____
_____
_____
_____
_____
_____

SCRIPTING

_____
_____
_____
_____
_____
_____
_____
_____
_____
_____
_____
_____
_____
_____
_____

_____
_____
_____
_____

RITUAL TIME   MINDFUL MINUTES

5
10
15
20
25
30

POSITIVE THOUGHT I AM CARRYING TO SLEEP

_____
_____

1 THING I DID TO MOVE FORWARD

_____
_____
_____

DAILY

I AM GRATEFUL FOR

_____
_____
_____

MOOD TRACKER

😠 😦 😐 🙂 😄

SELF-CARE

MY AFFIRMATION FOR THE DAY

_____
_____

MY DREAM JOURNAL

_____
_____
_____
_____
_____
_____
_____
_____

SCRIPTING

_____
_____
_____
_____
_____
_____
_____
_____
_____
_____
_____
_____
_____
_____
_____

_____
_____
_____
_____

RITUAL TIME   MINDFUL MINUTES

5
10
15
20
25
30

POSITIVE THOUGHT I AM CARRYING TO SLEEP

_____
_____

1 THING I DID TO MOVE FORWARD

_____
_____
_____

DAILY

I AM GRATEFUL FOR

_____
_____
_____

MOOD TRACKER

SELF-CARE

MY AFFIRMATION FOR THE DAY

_____
_____

MY DREAM JOURNAL

_____
_____
_____
_____
_____
_____
_____
_____
_____

SCRIPTING

_____
_____
_____
_____
_____
_____
_____
_____
_____
_____
_____
_____
_____
_____
_____
_____
_____

_____
_____
_____
_____

RITUAL TIME   MINDFUL MINUTES

5
10
15
20
25
30

POSITIVE THOUGHT I AM CARRYING TO SLEEP

_____
_____

1 THING I DID TO MOVE FORWARD

_____
_____
_____

DAILY

I AM GRATEFUL FOR

_____

_____

_____

MOOD TRACKER

😠 😞 😐 🙂 😄

SELF-CARE

MY AFFIRMATION FOR THE DAY

_____

_____

MY DREAM JOURNAL

_____

_____

_____

_____

_____

_____

_____

_____

SCRIPTING

_____

_____

_____

_____

_____

_____

_____

_____

_____

_____

_____

_____

_____

_____

_____

_____

_____

_____

_____

_____

_____

_____

RITUAL TIME

MINDFUL MINUTES

5
10
15
20
25
30

POSITIVE THOUGHT I AM CARRYING TO SLEEP

_____

_____

1 THING I DID TO MOVE FORWARD

_____

_____

_____

DAILY

I AM GRATEFUL FOR

_____

_____

_____

MOOD TRACKER

😠 😞 😐 🙂 😄

SELF-CARE

MY AFFIRMATION FOR THE DAY

_____

_____

MY DREAM JOURNAL

_____

_____

_____

_____

_____

_____

_____

SCRIPTING

_____

_____

_____

_____

_____

_____

_____

_____

_____

_____

_____

_____

_____

_____

_____

_____

_____

_____

_____

_____

_____

RITUAL TIME	MINDFUL MINUTES
	5
	10
	15
	20
	25
	30

POSITIVE THOUGHT I AM CARRYING TO SLEEP

_____

_____

1 THING I DID TO MOVE FORWARD

_____

_____

_____

DAILY

I AM GRATEFUL FOR

_____
_____
_____

MOOD TRACKER

SELF-CARE

MY AFFIRMATION FOR THE DAY

_____
_____

MY DREAM JOURNAL

_____
_____
_____
_____
_____
_____
_____
_____

SCRIPTING

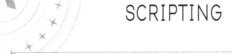

_____
_____
_____
_____
_____
_____
_____
_____
_____
_____
_____
_____
_____

_____
_____
_____
_____

RITUAL TIME   MINDFUL MINUTES

POSITIVE THOUGHT I AM CARRYING TO SLEEP

_____
_____

1 THING I DID TO MOVE FORWARD

_____
_____
_____

DAILY

I AM GRATEFUL FOR

_____

_____

_____

MOOD TRACKER

SELF-CARE

MY AFFIRMATION FOR THE DAY

_____

_____

MY DREAM JOURNAL

_____

_____

_____

_____

_____

_____

_____

SCRIPTING

_____

_____

_____

_____

_____

_____

_____

_____

_____

_____

_____

_____

_____

_____

_____

_____

_____

_____

_____

_____

_____

RITUAL TIME   MINDFUL MINUTES

5
10
15
20
25
30

POSITIVE THOUGHT I AM CARRYING TO SLEEP

_____

_____

1 THING I DID TO MOVE FORWARD

_____

_____

_____

WEEK AHEAD

Sunday

Thursday

Monday

Friday

Tuesday

Saturday

Wednesday

NOTES:

DAILY

I AM GRATEFUL FOR

_____
_____
_____

MOOD TRACKER

SELF-CARE

MY AFFIRMATION FOR THE DAY

_____
_____

MY DREAM JOURNAL

_____
_____
_____
_____
_____
_____
_____
_____

_____
_____
_____
_____

SCRIPTING

_____
_____
_____
_____
_____
_____
_____
_____
_____
_____
_____
_____
_____
_____
_____

RITUAL TIME

MINDFUL MINUTES

5
10
15
20
25
30

POSITIVE THOUGHT I AM CARRYING TO SLEEP

_____
_____

1 THING I DID TO MOVE FORWARD

_____
_____
_____

DAILY

I AM GRATEFUL FOR

_____
_____
_____

MOOD TRACKER

SELF-CARE

MY AFFIRMATION FOR THE DAY

_____
_____

MY DREAM JOURNAL

_____
_____
_____
_____
_____
_____
_____

SCRIPTING

_____
_____
_____
_____
_____
_____
_____
_____
_____
_____
_____
_____
_____
_____

_____
_____
_____
_____

RITUAL TIME   MINDFUL MINUTES

5
10
15
20
25
30

POSITIVE THOUGHT I AM CARRYING TO SLEEP

_____
_____

1 THING I DID TO MOVE FORWARD

_____
_____
_____

DAILY

I AM GRATEFUL FOR

_____

_____

_____

MOOD TRACKER

SELF-CARE

MY AFFIRMATION FOR THE DAY

_____

_____

MY DREAM JOURNAL

_____

_____

_____

_____

_____

_____

_____

_____

SCRIPTING

_____

_____

_____

_____

_____

_____

_____

_____

_____

_____

_____

_____

_____

_____

_____

_____

RITUAL TIME   MINDFUL MINUTES

5
10
15
20
25
30

POSITIVE THOUGHT I AM CARRYING TO SLEEP

_____

_____

1 THING I DID TO MOVE FORWARD

_____

_____

_____

DAILY

I AM GRATEFUL FOR

_____
_____
_____

MOOD TRACKER

SELF-CARE

MY AFFIRMATION FOR THE DAY

_____
_____

MY DREAM JOURNAL

_____
_____
_____
_____
_____
_____
_____
_____

SCRIPTING

_____
_____
_____
_____
_____
_____
_____
_____
_____
_____
_____
_____
_____
_____
_____
_____

_____
_____
_____
_____

RITUAL TIME   MINDFUL MINUTES

5
10
15
20
25
30

POSITIVE THOUGHT I AM CARRYING TO SLEEP

_____
_____

1 THING I DID TO MOVE FORWARD

_____
_____
_____

DAILY

I AM GRATEFUL FOR

_____
_____
_____

MOOD TRACKER

😠 😞 😐 🙂 😀

SELF-CARE

MY AFFIRMATION FOR THE DAY

_____
_____

MY DREAM JOURNAL

_____
_____
_____
_____
_____
_____
_____
_____

SCRIPTING

_____
_____
_____
_____
_____
_____
_____
_____
_____
_____
_____
_____
_____
_____
_____
_____

_____
_____
_____
_____

RITUAL TIME   MINDFUL MINUTES

5
10
15
20
25
30

POSITIVE THOUGHT I AM CARRYING TO SLEEP

_____
_____

1 THING I DID TO MOVE FORWARD

_____
_____

THIS LUNATION

☐ Full Moon   ☐ New Moon

The sign the moon is in _____ and transits the _____ house,
meaning _____
_____ for me.

Build your Moon ritual: _____

_____
_____
_____
_____
_____
_____
_____
_____
_____

CANDLES	CRYSTALS
HERBS	OTHER

Card 1	Card 2	Card 3
_____	_____	_____
Deck	Deck	Deck
_____	_____	_____
Card	Card	Card

Interpretation & Meaning _____

_____
_____
_____
_____
_____
_____

Intentions for this lunation: _____

_____
_____
_____
_____
_____
_____
_____

DAILY

I AM GRATEFUL FOR

_____
_____
_____

MOOD TRACKER

😠 😞 😐 🙂 😄

SELF-CARE

MY AFFIRMATION FOR THE DAY

_____
_____

MY DREAM JOURNAL

_____
_____
_____
_____
_____
_____
_____
_____

SCRIPTING

_____
_____
_____
_____
_____
_____
_____
_____
_____
_____
_____
_____
_____
_____

_____
_____
_____
_____

RITUAL TIME   MINDFUL MINUTES

5
10
15
20
25
30

POSITIVE THOUGHT I AM CARRYING TO SLEEP

_____
_____

1 THING I DID TO MOVE FORWARD

_____
_____
_____

DAILY

I AM GRATEFUL FOR

_____
_____
_____

MOOD TRACKER

😠 😟 😐 🙂 😄

SELF-CARE

MY AFFIRMATION FOR THE DAY

_____
_____

MY DREAM JOURNAL

_____
_____
_____
_____
_____
_____
_____

SCRIPTING

_____
_____
_____
_____
_____
_____
_____
_____
_____
_____
_____
_____

_____
_____
_____
_____

RITUAL TIME   MINDFUL MINUTES

5
10
15
20
25
30

POSITIVE THOUGHT I AM CARRYING TO SLEEP

_____
_____

1 THING I DID TO MOVE FORWARD

_____
_____
_____

WEEK AHEAD

Sunday

Thursday

Monday

Friday

Tuesday

Saturday

NOTES:

Wednesday

DAILY

I AM GRATEFUL FOR

_____
_____
_____

MOOD TRACKER

😠 😦 😐 🙂 😃

SELF-CARE

MY AFFIRMATION FOR THE DAY

_____
_____

MY DREAM JOURNAL

_____
_____
_____
_____
_____
_____
_____
_____

SCRIPTING

_____
_____
_____
_____
_____
_____
_____
_____
_____
_____
_____
_____
_____

_____
_____
_____
_____

RITUAL TIME   MINDFUL MINUTES

5
10
15
20
25
30

POSITIVE THOUGHT I AM CARRYING TO SLEEP

_____
_____

1 THING I DID TO MOVE FORWARD

_____
_____
_____

AUGUST

SUNDAY	MONDAY	TUESDAY	WEDNESDAY
	1	2	3
7	8	9	10
14	15	16	17
21	22	23	24 URANUS RETROGRADE VIRGO SEASON
28	29	30	31

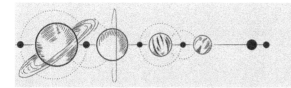

2022

THURSDAY	FRIDAY	SATURDAY	NOTES
4	5	6	
11	12	13	
PERSEIDS METEOR	FULL MOON IN AQUARIUS SHOWER		
18	19	20	
25	26	27	
		NEW MOON IN VIRGO	

SMART Goal & Action Plan

This month I will accomplish...

_____
_____
_____
_____
_____
_____
_____

Make your goals easier by making them SMART goals. Know what you want to accomplish and then simply word it to be specific, measureable, attainable, realistic, and time-specific.

Specific → **Measurable** → **Attainable** → **Realistic** → **Time-Specific**

My SMART Goal

_____
_____
_____
_____
_____

What I need to attract to do this

_____
_____
_____
_____

My Action Plan

_____
_____
_____
_____
_____

What I need to release to do this

_____
_____
_____
_____

CREATING THE REALITY YOU WANT

Scripting
Check-in

How has your scripting been going? Take some time at the beginning of the new month to look over last month's work. Did you use enough detail? Did you honestly believe the changes were possible? Did any of your scripting come true? Use this private space to be honest with yourself. Include changes you want to make to your scripting next month.

_____

_____

_____

_____

_____

_____

_____

_____

_____

_____

• •

Science tells us that it takes roughly 30 days to break or build habits. this wheel will help you keep track of how well you are showing up for your habits. Add up to 7 habits you want to track. whether you want to break old/unhealthy habits or build new/healthier ones.

To make it more interactive use the following key to color-code your habits. by adding the color of your choice. If there is a day you don't have a positive result simply don't color in that day.

From month to month evaluate how you are doing with your goals. look for patterns where you've had success or challenges.

☐ Habit 1   ☐ Habit 2   ☐ Habit 3

☐ Habit 4   ☐ Habit 5   ☐ Habit 6

☐ Habit 7

AUGUST-STURGEON MOON
CORRESPONDENCES

ENERGETIC:
GRATITUDE, FRIENDSHIP, BOUNTY,
PEACE, SYMMETRY, REFLECTION

MAGICAL:
CLEANSING, REAPING, HARVESTING

ZODIACS:
LEO, VIRGO

TREES:
HAZEL, ALDER, CEDAR

COLORS:
GOLD, YELLOW, GREEN

ELEMENTS:
EARTH, AIR

DEITIES:
DEMETER, CERES, HATHOR,
ISIS, VENUS, VESTA, DIANA,
HECATE, GANESHA, NEMESIS

CRYSTALS:
PERIDOT, ONYX, GREEN
SAPPHIRE, YELLOW CALCITE,
SUNSTONE, BRONZITE

ANIMALS:
LION, PHOENIX, SPHINX,
DRAGON

FLOWERS:
GLADIOLUS, POPPY,
GERANIUM

HERBS:
CHAMOMILE, ANGELICA, BAY, FENNEL, RUE,
ROSEMARY, JASMINE, LILAC, VIOLET, CALAMUS

RITUAL FOCUS:
THE STURGEON MOON IS A TIME FOR REFLECTING
ON WHAT YOU'VE BEEN MANIFESTING AND HOW IT IS
SHOWING UP FOR YOU. REVIEW YOUR
MANIFESTATIONS AND INTENTIONS FOR THE
PREVIOUS YEAR AND RECOMMIT IF YOU NEED TO.

OTHER COMMON NAMES:
BARLEY MOON
CORN MOON
GRAIN MOON
RED MOON

DIVINATION TRACKER

DATE	PULL	MESSAGE

DAILY

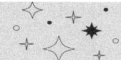

I AM GRATEFUL FOR

_____

_____

_____

MOOD TRACKER

SELF-CARE

MY AFFIRMATION FOR THE DAY

_____

_____

MY DREAM JOURNAL

_____

_____

_____

_____

_____

_____

_____

_____

_____

_____

_____

_____

SCRIPTING

_____

_____

_____

_____

_____

_____

_____

_____

_____

_____

_____

_____

_____

_____

_____

RITUAL TIME

MINDFUL MINUTES

5
10
15
20
25
30

POSITIVE THOUGHT I AM CARRYING TO SLEEP

_____

_____

1 THING I DID TO MOVE FORWARD

_____

_____

_____

DAILY

I AM GRATEFUL FOR

_____

_____

_____

MOOD TRACKER

SELF-CARE

MY AFFIRMATION FOR THE DAY

_____

_____

MY DREAM JOURNAL

_____

_____

_____

_____

_____

_____

_____

_____

_____

_____

_____

_____

SCRIPTING

_____

_____

_____

_____

_____

_____

_____

_____

_____

_____

_____

_____

_____

_____

_____

RITUAL TIME   MINDFUL MINUTES

5
10
15
20
25
30

POSITIVE THOUGHT I AM CARRYING TO SLEEP

_____

_____

1 THING I DID TO MOVE FORWARD

_____

_____

DAILY

I AM GRATEFUL FOR

_____
_____
_____

MOOD TRACKER

SELF-CARE

MY AFFIRMATION FOR THE DAY

_____
_____

MY DREAM JOURNAL

_____
_____
_____
_____
_____
_____
_____
_____
_____
_____

SCRIPTING

_____
_____
_____
_____
_____
_____
_____
_____
_____
_____
_____
_____
_____
_____
_____
_____
_____

RITUAL TIME   MINDFUL MINUTES

5
10
15
20
25
30

POSITIVE THOUGHT I AM CARRYING TO SLEEP

_____
_____

1 THING I DID TO MOVE FORWARD

_____
_____
_____

DAILY

I AM GRATEFUL FOR

_____
_____
_____

MOOD TRACKER

SELF-CARE

MY AFFIRMATION FOR THE DAY

_____
_____

MY DREAM JOURNAL

_____
_____
_____
_____
_____
_____
_____
_____

SCRIPTING

_____
_____
_____
_____
_____
_____
_____
_____
_____
_____
_____
_____
_____

_____
_____
_____

RITUAL TIME   MINDFUL MINUTES

5
10
15
20
25
30

POSITIVE THOUGHT I AM CARRYING TO SLEEP

_____
_____

1 THING I DID TO MOVE FORWARD

_____
_____
_____

DAILY

I AM GRATEFUL FOR

_____

_____

_____

MOOD TRACKER

SELF-CARE

MY AFFIRMATION FOR THE DAY

_____

_____

MY DREAM JOURNAL

_____

_____

_____

_____

_____

_____

_____

_____

SCRIPTING

_____

_____

_____

_____

_____

_____

_____

_____

_____

_____

_____

_____

_____

_____

_____

_____

_____

_____

_____

_____

_____

RITUAL TIME   MINDFUL MINUTES

5
10
15
20
25
30

POSITIVE THOUGHT I AM CARRYING TO SLEEP

_____

_____

1 THING I DID TO MOVE FORWARD

_____

_____

_____

DAILY

I AM GRATEFUL FOR

_____

_____

_____

MOOD TRACKER

SELF-CARE

MY AFFIRMATION FOR THE DAY

_____

_____

MY DREAM JOURNAL

_____

_____

_____

_____

_____

_____

_____

_____

SCRIPTING

_____

_____

_____

_____

_____

_____

_____

_____

_____

_____

_____

_____

_____

_____

_____

_____

_____

_____

RITUAL TIME   MINDFUL MINUTES

5
10
15
20
25
30

POSITIVE THOUGHT I AM CARRYING TO SLEEP

_____

_____

1 THING I DID TO MOVE FORWARD

_____

_____

_____

WEEK AHEAD

Sunday
_____
_____
_____
_____
_____
_____

Monday
_____
_____
_____
_____
_____
_____

Tuesday
_____
_____
_____
_____
_____
_____

Wednesday
_____
_____
_____
_____
_____
_____

Thursday
_____
_____
_____
_____
_____

Friday
_____
_____
_____
_____
_____

Saturday
_____
_____
_____
_____

NOTES:

DAILY

I AM GRATEFUL FOR

_____
_____
_____

MOOD TRACKER

SELF-CARE

MY AFFIRMATION FOR THE DAY

_____
_____

MY DREAM JOURNAL

_____
_____
_____
_____
_____
_____
_____
_____
_____
_____

SCRIPTING

_____
_____
_____
_____
_____
_____
_____
_____
_____
_____
_____
_____
_____
_____
_____

RITUAL TIME   MINDFUL MINUTES

5
10
15
20
25
30

POSITIVE THOUGHT I AM CARRYING TO SLEEP

_____
_____

1 THING I DID TO MOVE FORWARD

_____
_____
_____

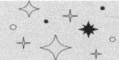

DAILY

I AM GRATEFUL FOR

_____
_____
_____

MOOD TRACKER

SELF-CARE

MY AFFIRMATION FOR THE DAY

_____
_____

MY DREAM JOURNAL

_____
_____
_____
_____
_____
_____
_____

SCRIPTING

_____
_____
_____
_____
_____
_____
_____
_____
_____
_____
_____
_____
_____
_____

_____
_____
_____
_____

RITUAL TIME

MINDFUL MINUTES

5
10
15
20
25
30

POSITIVE THOUGHT I AM CARRYING TO SLEEP

_____
_____

1 THING I DID TO MOVE FORWARD

_____
_____
_____

DAILY

I AM GRATEFUL FOR

_____
_____
_____

MOOD TRACKER

😠 🙁 😐 🙂 😃

SELF-CARE

MY AFFIRMATION FOR THE DAY

_____
_____

MY DREAM JOURNAL

_____
_____
_____
_____
_____
_____
_____
_____

SCRIPTING

_____
_____
_____
_____
_____
_____
_____
_____
_____
_____
_____
_____
_____

_____
_____
_____
_____

RITUAL TIME   MINDFUL MINUTES

5
10
15
20
25
30

POSITIVE THOUGHT I AM CARRYING TO SLEEP

_____
_____

1 THING I DID TO MOVE FORWARD

_____
_____
_____

DAILY

I AM GRATEFUL FOR

_____

_____

_____

MOOD TRACKER

SELF-CARE

MY AFFIRMATION FOR THE DAY

_____

_____

MY DREAM JOURNAL

_____

_____

_____

_____

_____

_____

_____

SCRIPTING

_____

_____

_____

_____

_____

_____

_____

_____

_____

_____

_____

_____

_____

_____

_____

_____

_____

_____

_____

_____

RITUAL TIME   MINDFUL MINUTES

5
10
15
20
25
30

POSITIVE THOUGHT I AM CARRYING TO SLEEP

_____

_____

1 THING I DID TO MOVE FORWARD

_____

_____

_____

DAILY

I AM GRATEFUL FOR

_____

_____

_____

MOOD TRACKER

SELF-CARE

MY AFFIRMATION FOR THE DAY

_____

_____

MY DREAM JOURNAL

_____

_____

_____

_____

_____

_____

_____

_____

_____

_____

_____

SCRIPTING

_____

_____

_____

_____

_____

_____

_____

_____

_____

_____

_____

_____

_____

RITUAL TIME   MINDFUL MINUTES

5
10
15
20
25
30

POSITIVE THOUGHT I AM CARRYING TO SLEEP

_____

_____

1 THING I DID TO MOVE FORWARD

_____

_____

_____

THIS LUNATION

☐ Full Moon ☐ New Moon

The sign the moon is in _____ and transits the _____ house, meaning _____ _____ for me.

Build your Moon ritual: _____
_____
_____
_____
_____
_____
_____
_____

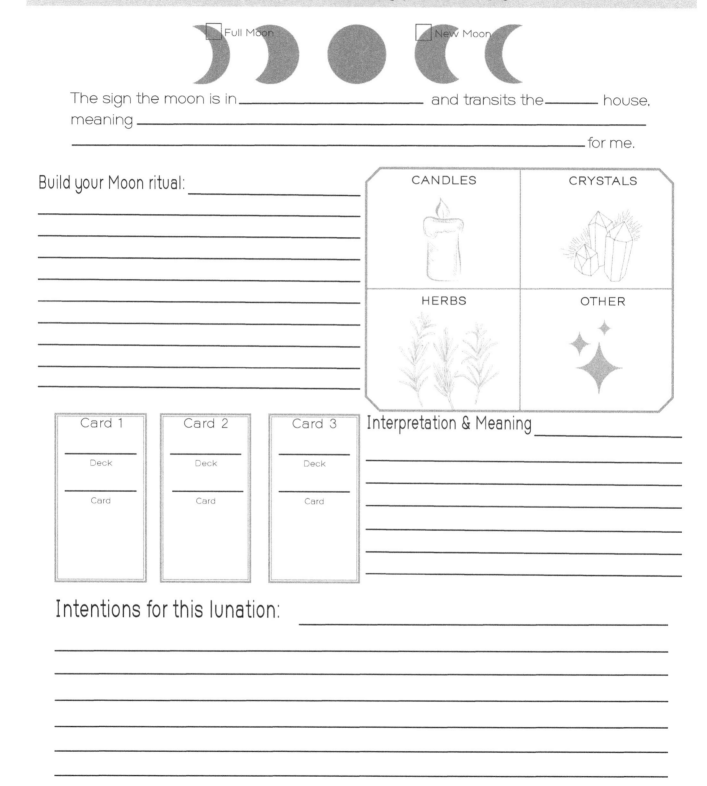

CANDLES	CRYSTALS
HERBS	OTHER

Card 1	Card 2	Card 3
_____	_____	_____
Deck	Deck	Deck
_____	_____	_____
Card	Card	Card

Interpretation & Meaning _____
_____
_____
_____
_____
_____
_____

Intentions for this lunation: _____
_____
_____
_____
_____
_____
_____
_____
_____

DAILY

I AM GRATEFUL FOR

_____

_____

_____

MOOD TRACKER

SELF-CARE

MY AFFIRMATION FOR THE DAY

_____

_____

MY DREAM JOURNAL

_____

_____

_____

_____

_____

_____

_____

_____

_____

_____

SCRIPTING

_____

_____

_____

_____

_____

_____

_____

_____

_____

_____

_____

_____

_____

_____

_____

RITUAL TIME

MINDFUL MINUTES

← 5
← 10
← 15
← 20
← 25
← 30

POSITIVE THOUGHT I AM CARRYING TO SLEEP

_____

_____

1 THING I DID TO MOVE FORWARD

_____

_____

_____

DAILY

I AM GRATEFUL FOR

_____
_____
_____

MOOD TRACKER

SELF-CARE

MY AFFIRMATION FOR THE DAY

_____
_____

MY DREAM JOURNAL

_____
_____
_____
_____
_____
_____
_____

SCRIPTING

_____
_____
_____
_____
_____
_____
_____
_____
_____
_____
_____
_____
_____
_____
_____
_____

_____
_____
_____
_____

RITUAL TIME

MINDFUL MINUTES

5
10
15
20
25
30

POSITIVE THOUGHT I AM CARRYING TO SLEEP

_____
_____

1 THING I DID TO MOVE FORWARD

_____
_____
_____

WEEK AHEAD

Sunday

Monday

Tuesday

Wednesday

Thursday

Friday

Saturday

NOTES:

DAILY

I AM GRATEFUL FOR

_____
_____
_____

MOOD TRACKER

😠 😟 😐 🙂 😃

SELF-CARE

MY AFFIRMATION FOR THE DAY

_____
_____

MY DREAM JOURNAL

_____
_____
_____
_____
_____
_____
_____
_____
_____
_____
_____
_____

SCRIPTING

_____
_____
_____
_____
_____
_____
_____
_____
_____
_____
_____
_____
_____
_____
_____

RITUAL TIME

MINDFUL MINUTES

5
10
15
20
25
30

POSITIVE THOUGHT I AM CARRYING TO SLEEP

_____
_____

1 THING I DID TO MOVE FORWARD

_____
_____
_____

DAILY

I AM GRATEFUL FOR

_____
_____
_____

MOOD TRACKER

SELF-CARE

MY AFFIRMATION FOR THE DAY

_____
_____

MY DREAM JOURNAL

_____
_____
_____
_____
_____
_____
_____
_____

SCRIPTING

_____
_____
_____
_____
_____
_____
_____
_____
_____
_____
_____
_____
_____
_____
_____

_____
_____
_____
_____

RITUAL TIME

MINDFUL MINUTES

5
10
15
20
25
30

POSITIVE THOUGHT I AM CARRYING TO SLEEP

_____
_____

1 THING I DID TO MOVE FORWARD

_____
_____
_____

DAILY

I AM GRATEFUL FOR

_____
_____
_____

MOOD TRACKER

😠 😦 😐 🙂 😄

SELF-CARE

MY AFFIRMATION FOR THE DAY

_____
_____

MY DREAM JOURNAL

_____
_____
_____
_____
_____
_____
_____
_____

_____
_____
_____
_____

SCRIPTING

_____
_____
_____
_____
_____
_____
_____
_____
_____
_____
_____
_____
_____
_____
_____

RITUAL TIME   MINDFUL MINUTES

← 5 →
← 10 →
← 15 →
← 20 →
← 25 →
← 30 →

POSITIVE THOUGHT I AM CARRYING TO SLEEP

_____
_____

1 THING I DID TO MOVE FORWARD

_____
_____
_____

DAILY

I AM GRATEFUL FOR

_____
_____
_____

MOOD TRACKER

SELF-CARE

MY AFFIRMATION FOR THE DAY

_____
_____

MY DREAM JOURNAL

_____
_____
_____
_____
_____
_____
_____

SCRIPTING

_____
_____
_____
_____
_____
_____
_____
_____
_____
_____
_____
_____
_____
_____

_____
_____
_____
_____

RITUAL TIME

MINDFUL MINUTES

5
10
15
20
25
30

POSITIVE THOUGHT I AM CARRYING TO SLEEP

_____
_____

1 THING I DID TO MOVE FORWARD

_____
_____
_____

DAILY

I AM GRATEFUL FOR

_____

_____

_____

MOOD TRACKER

SELF-CARE

MY AFFIRMATION FOR THE DAY

_____

_____

MY DREAM JOURNAL

_____

_____

_____

_____

_____

_____

_____

_____

_____

SCRIPTING

_____

_____

_____

_____

_____

_____

_____

_____

_____

_____

_____

_____

_____

_____

_____

_____

_____

_____

_____

_____

_____

_____

_____

_____

RITUAL TIME   MINDFUL MINUTES

5
10
15
20
25
30

POSITIVE THOUGHT I AM CARRYING TO SLEEP

_____

_____

1 THING I DID TO MOVE FORWARD

_____

_____

_____

DAILY

I AM GRATEFUL FOR

_____
_____
_____

MOOD TRACKER

😠 😟 😐 🙂 😀

SELF-CARE

MY AFFIRMATION FOR THE DAY

_____
_____

MY DREAM JOURNAL

_____
_____
_____
_____
_____
_____
_____
_____

SCRIPTING

_____
_____
_____
_____
_____
_____
_____
_____
_____
_____
_____
_____
_____
_____
_____
_____
_____

_____
_____
_____
_____

RITUAL TIME | MINDFUL MINUTES

5
10
15
20
25
30

POSITIVE THOUGHT I AM CARRYING TO SLEEP

_____
_____

1 THING I DID TO MOVE FORWARD

_____
_____
_____

DAILY

I AM GRATEFUL FOR

_____

_____

MOOD TRACKER

😠 😟 😐 🙂 😀

SELF-CARE

MY AFFIRMATION FOR THE DAY

_____

MY DREAM JOURNAL

_____

_____

_____

_____

_____

_____

_____

SCRIPTING

_____

_____

_____

_____

_____

_____

_____

_____

_____

_____

_____

_____

_____

_____

_____

_____

_____

RITUAL TIME   MINDFUL MINUTES

5
10
15
20
25
30

POSITIVE THOUGHT I AM CARRYING TO SLEEP

_____

_____

1 THING I DID TO MOVE FORWARD

_____

_____

WEEK AHEAD

Sunday
_____
_____
_____
_____
_____

Monday
_____
_____
_____
_____
_____

Tuesday
_____
_____
_____
_____
_____

Wednesday
_____
_____
_____
_____
_____

Thursday
_____
_____
_____
_____
_____

Friday
_____
_____
_____
_____
_____

Saturday
_____
_____
_____
_____
_____

NOTES:

DAILY

I AM GRATEFUL FOR

_____

_____

_____

MOOD TRACKER

😠 🙁 😐 🙂 😄

SELF-CARE

MY AFFIRMATION FOR THE DAY

_____

_____

MY DREAM JOURNAL

_____

_____

_____

_____

_____

_____

_____

_____

SCRIPTING

_____

_____

_____

_____

_____

_____

_____

_____

_____

_____

_____

_____

_____

_____

_____

_____

RITUAL TIME   MINDFUL MINUTES

5
10
15
20
25
30

POSITIVE THOUGHT I AM CARRYING TO SLEEP

_____

_____

1 THING I DID TO MOVE FORWARD

_____

_____

_____

DAILY

I AM GRATEFUL FOR

_____

_____

_____

MOOD TRACKER

SELF-CARE

MY AFFIRMATION FOR THE DAY

_____

_____

MY DREAM JOURNAL

_____

_____

_____

_____

_____

_____

_____

_____

SCRIPTING

_____

_____

_____

_____

_____

_____

_____

_____

_____

_____

_____

_____

_____

_____

_____

_____

RITUAL TIME

MINDFUL MINUTES

5
10
15
20
25
30

POSITIVE THOUGHT I AM CARRYING TO SLEEP

_____

_____

1 THING I DID TO MOVE FORWARD

_____

_____

_____

DAILY

I AM GRATEFUL FOR

_____
_____
_____

MOOD TRACKER

SELF-CARE

MY AFFIRMATION FOR THE DAY

_____
_____

MY DREAM JOURNAL

_____
_____
_____
_____
_____
_____
_____
_____
_____

SCRIPTING

_____
_____
_____
_____
_____
_____
_____
_____
_____
_____
_____
_____
_____
_____
_____
_____

_____
_____
_____
_____

RITUAL TIME   MINDFUL MINUTES

5
10
15
20
25
30

POSITIVE THOUGHT I AM CARRYING TO SLEEP

_____
_____

1 THING I DID TO MOVE FORWARD

_____
_____
_____

DAILY

I AM GRATEFUL FOR

_____

_____

_____

MOOD TRACKER

SELF-CARE

MY AFFIRMATION FOR THE DAY

_____

_____

MY DREAM JOURNAL

_____

_____

_____

_____

_____

_____

_____

SCRIPTING

_____

_____

_____

_____

_____

_____

_____

_____

_____

_____

_____

_____

_____

_____

_____

_____

_____

_____

_____

_____

RITUAL TIME

MINDFUL MINUTES

5
10
15
20
25
30

POSITIVE THOUGHT I AM CARRYING TO SLEEP

_____

_____

1 THING I DID TO MOVE FORWARD

_____

_____

_____

DAILY

I AM GRATEFUL FOR

_____

_____

_____

MOOD TRACKER

SELF-CARE

MY AFFIRMATION FOR THE DAY

_____

_____

MY DREAM JOURNAL

_____

_____

_____

_____

_____

_____

_____

_____

SCRIPTING

_____

_____

_____

_____

_____

_____

_____

_____

_____

_____

_____

_____

_____

_____

_____

_____

_____

_____

_____

RITUAL TIME   MINDFUL MINUTES

5
10
15
20
25
30

POSITIVE THOUGHT I AM CARRYING TO SLEEP

_____

_____

1 THING I DID TO MOVE FORWARD

_____

_____

_____

DAILY

I AM GRATEFUL FOR

_____
_____
_____

MOOD TRACKER

SELF-CARE

MY AFFIRMATION FOR THE DAY

_____
_____

MY DREAM JOURNAL

_____
_____
_____
_____
_____
_____
_____
_____

SCRIPTING

_____
_____
_____
_____
_____
_____
_____
_____
_____
_____
_____
_____

_____
_____
_____

RITUAL TIME

5
10
15
20
25
30

MINDFUL MINUTES

POSITIVE THOUGHT I AM CARRYING TO SLEEP

_____
_____

1 THING I DID TO MOVE FORWARD

_____
_____
_____

DAILY

I AM GRATEFUL FOR

_____
_____
_____

MOOD TRACKER

SELF-CARE

MY AFFIRMATION FOR THE DAY

_____
_____

MY DREAM JOURNAL

_____
_____
_____
_____
_____
_____
_____
_____

SCRIPTING

_____
_____
_____
_____
_____
_____
_____
_____
_____
_____
_____
_____
_____
_____
_____

_____
_____
_____
_____

RITUAL TIME

MINDFUL MINUTES

5
10
15
20
25
30

POSITIVE THOUGHT I AM CARRYING TO SLEEP

_____
_____

1 THING I DID TO MOVE FORWARD

_____
_____
_____

THIS LUNATION

☐ Full Moon   ☐ New Moon

The sign the moon is in _____ and transits the _____ house,
meaning _____
_____ for me.

Build your Moon ritual: _____
_____
_____
_____
_____
_____
_____
_____
_____
_____

CANDLES	CRYSTALS
HERBS	OTHER

Card 1	Card 2	Card 3
_____	_____	_____
Deck	Deck	Deck
_____	_____	_____
Card	Card	Card

Interpretation & Meaning _____
_____
_____
_____
_____
_____
_____

Intentions for this lunation: _____
_____
_____
_____
_____
_____
_____
_____

WEEK AHEAD

Sunday

Monday

Tuesday

Wednesday

Thursday

Friday

Saturday

NOTES:

DAILY

I AM GRATEFUL FOR

_____
_____
_____

MOOD TRACKER

SELF-CARE

MY AFFIRMATION FOR THE DAY

_____
_____

MY DREAM JOURNAL

_____
_____
_____
_____
_____
_____
_____

SCRIPTING

_____
_____
_____
_____
_____
_____
_____
_____
_____
_____
_____
_____
_____
_____
_____
_____

_____
_____
_____
_____

RITUAL TIME   MINDFUL MINUTES

5
10
15
20
25
30

POSITIVE THOUGHT I AM CARRYING TO SLEEP

_____
_____

1 THING I DID TO MOVE FORWARD

_____
_____
_____

DAILY

I AM GRATEFUL FOR

_____
_____
_____

MOOD TRACKER

SELF-CARE

MY AFFIRMATION FOR THE DAY

_____
_____

MY DREAM JOURNAL

_____
_____
_____
_____
_____
_____
_____
_____

SCRIPTING

_____
_____
_____
_____
_____
_____
_____
_____
_____
_____
_____
_____
_____
_____
_____

_____
_____
_____

RITUAL TIME   MINDFUL MINUTES

5
10
15
20
25
30

POSITIVE THOUGHT I AM CARRYING TO SLEEP

_____
_____

1 THING I DID TO MOVE FORWARD

_____
_____
_____

DAILY

I AM GRATEFUL FOR

_____
_____
_____

MOOD TRACKER

SELF-CARE

MY AFFIRMATION FOR THE DAY

_____
_____

MY DREAM JOURNAL

_____
_____
_____
_____
_____
_____
_____
_____

SCRIPTING

_____
_____
_____
_____
_____
_____
_____
_____
_____
_____
_____
_____
_____
_____

_____
_____
_____

RITUAL TIME   MINDFUL MINUTES

5
10
15
20
25
30

POSITIVE THOUGHT I AM CARRYING TO SLEEP

_____
_____

1 THING I DID TO MOVE FORWARD

_____
_____
_____

DAILY

I AM GRATEFUL FOR

_____
_____
_____

MOOD TRACKER

SELF-CARE

MY AFFIRMATION FOR THE DAY

_____
_____

MY DREAM JOURNAL

_____
_____
_____
_____
_____
_____
_____
_____

SCRIPTING

_____
_____
_____
_____
_____
_____
_____
_____
_____
_____
_____
_____
_____
_____
_____

_____
_____
_____

RITUAL TIME   MINDFUL MINUTES

5
10
15
20
25
30

POSITIVE THOUGHT I AM CARRYING TO SLEEP

_____
_____

1 THING I DID TO MOVE FORWARD

_____
_____
_____

NOTES

SEPTEMBER

SUNDAY	MONDAY	TUESDAY	WEDNESDAY
4	5 LABOR DAY	6	7
11	12	13	14
18	19	20	21
25 NEW MOON IN LIBRA	26	27	28

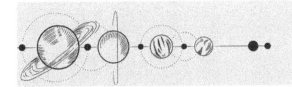

2022

THURSDAY	FRIDAY	SATURDAY	NOTES
1	2	3	
8	9	10 FULL MOON IN PISCES MERCURY RETROGRADE BEGINS	
15	16	17	
22	23	24 LIBRA SEASON	
29	30		

SMART Goal & Action Plan

This month I will accomplish...

_____
_____
_____
_____
_____
_____
_____

Make your goals easier by making them SMART goals. Know what you want to accomplish and then simply word it to be specific, measureable, attainable, realistic, and time-specific.

Specific → Measurable → Attainable → Realistic → Time-Specific

My SMART Goal

_____
_____
_____
_____
_____

What I need to attract to do this

_____
_____
_____
_____
_____

My Action Plan

_____
_____
_____
_____
_____

What I need to release to do this

_____
_____
_____
_____
_____

CREATING THE REALITY YOU WANT

Scripting
Check-in

How has your scripting been going? Take some time at the beginning of the new month to look over last month's work. Did you use enough detail? Did you honestly believe the changes were possible? Did any of your scripting come true? Use this private space to be honest with yourself. Include changes you want to make to your scripting next month.

_____

_____

_____

_____

_____

_____

_____

_____

_____

_____

Science tells us that it takes roughly 30 days to break or build habits, this wheel will help you keep track of how well you are showing up for your habits. Add up to 7 habits you want to track, whether you want to break old/unhealthy habits or build new/healthier ones.

To make it more interactive use the following key to color-code your habits, by adding the color of your choice. If there is a day you don't have a positive result simply don't color in that day. From month to month evaluate how you are doing with your goals, look for patterns where you've had success or challenges.

☐ Habit 1   ☐ Habit 2   ☐ Habit 3

☐ Habit 4   ☐ Habit 5   ☐ Habit 6

☐ Habit 7

SEPTEMBER-CORN MOON

ELEMENT: AIR, EARTH

COLOR: BROWN, YELLOW, AMBER, DEEP RED, EARTH

FLOWERS: ASTER, MORNING GLORY, FORGET-ME-NOT

ZODIAC: VIRGO, LIBRA

ANIMALS: SNAKE, JACKAL

HERB: COPAL, FENNEL, VALERIAN, RYE, LILAC, MUGWORT, ROSE, THYME

DEITIES: DEMETER, CERES, ISIS, FREYJA, NEPHTHYS, PERSEPHONE.

CRYSTAL: CITRINE, AMBER, QUARTZ, AVENTURINE, GOLD, RUBY, TIGER'S EYE, BLOODSTONE, RAINBOW OBSIDIAN

ENERGY: GRATITUDE, ABUNDANCE, HARVEST, TRANSITION, BALANCE, HOME, HEARTH, REST, REFLECTION

RITUAL FOCUS: THE CORN MOON IS A GOOD TIME TO REFRESH THE ENERGY IN YOUR HOME! EVALUATE WHETHER OR NOT THE THINGS IN YOUR HOME OR SPACE ARE HELPING YOU TO MOVE FORWARD, OR ARE HOLDING YOU BACK.

OTHER NAMES:
FALL MOON, BARLEY MOON, NUT MOON, AUTUMN MOON, SINGING MOON, HARVEST MOON

DIVINATION TRACKER

DATE	PULL	MESSAGE

DAILY

I AM GRATEFUL FOR

_____
_____
_____

MOOD TRACKER

SELF-CARE

MY AFFIRMATION FOR THE DAY

_____
_____

MY DREAM JOURNAL

_____
_____
_____
_____
_____
_____
_____
_____

SCRIPTING

_____
_____
_____
_____
_____
_____
_____
_____
_____
_____
_____
_____
_____
_____

_____
_____
_____
_____

RITUAL TIME

MINDFUL MINUTES

5
10
15
20
25
30

POSITIVE THOUGHT I AM CARRYING TO SLEEP

_____
_____

1 THING I DID TO MOVE FORWARD

_____
_____
_____

DAILY

I AM GRATEFUL FOR

_____
_____
_____

MOOD TRACKER

SELF-CARE

MY AFFIRMATION FOR THE DAY

_____
_____

MY DREAM JOURNAL

_____
_____
_____
_____
_____
_____
_____

SCRIPTING

_____
_____
_____
_____
_____
_____
_____
_____
_____
_____
_____
_____
_____
_____

_____
_____
_____
_____

RITUAL TIME   MINDFUL MINUTES

5
10
15
20
25
30

POSITIVE THOUGHT I AM CARRYING TO SLEEP

_____
_____

1 THING I DID TO MOVE FORWARD

_____
_____
_____

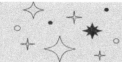

DAILY

I AM GRATEFUL FOR

_____
_____
_____

MOOD TRACKER

SELF-CARE

MY AFFIRMATION FOR THE DAY

_____
_____

MY DREAM JOURNAL

_____
_____
_____
_____
_____
_____
_____
_____

SCRIPTING

_____
_____
_____
_____
_____
_____
_____
_____
_____
_____
_____
_____
_____

_____
_____
_____
_____

RITUAL TIME   MINDFUL MINUTES

5
10
15
20
25
30

POSITIVE THOUGHT I AM CARRYING TO SLEEP

_____
_____

1 THING I DID TO MOVE FORWARD

_____
_____
_____

WEEK AHEAD

Sunday
_____
_____
_____
_____
_____

Monday
_____
_____
_____
_____
_____

Tuesday
_____
_____
_____
_____
_____

Wednesday
_____
_____
_____
_____
_____

Thursday
_____
_____
_____
_____
_____

Friday
_____
_____
_____
_____
_____

Saturday
_____
_____
_____
_____
_____

NOTES:

DAILY

I AM GRATEFUL FOR

_____
_____
_____

MOOD TRACKER

SELF-CARE

MY AFFIRMATION FOR THE DAY

_____
_____

MY DREAM JOURNAL

_____
_____
_____
_____
_____
_____
_____
_____

SCRIPTING

_____
_____
_____
_____
_____
_____
_____
_____
_____
_____
_____
_____
_____
_____
_____
_____

_____
_____
_____
_____

RITUAL TIME

MINDFUL MINUTES

5
10
15
20
25
30

POSITIVE THOUGHT I AM CARRYING TO SLEEP

_____
_____

1 THING I DID TO MOVE FORWARD

_____
_____
_____

DAILY

I AM GRATEFUL FOR

_____
_____
_____

MOOD TRACKER

😠 ☹️ 😐 🙂 😁

SELF-CARE

MY AFFIRMATION FOR THE DAY

_____
_____

MY DREAM JOURNAL

_____
_____
_____
_____
_____
_____
_____
_____

SCRIPTING

_____
_____
_____
_____
_____
_____
_____
_____
_____
_____
_____
_____
_____
_____
_____

RITUAL TIME   MINDFUL MINUTES

5
10
15
20
25
30

POSITIVE THOUGHT I AM CARRYING TO SLEEP

_____
_____

1 THING I DID TO MOVE FORWARD

_____
_____
_____

DAILY

I AM GRATEFUL FOR

_____
_____
_____

MOOD TRACKER

😠 😟 😐 🙂 😄

SELF-CARE

MY AFFIRMATION FOR THE DAY

_____
_____

MY DREAM JOURNAL

_____
_____
_____
_____
_____
_____
_____
_____
_____
_____
_____
_____
_____

SCRIPTING

_____
_____
_____
_____
_____
_____
_____
_____
_____
_____
_____
_____
_____
_____
_____
_____

RITUAL TIME   MINDFUL MINUTES

5
10
15
20
25
30

POSITIVE THOUGHT I AM CARRYING TO SLEEP

_____
_____

1 THING I DID TO MOVE FORWARD

_____
_____
_____

DAILY

I AM GRATEFUL FOR

_____
_____
_____

MOOD TRACKER

SELF-CARE

MY AFFIRMATION FOR THE DAY

_____
_____

MY DREAM JOURNAL

_____
_____
_____
_____
_____
_____
_____
_____

SCRIPTING

_____
_____
_____
_____
_____
_____
_____
_____
_____
_____
_____
_____

_____
_____
_____

RITUAL TIME

5
10
15
20
25
30

MINDFUL MINUTES

POSITIVE THOUGHT I AM CARRYING TO SLEEP

_____
_____

1 THING I DID TO MOVE FORWARD

_____
_____
_____

DAILY

I AM GRATEFUL FOR

_____
_____
_____

MOOD TRACKER

SELF-CARE

MY AFFIRMATION FOR THE DAY

_____
_____

MY DREAM JOURNAL

_____
_____
_____
_____
_____
_____
_____
_____

SCRIPTING

_____
_____
_____
_____
_____
_____
_____
_____
_____
_____
_____
_____
_____
_____

_____
_____
_____
_____

RITUAL TIME

MINDFUL MINUTES

5
10
15
20
25
30

POSITIVE THOUGHT I AM CARRYING TO SLEEP

_____
_____

1 THING I DID TO MOVE FORWARD

_____
_____
_____

DAILY

I AM GRATEFUL FOR

_____
_____
_____

MOOD TRACKER

SELF-CARE

MY AFFIRMATION FOR THE DAY

_____
_____

MY DREAM JOURNAL

_____
_____
_____
_____
_____
_____
_____

_____
_____
_____

SCRIPTING

_____
_____
_____
_____
_____
_____
_____
_____
_____
_____
_____
_____
_____
_____
_____
_____

RITUAL TIME   MINDFUL MINUTES

5
10
15
20
25
30

POSITIVE THOUGHT I AM CARRYING TO SLEEP

_____
_____

1 THING I DID TO MOVE FORWARD

_____
_____
_____

DAILY

I AM GRATEFUL FOR

_____
_____
_____

MOOD TRACKER

SELF-CARE

MY AFFIRMATION FOR THE DAY

_____
_____

MY DREAM JOURNAL

_____
_____
_____
_____
_____
_____
_____
_____
_____

SCRIPTING

_____
_____
_____
_____
_____
_____
_____
_____
_____
_____
_____
_____
_____
_____

RITUAL TIME   MINDFUL MINUTES

5
10
15
20
25
30

POSITIVE THOUGHT I AM CARRYING TO SLEEP

_____
_____

1 THING I DID TO MOVE FORWARD

_____
_____
_____

THIS LUNATION

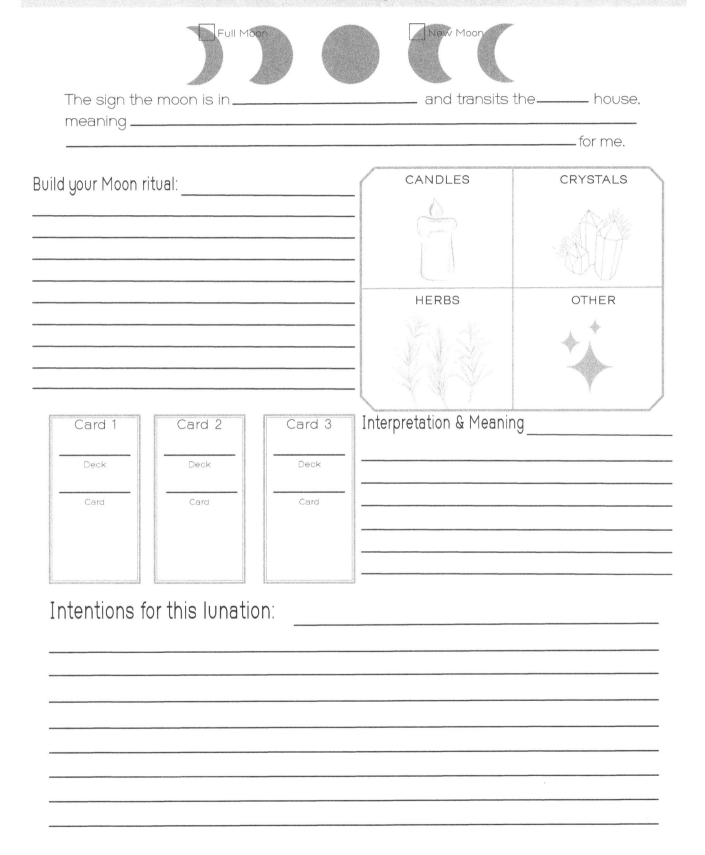

☐ Full Moon   ☐ New Moon

The sign the moon is in _____ and transits the _____ house,
meaning _____
_____ for me.

Build your Moon ritual: _____

_____
_____
_____
_____
_____
_____
_____
_____

| CANDLES | CRYSTALS |
| HERBS | OTHER |

Card 1	Card 2	Card 3
___ Deck	___ Deck	___ Deck
___ Card	___ Card	___ Card

Interpretation & Meaning _____

_____
_____
_____
_____
_____
_____

Intentions for this lunation: _____

_____
_____
_____
_____
_____
_____
_____

WEEK AHEAD

Sunday
_____
_____
_____
_____
_____
_____

Monday
_____
_____
_____
_____
_____
_____

Tuesday
_____
_____
_____
_____
_____
_____

Wednesday
_____
_____
_____
_____
_____
_____

Thursday
_____
_____
_____
_____
_____
_____

Friday
_____
_____
_____
_____
_____
_____

Saturday
_____
_____
_____
_____
_____
_____

NOTES:

DAILY

I AM GRATEFUL FOR

_____
_____
_____

MOOD TRACKER

SELF-CARE

MY AFFIRMATION FOR THE DAY

_____
_____

MY DREAM JOURNAL

_____
_____
_____
_____
_____
_____
_____
_____

SCRIPTING

_____
_____
_____
_____
_____
_____
_____
_____
_____
_____
_____
_____
_____
_____
_____
_____

_____
_____
_____
_____

RITUAL TIME

MINDFUL MINUTES

5
10
15
20
25
30

POSITIVE THOUGHT I AM CARRYING TO SLEEP

_____
_____

1 THING I DID TO MOVE FORWARD

_____
_____
_____

DAILY

I AM GRATEFUL FOR

_____
_____
_____

MOOD TRACKER

SELF-CARE

MY AFFIRMATION FOR THE DAY

_____
_____

MY DREAM JOURNAL

_____
_____
_____
_____
_____
_____
_____
_____

_____
_____
_____
_____

SCRIPTING

_____
_____
_____
_____
_____
_____
_____
_____
_____
_____
_____
_____
_____
_____
_____
_____

RITUAL TIME   MINDFUL MINUTES

5
10
15
20
25
30

POSITIVE THOUGHT I AM CARRYING TO SLEEP

_____
_____

1 THING I DID TO MOVE FORWARD

_____
_____
_____

DAILY

I AM GRATEFUL FOR

_____
_____
_____

MOOD TRACKER

SELF-CARE

MY AFFIRMATION FOR THE DAY

_____
_____

MY DREAM JOURNAL

_____
_____
_____
_____
_____
_____
_____
_____

SCRIPTING

_____
_____
_____
_____
_____
_____
_____
_____
_____
_____
_____
_____
_____
_____

_____
_____
_____

RITUAL TIME

MINDFUL MINUTES

5
10
15
20
25
30

POSITIVE THOUGHT I AM CARRYING TO SLEEP

_____
_____

1 THING I DID TO MOVE FORWARD

_____
_____
_____

DAILY

I AM GRATEFUL FOR

_____
_____
_____

MOOD TRACKER

SELF-CARE

MY AFFIRMATION FOR THE DAY

_____
_____

MY DREAM JOURNAL

_____
_____
_____
_____
_____
_____
_____

_____
_____
_____

SCRIPTING

_____
_____
_____
_____
_____
_____
_____
_____
_____
_____
_____
_____
_____
_____

RITUAL TIME   MINDFUL MINUTES

5
10
15
20
25
30

POSITIVE THOUGHT I AM CARRYING TO SLEEP

_____
_____

1 THING I DID TO MOVE FORWARD

_____
_____
_____

DAILY

I AM GRATEFUL FOR

_____
_____
_____

MOOD TRACKER

SELF-CARE

MY AFFIRMATION FOR THE DAY

_____
_____

MY DREAM JOURNAL

_____
_____
_____
_____
_____
_____
_____
_____

SCRIPTING

_____
_____
_____
_____
_____
_____
_____
_____
_____
_____
_____
_____
_____
_____
_____
_____
_____

_____
_____
_____
_____

RITUAL TIME

MINDFUL MINUTES

5
10
15
20
25
30

POSITIVE THOUGHT I AM CARRYING TO SLEEP

_____
_____

1 THING I DID TO MOVE FORWARD

_____
_____
_____

DAILY

I AM GRATEFUL FOR

_____
_____
_____

MOOD TRACKER

SELF-CARE

MY AFFIRMATION FOR THE DAY

_____
_____

MY DREAM JOURNAL

_____
_____
_____
_____
_____
_____
_____
_____

_____
_____
_____
_____

SCRIPTING

_____
_____
_____
_____
_____
_____
_____
_____
_____
_____
_____
_____
_____
_____

RITUAL TIME   MINDFUL MINUTES

5
10
15
20
25
30

POSITIVE THOUGHT I AM CARRYING TO SLEEP

_____
_____

1 THING I DID TO MOVE FORWARD

_____
_____

DAILY

I AM GRATEFUL FOR

_____
_____
_____

MOOD TRACKER

😠 🙁 😐 🙂 😄

SELF-CARE

MY AFFIRMATION FOR THE DAY

_____
_____

MY DREAM JOURNAL

_____
_____
_____
_____
_____
_____
_____
_____

SCRIPTING

_____
_____
_____
_____
_____
_____
_____
_____
_____
_____
_____
_____
_____

_____
_____
_____
_____

RITUAL TIME

MINDFUL MINUTES

5
10
15
20
25
30

POSITIVE THOUGHT I AM CARRYING TO SLEEP

_____
_____

1 THING I DID TO MOVE FORWARD

_____
_____
_____

WEEK AHEAD

Sunday

Thursday

Monday

Friday

Tuesday

Saturday

Wednesday

NOTES:

DAILY

I AM GRATEFUL FOR

_____
_____
_____

MOOD TRACKER

SELF-CARE

MY AFFIRMATION FOR THE DAY

_____
_____

MY DREAM JOURNAL

_____
_____
_____
_____
_____
_____
_____
_____

SCRIPTING

_____
_____
_____
_____
_____
_____
_____
_____
_____
_____
_____
_____
_____
_____
_____
_____
_____

_____
_____
_____
_____

RITUAL TIME

MINDFUL MINUTES

5
10
15
20
25
30

POSITIVE THOUGHT I AM CARRYING TO SLEEP

_____
_____

1 THING I DID TO MOVE FORWARD

_____
_____
_____

DAILY

I AM GRATEFUL FOR

_____

_____

_____

MOOD TRACKER

😠 🙁 😐 🙂 😃

SELF-CARE

MY AFFIRMATION FOR THE DAY

_____

_____

MY DREAM JOURNAL

_____

_____

_____

_____

_____

_____

_____

_____

_____

SCRIPTING

_____

_____

_____

_____

_____

_____

_____

_____

_____

_____

_____

_____

_____

_____

_____

_____

_____

RITUAL TIME   MINDFUL MINUTES

← 5 →
← 10 →
← 15 →
← 20 →
← 25 →
← 30 →

POSITIVE THOUGHT I AM CARRYING TO SLEEP

_____

_____

1 THING I DID TO MOVE FORWARD

_____

_____

_____

DAILY

I AM GRATEFUL FOR

_____
_____
_____

MOOD TRACKER

SELF-CARE

MY AFFIRMATION FOR THE DAY

_____
_____

MY DREAM JOURNAL

_____
_____
_____
_____
_____
_____
_____
_____

_____
_____
_____

SCRIPTING

_____
_____
_____
_____
_____
_____
_____
_____
_____
_____
_____
_____
_____
_____
_____

RITUAL TIME   MINDFUL MINUTES

5
10
15
20
25
30

POSITIVE THOUGHT I AM CARRYING TO SLEEP

_____
_____

1 THING I DID TO MOVE FORWARD

_____
_____
_____

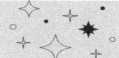

DAILY

I AM GRATEFUL FOR

_____
_____
_____

MOOD TRACKER

😠 😦 😐 🙂 😀

SELF-CARE

MY AFFIRMATION FOR THE DAY

_____
_____

MY DREAM JOURNAL

_____
_____
_____
_____
_____
_____
_____
_____

SCRIPTING

_____
_____
_____
_____
_____
_____
_____
_____
_____
_____
_____
_____
_____
_____

_____
_____
_____
_____

RITUAL TIME   MINDFUL MINUTES

5
10
15
20
25
30

POSITIVE THOUGHT I AM CARRYING TO SLEEP

_____
_____

1 THING I DID TO MOVE FORWARD

_____
_____
_____

DAILY

I AM GRATEFUL FOR

_____
_____
_____

MOOD TRACKER

😠 😦 😐 🙂 😄

SELF-CARE

MY AFFIRMATION FOR THE DAY

_____
_____

MY DREAM JOURNAL

_____
_____
_____
_____
_____
_____
_____
_____

SCRIPTING

_____
_____
_____
_____
_____
_____
_____
_____
_____
_____
_____
_____
_____

RITUAL TIME

5
10
15
20
25
30

MINDFUL MINUTES

POSITIVE THOUGHT I AM CARRYING TO SLEEP

_____
_____

1 THING I DID TO MOVE FORWARD

_____
_____
_____

DAILY

I AM GRATEFUL FOR

_____
_____
_____

MOOD TRACKER

SELF-CARE

MY AFFIRMATION FOR THE DAY

_____
_____

MY DREAM JOURNAL

_____
_____
_____
_____
_____
_____
_____
_____
_____
_____
_____
_____

SCRIPTING

_____

RITUAL TIME   MINDFUL MINUTES

5
10
15
20
25
30

POSITIVE THOUGHT I AM CARRYING TO SLEEP

_____
_____

1 THING I DID TO MOVE FORWARD

_____
_____
_____

DAILY

I AM GRATEFUL FOR

_____
_____
_____

MOOD TRACKER

😣 😟 😐 🙂 😄

SELF-CARE

MY AFFIRMATION FOR THE DAY

_____
_____

MY DREAM JOURNAL

_____
_____
_____
_____
_____
_____
_____

SCRIPTING

_____
_____
_____
_____
_____
_____
_____
_____
_____
_____
_____
_____

_____
_____
_____

RITUAL TIME   MINDFUL MINUTES

5
10
15
20
25
30

POSITIVE THOUGHT I AM CARRYING TO SLEEP

_____
_____

1 THING I DID TO MOVE FORWARD

_____
_____
_____

WEEK AHEAD

Sunday

Monday

Tuesday

Wednesday

Thursday

Friday

Saturday

NOTES:

DAILY

I AM GRATEFUL FOR

_____
_____
_____

MOOD TRACKER

SELF-CARE

MY AFFIRMATION FOR THE DAY

_____
_____

MY DREAM JOURNAL

_____
_____
_____
_____
_____
_____
_____

_____
_____
_____
_____

SCRIPTING

_____
_____
_____
_____
_____
_____
_____
_____
_____
_____
_____
_____
_____
_____
_____
_____
_____
_____
_____
_____
_____

RITUAL TIME   MINDFUL MINUTES

5
10
15
20
25
30

POSITIVE THOUGHT I AM CARRYING TO SLEEP

_____
_____

1 THING I DID TO MOVE FORWARD

_____
_____
_____

THIS LUNATION

☐ Full Moon   ☐ New Moon

The sign the moon is in _____ and transits the _____ house,
meaning _____
_____ for me.

Build your Moon ritual: _____
_____
_____
_____
_____
_____
_____
_____

CANDLES	CRYSTALS
HERBS	OTHER

Card 1	Card 2	Card 3
_____	_____	_____
Deck	Deck	Deck
_____	_____	_____
Card	Card	Card

Interpretation & Meaning _____
_____
_____
_____
_____
_____
_____

Intentions for this lunation: _____
_____
_____
_____
_____
_____
_____
_____

DAILY

I AM GRATEFUL FOR

_____

_____

_____

MOOD TRACKER

😠 😟 😐 🙂 😃

SELF-CARE

MY AFFIRMATION FOR THE DAY

_____

_____

MY DREAM JOURNAL

_____

_____

_____

_____

_____

_____

_____

_____

SCRIPTING

_____

_____

_____

_____

_____

_____

_____

_____

_____

_____

_____

_____

_____

_____

_____

_____

_____

_____

_____

_____

_____

_____

RITUAL TIME

5
10
15
20
25
30

MINDFUL MINUTES

POSITIVE THOUGHT I AM CARRYING TO SLEEP

_____

_____

1 THING I DID TO MOVE FORWARD

_____

_____

_____

DAILY

I AM GRATEFUL FOR

_____
_____
_____

MOOD TRACKER

SELF-CARE

MY AFFIRMATION FOR THE DAY

_____
_____

MY DREAM JOURNAL

_____
_____
_____
_____
_____
_____
_____
_____
_____

_____
_____
_____
_____

SCRIPTING

_____
_____
_____
_____
_____
_____
_____
_____
_____
_____
_____
_____
_____
_____
_____

RITUAL TIME   MINDFUL MINUTES

5
10
15
20
25
30

POSITIVE THOUGHT I AM CARRYING TO SLEEP

_____
_____

1 THING I DID TO MOVE FORWARD

_____
_____

DAILY

I AM GRATEFUL FOR

_____
_____
_____

MOOD TRACKER

SELF-CARE

MY AFFIRMATION FOR THE DAY

_____
_____

MY DREAM JOURNAL

_____
_____
_____
_____
_____
_____
_____

SCRIPTING

_____
_____
_____
_____
_____
_____
_____
_____
_____
_____
_____
_____
_____

_____
_____
_____
_____

RITUAL TIME   MINDFUL MINUTES

5
10
15
20
25
30

POSITIVE THOUGHT I AM CARRYING TO SLEEP

_____
_____

1 THING I DID TO MOVE FORWARD

_____
_____
_____

DAILY

I AM GRATEFUL FOR

_____

_____

_____

MOOD TRACKER

SELF-CARE

MY AFFIRMATION FOR THE DAY

_____

_____

MY DREAM JOURNAL

_____

_____

_____

_____

_____

_____

_____

_____

_____

_____

_____

_____

SCRIPTING

_____

_____

_____

_____

_____

_____

_____

_____

_____

_____

_____

_____

_____

_____

_____

_____

_____

_____

RITUAL TIME   MINDFUL MINUTES

5
10
15
20
25
30

POSITIVE THOUGHT I AM CARRYING TO SLEEP

_____

_____

1 THING I DID TO MOVE FORWARD

_____

_____

_____

DAILY

I AM GRATEFUL FOR

_____
_____
_____

MOOD TRACKER

SELF-CARE

MY AFFIRMATION FOR THE DAY

_____
_____

MY DREAM JOURNAL

_____
_____
_____
_____
_____
_____
_____

_____
_____
_____
_____

SCRIPTING

_____
_____
_____
_____
_____
_____
_____
_____
_____
_____
_____
_____
_____
_____
_____

RITUAL TIME   MINDFUL MINUTES

5
10
15
20
25
30

POSITIVE THOUGHT I AM CARRYING TO SLEEP

_____
_____

1 THING I DID TO MOVE FORWARD

_____
_____
_____

OCTOBER

SUNDAY	MONDAY	TUESDAY	WEDNESDAY
2 MERCURY RETROGRADE ENDS	3	4	5
9 FULL MOON IN ARIES DRACONIS METEOR SHOWER	10	11	12
16	17	18	19
23 SATURN RETROGRADE ENDS	24 SCORPIO SEASON	25 NEW MOON IN SCORPIO PARTIAL SOLAR ECLIPSE	26
30 MARS RETROGRADE BEGINS	31 HALLOWEEN		

THURSDAY	FRIDAY	SATURDAY	NOTES
		1	
6	7	8	
	PERSEIDS METEOR SHOWER	PLUTO RETROGRADE ENDS	
13	14	15	
20	21	22	
ORIONIDS METEOR SHOWER			
27	28	29	

SMART Goal & Action Plan

This month I will accomplish...

_____
_____
_____
_____
_____
_____
_____

Make your goals easier by making them SMART goals. Know what you want to accomplish and then simply word it to be specific, measureable, attainable, realistic, and time-specific.

Specific → **Measurable** → **Attainable** → **Realistic** → **Time-Specific**

My SMART Goal

_____
_____
_____
_____

What I need to attract to do this

_____
_____
_____
_____

My Action Plan

_____
_____
_____
_____

What I need to release to do this

_____
_____
_____
_____

CREATING THE REALITY YOU WANT

Scripting
Check-in

How has your scripting been going? Take some time at the beginning of the new month to look over last month's work. Did you use enough detail? Did you honestly believe the changes were possible? Did any of your scripting come true? Use this private space to be honest with yourself. Include changes you want to make to your scripting next month.

_____
_____
_____
_____
_____
_____
_____
_____
_____

• •

Science tells us that it takes roughly 30 days to break or build habits. this wheel will help you keep track of how well you are showing up for your habits. Add up to 7 habits you want to track. whether you want to break old/unhealthy habits or build new/healthier ones.

To make it more interactive use the following key to color-code your habits. by adding the color of your choice. If there is a day you don't have a positive result simply don't color in that day. From month to month evaluate how you are doing with your goals. look for patterns where you've had success or challenges.

☐ Habit 1   ☐ Habit 2   ☐ Habit 3

☐ Habit 4   ☐ Habit 5   ☐ Habit 6

☐ Habit 7

OCTOBER-HUNTER MOON

COLORS: RED, PURPLE, BLACK, SILVER, NAVY

ANIMALS: STAG, ELEPHANT, SCORPION, RAM, WOLF

HERBS: ROSEMARY, SAGE, CATNIP, THYME, PENNYROYAL, BURDOCK, GINGER

ENERGY: BALANCE, GRATITUDE, TRANSITIONS, DIVINATION WORK, AFTERLIFE, SHADOW WORK

DEITIES: HECATE, HERMES, ANUBIS, SHIVA, AZREAL,

RITUAL: ANCESTRAL MAGIC, DIVINATION, AMBITION

OTHER NAMES: BLOOD MOON, HUNTING MOON, LEAF FALLING MOON, RUTTING MOON, LEAF FALLING MOON

CRYSTAL:AMETHYST, OBSIDIAN, BLACK TOURMALINE, MOONSTONE, BLOODSTONE, CARNELIAN, LABRADORITE

ZODIAC: LIBRA, SCORPIO

ELEMENT: AIR, WATER

EMBRACE THE MOON: The season for deep internal work and journaling or working in your grimoire. Look into the darkness and figure out what it wants to show you about who you are! With the veil thin take some time to contemplate the natural cycle of life, observe the natural cycle of life and death. It is also important during this season is traditionally a time for protection magic as well. Enjoy quiet connection during deep meditation.

DIVINATION TRACKER

DATE	PULL	MESSAGE

DAILY

I AM GRATEFUL FOR

_____

_____

_____

MOOD TRACKER

SELF-CARE

MY AFFIRMATION FOR THE DAY

_____

_____

MY DREAM JOURNAL

_____

_____

_____

_____

_____

_____

_____

SCRIPTING

_____

_____

_____

_____

_____

_____

_____

_____

_____

_____

_____

_____

_____

_____

_____

_____

_____

_____

RITUAL TIME   MINDFUL MINUTES

5
10
15
20
25
30

POSITIVE THOUGHT I AM CARRYING TO SLEEP

_____

_____

1 THING I DID TO MOVE FORWARD

_____

_____

WEEK AHEAD

Sunday

_____
_____
_____
_____
_____

Monday

_____
_____
_____
_____
_____

Tuesday

_____
_____
_____
_____
_____

Wednesday

_____
_____
_____
_____
_____

Thursday

_____
_____
_____
_____
_____

Friday

_____
_____
_____
_____
_____

Saturday

_____
_____
_____
_____
_____

NOTES:

DAILY

I AM GRATEFUL FOR

_____
_____
_____

MOOD TRACKER

SELF-CARE

MY AFFIRMATION FOR THE DAY

_____
_____

MY DREAM JOURNAL

_____
_____
_____
_____
_____
_____
_____
_____

_____
_____
_____
_____

SCRIPTING

_____
_____
_____
_____
_____
_____
_____
_____
_____
_____
_____
_____
_____
_____
_____
_____

RITUAL TIME   MINDFUL MINUTES

5
10
15
20
25
30

POSITIVE THOUGHT I AM CARRYING TO SLEEP

_____
_____

1 THING I DID TO MOVE FORWARD

_____
_____
_____

DAILY

I AM GRATEFUL FOR

_____
_____
_____

MOOD TRACKER

SELF-CARE

MY AFFIRMATION FOR THE DAY

_____
_____

MY DREAM JOURNAL

_____
_____
_____
_____
_____
_____
_____
_____

SCRIPTING

_____
_____
_____
_____
_____
_____
_____
_____
_____
_____
_____
_____
_____
_____

_____
_____
_____

RITUAL TIME   MINDFUL MINUTES

5
10
15
20
25
30

POSITIVE THOUGHT I AM CARRYING TO SLEEP

_____
_____

1 THING I DID TO MOVE FORWARD

_____
_____
_____

DAILY

I AM GRATEFUL FOR

_____
_____
_____

MOOD TRACKER

SELF-CARE

MY AFFIRMATION FOR THE DAY

_____
_____

MY DREAM JOURNAL

_____
_____
_____
_____
_____
_____
_____
_____
_____
_____
_____
_____

SCRIPTING

_____
_____
_____
_____
_____
_____
_____
_____
_____
_____
_____
_____
_____
_____
_____

RITUAL TIME

MINDFUL MINUTES

5
10
15
20
25
30

POSITIVE THOUGHT I AM CARRYING TO SLEEP

_____
_____

1 THING I DID TO MOVE FORWARD

_____
_____
_____

DAILY

I AM GRATEFUL FOR

_____

_____

_____

MOOD TRACKER

SELF-CARE

MY AFFIRMATION FOR THE DAY

_____

_____

MY DREAM JOURNAL

_____

_____

_____

_____

_____

_____

_____

_____

_____

_____

_____

_____

SCRIPTING

_____

_____

_____

_____

_____

_____

_____

_____

_____

_____

_____

_____

_____

_____

_____

_____

_____

RITUAL TIME   MINDFUL MINUTES

5
10
15
20
25
30

POSITIVE THOUGHT I AM CARRYING TO SLEEP

_____

_____

1 THING I DID TO MOVE FORWARD

_____

_____

_____

DAILY

I AM GRATEFUL FOR

_____
_____
_____

MOOD TRACKER

SELF-CARE

MY AFFIRMATION FOR THE DAY

_____
_____

MY DREAM JOURNAL

_____
_____
_____
_____
_____
_____
_____
_____

SCRIPTING

_____
_____
_____
_____
_____
_____
_____
_____
_____
_____
_____
_____
_____

_____
_____
_____
_____

RITUAL TIME   MINDFUL MINUTES

5
10
15
20
25
30

POSITIVE THOUGHT I AM CARRYING TO SLEEP

_____
_____

1 THING I DID TO MOVE FORWARD

_____
_____
_____

DAILY

I AM GRATEFUL FOR

_____
_____
_____

MOOD TRACKER

😠 😟 😐 🙂 😄

SELF-CARE

MY AFFIRMATION FOR THE DAY

_____
_____

MY DREAM JOURNAL

_____
_____
_____
_____
_____
_____
_____
_____

_____
_____
_____
_____

SCRIPTING

_____
_____
_____
_____
_____
_____
_____
_____
_____
_____
_____
_____
_____
_____
_____
_____
_____

RITUAL TIME   MINDFUL MINUTES

5
10
15
20
25
30

POSITIVE THOUGHT I AM CARRYING TO SLEEP

_____
_____

1 THING I DID TO MOVE FORWARD

_____
_____
_____

DAILY

I AM GRATEFUL FOR

_____

_____

_____

MOOD TRACKER

SELF-CARE

MY AFFIRMATION FOR THE DAY

_____

_____

MY DREAM JOURNAL

_____

_____

_____

_____

_____

_____

_____

_____

SCRIPTING

_____

_____

_____

_____

_____

_____

_____

_____

_____

_____

_____

_____

_____

_____

_____

_____

_____

_____

_____

_____

_____

_____

RITUAL TIME   MINDFUL MINUTES

5
10
15
20
25
30

POSITIVE THOUGHT I AM CARRYING TO SLEEP

_____

_____

1 THING I DID TO MOVE FORWARD

_____

_____

WEEK AHEAD

Sunday

Thursday

Monday

Friday

Tuesday

Saturday

Wednesday

NOTES:

DAILY

I AM GRATEFUL FOR

_____

_____

_____

MOOD TRACKER

SELF-CARE

MY AFFIRMATION FOR THE DAY

_____

_____

MY DREAM JOURNAL

_____

_____

_____

_____

_____

_____

_____

_____

SCRIPTING

_____

_____

_____

_____

_____

_____

_____

_____

_____

_____

_____

_____

_____

_____

_____

_____

RITUAL TIME

MINDFUL MINUTES

5
10
15
20
25
30

POSITIVE THOUGHT I AM CARRYING TO SLEEP

_____

_____

1 THING I DID TO MOVE FORWARD

_____

_____

THIS LUNATION

☐ Full Moon   ☐ New Moon

The sign the moon is in _____ and transits the _____ house,
meaning _____
_____ for me.

Build your Moon ritual: _____
_____
_____
_____
_____
_____
_____
_____
_____

CANDLES	CRYSTALS
HERBS	OTHER

Card 1	Card 2	Card 3
_____	_____	_____
Deck	Deck	Deck
_____	_____	_____
Card	Card	Card

Interpretation & Meaning _____
_____
_____
_____
_____
_____
_____

Intentions for this lunation: _____
_____
_____
_____
_____
_____
_____
_____

DAILY

I AM GRATEFUL FOR

_____
_____
_____

MOOD TRACKER

SELF-CARE

MY AFFIRMATION FOR THE DAY

_____
_____

MY DREAM JOURNAL

_____
_____
_____
_____
_____
_____
_____

_____
_____
_____

SCRIPTING

_____
_____
_____
_____
_____
_____
_____
_____
_____
_____
_____
_____
_____
_____
_____

RITUAL TIME   MINDFUL MINUTES

5
10
15
20
25
30

POSITIVE THOUGHT I AM CARRYING TO SLEEP

_____
_____

1 THING I DID TO MOVE FORWARD

_____
_____

DAILY

I AM GRATEFUL FOR

_____

_____

_____

MOOD TRACKER

SELF-CARE

MY AFFIRMATION FOR THE DAY

_____

_____

MY DREAM JOURNAL

_____

_____

_____

_____

_____

_____

_____

_____

SCRIPTING

_____

_____

_____

_____

_____

_____

_____

_____

_____

_____

_____

_____

_____

_____

RITUAL TIME   MINDFUL MINUTES

5
10
15
20
25
30

POSITIVE THOUGHT I AM CARRYING TO SLEEP

_____

_____

1 THING I DID TO MOVE FORWARD

_____

_____

_____

DAILY

I AM GRATEFUL FOR

_____
_____
_____

MOOD TRACKER

SELF-CARE

MY AFFIRMATION FOR THE DAY

_____
_____

MY DREAM JOURNAL

_____
_____
_____
_____
_____
_____
_____

SCRIPTING

_____
_____
_____
_____
_____
_____
_____
_____
_____
_____
_____
_____
_____
_____
_____
_____

_____
_____
_____

RITUAL TIME   MINDFUL MINUTES

5
10
15
20
25
30

POSITIVE THOUGHT I AM CARRYING TO SLEEP

_____
_____

1 THING I DID TO MOVE FORWARD

_____
_____
_____

DAILY

I AM GRATEFUL FOR

_____
_____
_____

MOOD TRACKER

SELF-CARE

MY AFFIRMATION FOR THE DAY

_____
_____

MY DREAM JOURNAL

_____
_____
_____
_____
_____
_____
_____
_____

SCRIPTING

_____
_____
_____
_____
_____
_____
_____
_____
_____
_____
_____
_____
_____
_____

_____
_____
_____

RITUAL TIME

5
10
15
20
25
30

MINDFUL MINUTES

POSITIVE THOUGHT I AM CARRYING TO SLEEP

_____
_____

1 THING I DID TO MOVE FORWARD

_____
_____
_____

DAILY

I AM GRATEFUL FOR

_____
_____
_____

MOOD TRACKER

SELF-CARE

MY AFFIRMATION FOR THE DAY

_____
_____

MY DREAM JOURNAL

_____
_____
_____
_____
_____
_____
_____
_____

SCRIPTING

_____
_____
_____
_____
_____
_____
_____
_____
_____
_____
_____
_____
_____
_____

_____
_____
_____
_____

RITUAL TIME

MINDFUL MINUTES

5
10
15
20
25
30

POSITIVE THOUGHT I AM CARRYING TO SLEEP

_____
_____

1 THING I DID TO MOVE FORWARD

_____
_____

DAILY

I AM GRATEFUL FOR

_____
_____
_____

MOOD TRACKER

SELF-CARE

MY AFFIRMATION FOR THE DAY

_____
_____

MY DREAM JOURNAL

_____
_____
_____
_____
_____
_____
_____
_____

_____
_____
_____
_____

SCRIPTING

_____
_____
_____
_____
_____
_____
_____
_____
_____
_____
_____
_____
_____
_____
_____

RITUAL TIME   MINDFUL MINUTES

5
10
15
20
25
30

POSITIVE THOUGHT I AM CARRYING TO SLEEP

_____
_____

1 THING I DID TO MOVE FORWARD

_____
_____
_____

WEEK AHEAD

Sunday
_____
_____
_____
_____
_____
_____

Monday
_____
_____
_____
_____
_____
_____

Tuesday
_____
_____
_____
_____
_____
_____

Wednesday
_____
_____
_____
_____
_____
_____

Thursday
_____
_____
_____
_____
_____
_____

Friday
_____
_____
_____
_____
_____
_____

Saturday
_____
_____
_____
_____
_____

NOTES:

DAILY

I AM GRATEFUL FOR

_____
_____
_____

MOOD TRACKER

SELF-CARE

MY AFFIRMATION FOR THE DAY

_____
_____

MY DREAM JOURNAL

_____
_____
_____
_____
_____
_____
_____
_____
_____
_____

SCRIPTING

_____
_____
_____
_____
_____
_____
_____
_____
_____
_____
_____
_____
_____
_____

RITUAL TIME   MINDFUL MINUTES

5
10
15
20
25
30

POSITIVE THOUGHT I AM CARRYING TO SLEEP

_____
_____

1 THING I DID TO MOVE FORWARD

_____
_____
_____

DAILY

I AM GRATEFUL FOR

_____

_____

_____

MOOD TRACKER

SELF-CARE

MY AFFIRMATION FOR THE DAY

_____

_____

MY DREAM JOURNAL

_____

_____

_____

_____

_____

_____

_____

_____

SCRIPTING

_____

_____

_____

_____

_____

_____

_____

_____

_____

_____

_____

_____

_____

_____

_____

_____

_____

_____

_____

_____

RITUAL TIME   MINDFUL MINUTES

5
10
15
20
25
30

POSITIVE THOUGHT I AM CARRYING TO SLEEP

_____

_____

1 THING I DID TO MOVE FORWARD

_____

_____

_____

DAILY

I AM GRATEFUL FOR

_____
_____
_____

MOOD TRACKER

SELF-CARE

MY AFFIRMATION FOR THE DAY

_____
_____

MY DREAM JOURNAL

_____
_____
_____
_____
_____
_____
_____
_____

_____
_____
_____
_____

SCRIPTING

RITUAL TIME   MINDFUL MINUTES

5
10
15
20
25
30

POSITIVE THOUGHT I AM CARRYING TO SLEEP

_____
_____

1 THING I DID TO MOVE FORWARD

_____
_____
_____

DAILY

I AM GRATEFUL FOR

_____
_____
_____

MOOD TRACKER

SELF-CARE

MY AFFIRMATION FOR THE DAY

_____
_____

MY DREAM JOURNAL

_____
_____
_____
_____
_____
_____
_____
_____

SCRIPTING

_____
_____
_____
_____
_____
_____
_____
_____
_____
_____
_____
_____
_____
_____
_____
_____

_____
_____
_____

RITUAL TIME   MINDFUL MINUTES

5
10
15
20
25
30

POSITIVE THOUGHT I AM CARRYING TO SLEEP

_____
_____

1 THING I DID TO MOVE FORWARD

_____
_____
_____

DAILY

I AM GRATEFUL FOR

_____

_____

_____

MOOD TRACKER

SELF-CARE

MY AFFIRMATION FOR THE DAY

_____

_____

MY DREAM JOURNAL

_____

_____

_____

_____

_____

_____

_____

_____

_____

_____

SCRIPTING

RITUAL TIME   MINDFUL MINUTES

5
10
15
20
25
30

POSITIVE THOUGHT I AM CARRYING TO SLEEP

_____

_____

1 THING I DID TO MOVE FORWARD

_____

_____

_____

DAILY

I AM GRATEFUL FOR

_____
_____
_____

MOOD TRACKER

SELF-CARE

MY AFFIRMATION FOR THE DAY

_____
_____

MY DREAM JOURNAL

_____
_____
_____
_____
_____
_____
_____
_____

_____
_____
_____

SCRIPTING

RITUAL TIME   MINDFUL MINUTES

5
10
15
20
25
30

POSITIVE THOUGHT I AM CARRYING TO SLEEP

_____
_____

1 THING I DID TO MOVE FORWARD

_____
_____
_____

DAILY

I AM GRATEFUL FOR

_____
_____
_____

MOOD TRACKER

SELF-CARE

MY AFFIRMATION FOR THE DAY

_____
_____

MY DREAM JOURNAL

_____
_____
_____
_____
_____
_____
_____
_____

SCRIPTING

_____
_____
_____
_____
_____
_____
_____
_____
_____
_____
_____
_____
_____

_____
_____
_____

RITUAL TIME

MINDFUL MINUTES

5
10
15
20
25
30

POSITIVE THOUGHT I AM CARRYING TO SLEEP

_____
_____

1 THING I DID TO MOVE FORWARD

_____
_____
_____

WEEK AHEAD

Sunday

Monday

Tuesday

Wednesday

Thursday

Friday

Saturday

NOTES:

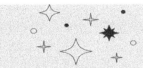

DAILY

I AM GRATEFUL FOR

_____
_____
_____

MOOD TRACKER

SELF-CARE

MY AFFIRMATION FOR THE DAY

_____
_____

MY DREAM JOURNAL

_____
_____
_____
_____
_____
_____
_____
_____
_____

SCRIPTING

_____
_____
_____
_____
_____
_____
_____
_____
_____
_____
_____
_____
_____
_____
_____

_____
_____
_____
_____

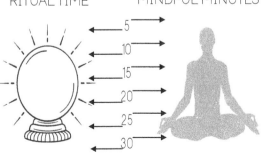

RITUAL TIME   MINDFUL MINUTES

5
10
15
20
25
30

POSITIVE THOUGHT I AM CARRYING TO SLEEP

_____
_____

1 THING I DID TO MOVE FORWARD

_____
_____
_____

DAILY

I AM GRATEFUL FOR

_____
_____
_____

MOOD TRACKER

😠 😦 😐 🙂 😃

SELF-CARE

MY AFFIRMATION FOR THE DAY

_____
_____

MY DREAM JOURNAL

_____
_____
_____
_____
_____
_____
_____
_____

_____
_____
_____
_____

SCRIPTING

_____
_____
_____
_____
_____
_____
_____
_____
_____
_____
_____
_____
_____
_____
_____

RITUAL TIME   MINDFUL MINUTES

5
10
15
20
25
30

POSITIVE THOUGHT I AM CARRYING TO SLEEP

_____
_____

1 THING I DID TO MOVE FORWARD

_____
_____
_____

DAILY

I AM GRATEFUL FOR

_____

_____

_____

MOOD TRACKER

😠 🙁 😐 🙂 😄

SELF-CARE

MY AFFIRMATION FOR THE DAY

_____

_____

MY DREAM JOURNAL

_____

_____

_____

_____

_____

_____

_____

_____

_____

_____

_____

SCRIPTING

_____

_____

_____

_____

_____

_____

_____

_____

_____

_____

_____

_____

_____

_____

_____

RITUAL TIME   MINDFUL MINUTES

5
10
15
20
25
30

POSITIVE THOUGHT I AM CARRYING TO SLEEP

_____

_____

1 THING I DID TO MOVE FORWARD

_____

_____

_____

THIS LUNATION

☐ Full Moon   ☐ New Moon

The sign the moon is in _____ and transits the _____ house,
meaning _____
_____ for me.

Build your Moon ritual: _____

_____
_____
_____
_____
_____
_____
_____
_____

CANDLES	CRYSTALS
HERBS	OTHER

Card 1	Card 2	Card 3
_____	_____	_____
Deck	Deck	Deck
_____	_____	_____
Card	Card	Card

Interpretation & Meaning _____

_____
_____
_____
_____
_____
_____

Intentions for this lunation: _____

_____
_____
_____
_____
_____
_____
_____

DAILY

I AM GRATEFUL FOR

_____
_____
_____

MOOD TRACKER

SELF-CARE

MY AFFIRMATION FOR THE DAY

_____
_____

MY DREAM JOURNAL

_____
_____
_____
_____
_____
_____
_____

SCRIPTING

_____
_____
_____
_____
_____
_____
_____
_____
_____
_____
_____
_____
_____
_____
_____
_____

_____
_____
_____
_____

RITUAL TIME

MINDFUL MINUTES

5
10
15
20
25
30

POSITIVE THOUGHT I AM CARRYING TO SLEEP

_____
_____

1 THING I DID TO MOVE FORWARD

_____
_____
_____

DAILY

I AM GRATEFUL FOR

_____
_____
_____

MOOD TRACKER

😣 😟 😐 🙂 😃

SELF-CARE

MY AFFIRMATION FOR THE DAY

_____
_____

MY DREAM JOURNAL

_____
_____
_____
_____
_____
_____
_____
_____

SCRIPTING

_____
_____
_____
_____
_____
_____
_____
_____
_____
_____
_____
_____
_____
_____

_____
_____
_____
_____

RITUAL TIME   MINDFUL MINUTES

→ 5
→ 10
→ 15
→ 20
→ 25
→ 30

POSITIVE THOUGHT I AM CARRYING TO SLEEP

_____
_____

1 THING I DID TO MOVE FORWARD

_____
_____
_____

DAILY

I AM GRATEFUL FOR

_____
_____
_____

MOOD TRACKER

SELF-CARE

MY AFFIRMATION FOR THE DAY

_____
_____

MY DREAM JOURNAL

_____
_____
_____
_____
_____
_____
_____
_____

SCRIPTING

_____
_____
_____
_____
_____
_____
_____
_____
_____
_____
_____
_____
_____
_____

_____
_____
_____
_____

RITUAL TIME   MINDFUL MINUTES

5
10
15
20
25
30

POSITIVE THOUGHT I AM CARRYING TO SLEEP

_____
_____

1 THING I DID TO MOVE FORWARD

_____
_____
_____

DAILY

I AM GRATEFUL FOR

_____
_____
_____

MOOD TRACKER

😠 🙁 😐 🙂 😄

SELF-CARE

MY AFFIRMATION FOR THE DAY

_____
_____

MY DREAM JOURNAL

_____
_____
_____
_____
_____
_____
_____
_____

SCRIPTING

_____
_____
_____
_____
_____
_____
_____
_____
_____
_____
_____
_____
_____
_____
_____
_____

_____
_____
_____

RITUAL TIME

MINDFUL MINUTES

5
10
15
20
25
30

POSITIVE THOUGHT I AM CARRYING TO SLEEP

_____
_____

1 THING I DID TO MOVE FORWARD

_____
_____
_____

WEEK AHEAD

Sunday

Monday

Tuesday

Wednesday

Thursday

Friday

Saturday

NOTES:

DAILY

I AM GRATEFUL FOR

_____

_____

_____

MOOD TRACKER

SELF-CARE

MY AFFIRMATION FOR THE DAY

_____

_____

MY DREAM JOURNAL

_____

_____

_____

_____

_____

_____

_____

SCRIPTING

_____

_____

_____

_____

_____

_____

_____

_____

_____

_____

_____

_____

_____

_____

_____

_____

_____

_____

_____

_____

_____

_____

RITUAL TIME   MINDFUL MINUTES

5
10
15
20
25
30

POSITIVE THOUGHT I AM CARRYING TO SLEEP

_____

_____

1 THING I DID TO MOVE FORWARD

_____

_____

_____

DAILY

I AM GRATEFUL FOR

_____
_____
_____

MOOD TRACKER

SELF-CARE

MY AFFIRMATION FOR THE DAY

_____
_____

MY DREAM JOURNAL

_____
_____
_____
_____
_____
_____
_____
_____

SCRIPTING

_____
_____
_____
_____
_____
_____
_____
_____
_____
_____
_____
_____
_____
_____
_____
_____

RITUAL TIME   MINDFUL MINUTES

5
10
15
20
25
30

POSITIVE THOUGHT I AM CARRYING TO SLEEP

_____
_____

1 THING I DID TO MOVE FORWARD

_____
_____
_____

NOVEMBER

SUNDAY	MONDAY	TUESDAY	WEDNESDAY
		1	2
6	7	8 FULL MOON IN TAURUS LUNAR ECLIPSE	9
13	14	15	16
20	21	22	23 JUPITER RETROGRADE ENDS SAGITTARIUS SEASON NEW MOON IN SAGITTARIUS
27	28	29	30

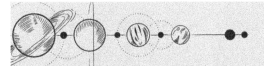

2022

THURSDAY	FRIDAY	SATURDAY	NOTES
	3	4	5
10	11 VETERANS DAY	12	
17	18	19	
24 THANKSGIVING DAY	25	26	

SMART Goal & Action Plan

This month I will accomplish...

_____
_____
_____
_____
_____
_____
_____

Make your goals easier by making them SMART goals. Know what you want to accomplish and then simply word it to be specific, measureable, attainable, realistic, and time-specific.

Specific → Measurable → Attainable → Realistic → Time-Specific

My SMART Goal

_____
_____
_____
_____
_____

What I need to attract to do this

_____
_____
_____
_____

My Action Plan

_____
_____
_____
_____
_____

What I need to release to do this

_____
_____
_____
_____

CREATING THE REALITY YOU WANT

Scripting
Check-in

How has your scripting been going? Take some time at the beginning of the new month to look over last month's work. Did you use enough detail? Did you honestly believe the changes were possible? Did any of your scripting come true? Use this private space to be honest with yourself. Include changes you want to make to your scripting next month.

_____

_____

_____

_____

_____

_____

_____

_____

_____

Science tells us that it takes roughly 30 days to break or build habits. this wheel will help you keep track of how well you are showing up for your habits. Add up to 7 habits you want to track. whether you want to break old/unhealthy habits or build new/healthier ones.

To make it more interactive use the following key to color-code your habits. by adding the color of your choice. If there is a day you don't have a positive result simply don't color in that day. From month to month evaluate how you are doing with your goals. look for patterns where you've had success or challenges.

☐ Habit 1   ☐ Habit 2   ☐ Habit 3

☐ Habit 4   ☐ Habit 5   ☐ Habit 6

☐ Habit 7

NOVEMBER

ZODIAC SIGNS

SCORPIO & SAGITTARIUS

ELEMENTS

WATER FIRE

OTHER NAMES: SNOW MOON, HARVEST MOON, MOURNING MOON

SCENTS: ROSEMARY, DRAGONS BLOOD, LILAC, PINE, CEDAR, HYACINTH, PEPPERMINT

CRYSTALS
- TOPAZ
- OBSIDIAN
- ONYX
- APACHE TEAR
- CITRINE
- LABRADORITE
- HOWLITE

HERBS
- MUGWORT
- GINGER
- WORMWOOD
- HYSSOP
- PATCHOOULI
- STAR ANISE
- SAGE
- NUTMEG

DEITIES
- ASTARTE
- CAILLEACH
- CIRCE
- HEL
- HOLDA
- KALI
- BAST
- OSIRIS
- SARASVATI

COLORS: DARK BLUE, DARK PURPLE, SAGE GREEN, BLACK

FLOWERS: WHITE LILY, DAHLIA, CHRYSANTHEMUM

ENERGIES OF THE MONTH

RELEASE, CLEANSING, EMPATHY, TRANSFORMATION

POTENTIAL OF THE MONTH

RELEASE, PROTECTION MAGIC, DIVINE CONNECTION

DIVINATION TRACKER

DATE	PULL	MESSAGE

DAILY

I AM GRATEFUL FOR

_____
_____
_____

MOOD TRACKER

SELF-CARE

MY AFFIRMATION FOR THE DAY

_____
_____

MY DREAM JOURNAL

_____
_____
_____
_____
_____
_____
_____
_____
_____

SCRIPTING

_____
_____
_____
_____
_____
_____
_____
_____
_____
_____
_____
_____
_____
_____
_____
_____

_____
_____
_____

RITUAL TIME   MINDFUL MINUTES

5
10
15
20
25
30

POSITIVE THOUGHT I AM CARRYING TO SLEEP

_____
_____

1 THING I DID TO MOVE FORWARD

_____
_____
_____

DAILY

I AM GRATEFUL FOR

_____
_____
_____

MOOD TRACKER

😠 ☹️ 😐 🙂 😄

SELF-CARE

MY AFFIRMATION FOR THE DAY

_____
_____

MY DREAM JOURNAL

_____
_____
_____
_____
_____
_____
_____

SCRIPTING

_____
_____
_____
_____
_____
_____
_____
_____
_____
_____
_____
_____

_____
_____
_____
_____

RITUAL TIME   MINDFUL MINUTES

5
10
15
20
25
30

POSITIVE THOUGHT I AM CARRYING TO SLEEP

_____
_____

1 THING I DID TO MOVE FORWARD

_____
_____
_____

DAILY

I AM GRATEFUL FOR

_____
_____
_____

MOOD TRACKER

SELF-CARE

MY AFFIRMATION FOR THE DAY

_____
_____

MY DREAM JOURNAL

_____
_____
_____
_____
_____
_____
_____
_____
_____
_____
_____

SCRIPTING

_____
_____
_____
_____
_____
_____
_____
_____
_____
_____
_____
_____
_____
_____
_____

RITUAL TIME   MINDFUL MINUTES

5
10
15
20
25
30

POSITIVE THOUGHT I AM CARRYING TO SLEEP

_____
_____

1 THING I DID TO MOVE FORWARD

_____
_____
_____

DAILY

I AM GRATEFUL FOR

_____
_____
_____

MOOD TRACKER

SELF-CARE

MY AFFIRMATION FOR THE DAY

_____
_____

MY DREAM JOURNAL

_____
_____
_____
_____
_____
_____
_____
_____

SCRIPTING

_____
_____
_____
_____
_____
_____
_____
_____
_____
_____
_____
_____
_____

_____
_____
_____
_____

RITUAL TIME   MINDFUL MINUTES

5
10
15
20
25
30

POSITIVE THOUGHT I AM CARRYING TO SLEEP

_____
_____

1 THING I DID TO MOVE FORWARD

_____
_____

DAILY

I AM GRATEFUL FOR

_____
_____
_____

MOOD TRACKER

😠 🙁 😐 🙂 😃

SELF-CARE

MY AFFIRMATION FOR THE DAY

_____
_____

MY DREAM JOURNAL

_____
_____
_____
_____
_____
_____
_____
_____
_____

SCRIPTING

_____
_____
_____
_____
_____
_____
_____
_____
_____
_____
_____
_____
_____

_____
_____
_____
_____

RITUAL TIME   MINDFUL MINUTES

5
10
15
20
25
30

POSITIVE THOUGHT I AM CARRYING TO SLEEP

_____
_____

1 THING I DID TO MOVE FORWARD

_____
_____
_____

WEEK AHEAD

Sunday

Monday

Tuesday

Wednesday

Thursday

Friday

Saturday

NOTES:

DAILY

I AM GRATEFUL FOR

_____
_____
_____

MOOD TRACKER

SELF-CARE

MY AFFIRMATION FOR THE DAY

_____
_____

MY DREAM JOURNAL

_____
_____
_____
_____
_____
_____
_____
_____

SCRIPTING

_____
_____
_____
_____
_____
_____
_____
_____
_____
_____
_____
_____
_____
_____
_____
_____

_____
_____
_____
_____

RITUAL TIME   MINDFUL MINUTES

5
10
15
20
25
30

POSITIVE THOUGHT I AM CARRYING TO SLEEP

_____
_____

1 THING I DID TO MOVE FORWARD

_____
_____
_____

DAILY

I AM GRATEFUL FOR

_____
_____
_____

MOOD TRACKER

SELF-CARE

MY AFFIRMATION FOR THE DAY

_____
_____

MY DREAM JOURNAL

_____
_____
_____
_____
_____
_____
_____

SCRIPTING

_____
_____
_____
_____
_____
_____
_____
_____
_____
_____
_____
_____
_____
_____
_____

_____
_____
_____
_____

RITUAL TIME   MINDFUL MINUTES

5
10
15
20
25
30

POSITIVE THOUGHT I AM CARRYING TO SLEEP

_____
_____

1 THING I DID TO MOVE FORWARD

_____
_____
_____

DAILY

I AM GRATEFUL FOR

_____

_____

_____

MOOD TRACKER

SELF-CARE

MY AFFIRMATION FOR THE DAY

_____

_____

MY DREAM JOURNAL

_____

_____

_____

_____

_____

_____

_____

SCRIPTING

_____

_____

_____

_____

_____

_____

_____

_____

_____

_____

_____

_____

_____

_____

_____

_____

_____

_____

_____

_____

_____

RITUAL TIME

5
10
15
20
25
30

MINDFUL MINUTES

POSITIVE THOUGHT I AM CARRYING TO SLEEP

_____

_____

1 THING I DID TO MOVE FORWARD

_____

_____

_____

THIS LUNATION

☐ Full Moon   ☐ New Moon

The sign the moon is in _____ and transits the _____ house,
meaning _____
_____ for me.

Build your Moon ritual: _____

_____
_____
_____
_____
_____
_____
_____
_____

CANDLES	CRYSTALS
HERBS	OTHER

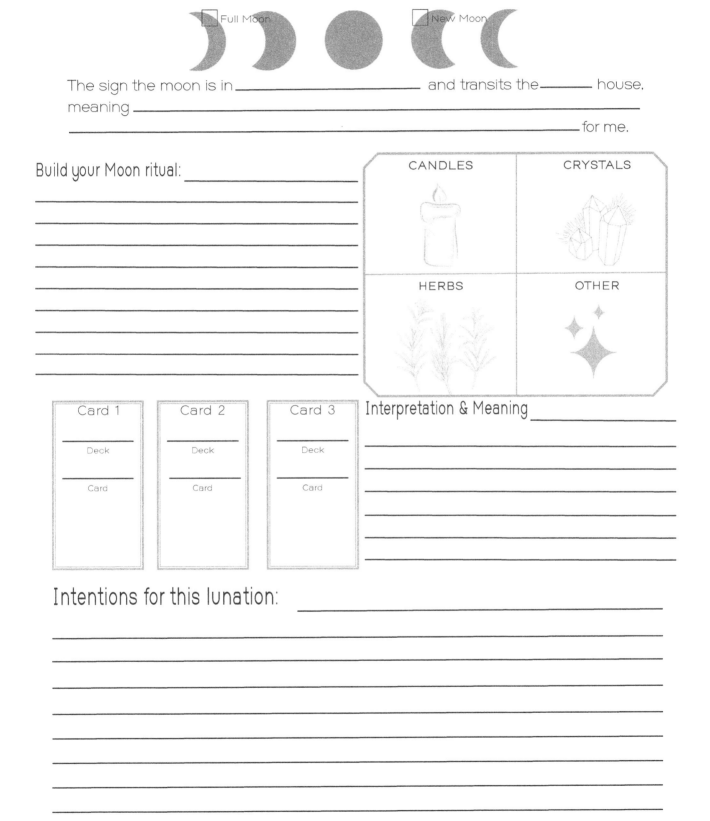

Card 1	Card 2	Card 3
_____	_____	_____
Deck	Deck	Deck
_____	_____	_____
Card	Card	Card

Interpretation & Meaning _____

_____
_____
_____
_____
_____
_____
_____

Intentions for this lunation: _____

_____
_____
_____
_____
_____
_____
_____

DAILY

I AM GRATEFUL FOR

_____
_____
_____

MOOD TRACKER

SELF-CARE

MY AFFIRMATION FOR THE DAY

_____
_____

MY DREAM JOURNAL

_____
_____
_____
_____
_____
_____
_____
_____

SCRIPTING

_____
_____
_____
_____
_____
_____
_____
_____
_____
_____
_____
_____
_____
_____

_____
_____
_____
_____

RITUAL TIME   MINDFUL MINUTES

5
10
15
20
25
30

POSITIVE THOUGHT I AM CARRYING TO SLEEP

_____
_____

1 THING I DID TO MOVE FORWARD

_____
_____
_____

DAILY

I AM GRATEFUL FOR

_____

_____

_____

MOOD TRACKER

SELF-CARE

MY AFFIRMATION FOR THE DAY

_____

_____

MY DREAM JOURNAL

_____

_____

_____

_____

_____

_____

_____

_____

_____

_____

SCRIPTING

_____

_____

_____

_____

_____

_____

_____

_____

_____

_____

_____

_____

_____

_____

RITUAL TIME

5
10
15
20
25
30

MINDFUL MINUTES

POSITIVE THOUGHT I AM CARRYING TO SLEEP

_____

_____

1 THING I DID TO MOVE FORWARD

_____

_____

_____

DAILY

I AM GRATEFUL FOR

_____
_____
_____

MOOD TRACKER

SELF-CARE

MY AFFIRMATION FOR THE DAY

_____
_____

MY DREAM JOURNAL

_____
_____
_____
_____
_____
_____
_____
_____

SCRIPTING

_____
_____
_____
_____
_____
_____
_____
_____
_____
_____
_____
_____
_____
_____
_____
_____
_____
_____
_____

_____
_____
_____
_____

RITUAL TIME   MINDFUL MINUTES

5
10
15
20
25
30

POSITIVE THOUGHT I AM CARRYING TO SLEEP

_____
_____

1 THING I DID TO MOVE FORWARD

_____
_____
_____

DAILY

I AM GRATEFUL FOR

_____
_____
_____

MOOD TRACKER

SELF-CARE

MY AFFIRMATION FOR THE DAY

_____
_____

MY DREAM JOURNAL

_____
_____
_____
_____
_____
_____
_____
_____
_____

SCRIPTING

_____
_____
_____
_____
_____
_____
_____
_____
_____
_____
_____
_____
_____

_____
_____
_____
_____

RITUAL TIME   MINDFUL MINUTES

5
10
15
20
25
30

POSITIVE THOUGHT I AM CARRYING TO SLEEP

_____
_____

1 THING I DID TO MOVE FORWARD

_____
_____
_____

WEEK AHEAD

Sunday
_____
_____
_____
_____
_____
_____

Monday
_____
_____
_____
_____
_____
_____

Tuesday
_____
_____
_____
_____
_____
_____

Wednesday
_____
_____
_____
_____
_____
_____

Thursday
_____
_____
_____
_____
_____
_____

Friday
_____
_____
_____
_____
_____
_____

Saturday
_____
_____
_____
_____
_____
_____

NOTES:

DAILY

I AM GRATEFUL FOR

_____

_____

_____

MOOD TRACKER

😠 😞 😐 🙂 😄

SELF-CARE

MY AFFIRMATION FOR THE DAY

_____

_____

MY DREAM JOURNAL

_____

_____

_____

_____

_____

_____

_____

SCRIPTING

_____

_____

_____

_____

_____

_____

_____

_____

_____

_____

_____

_____

_____

_____

_____

_____

_____

RITUAL TIME   MINDFUL MINUTES

5
10
15
20
25
30

POSITIVE THOUGHT I AM CARRYING TO SLEEP

_____

_____

1 THING I DID TO MOVE FORWARD

_____

_____

_____

DAILY

I AM GRATEFUL FOR

_____
_____
_____

MOOD TRACKER

😠 😟 😐 🙂 😄

SELF-CARE

MY AFFIRMATION FOR THE DAY

_____
_____

MY DREAM JOURNAL

_____
_____
_____
_____
_____
_____
_____
_____
_____
_____
_____

SCRIPTING

_____
_____
_____
_____
_____
_____
_____
_____
_____
_____
_____
_____
_____
_____

RITUAL TIME   MINDFUL MINUTES

5
10
15
20
25
30

POSITIVE THOUGHT I AM CARRYING TO SLEEP

_____
_____

1 THING I DID TO MOVE FORWARD

_____
_____
_____

DAILY

I AM GRATEFUL FOR

_____
_____
_____

MOOD TRACKER

SELF-CARE

MY AFFIRMATION FOR THE DAY

_____
_____

MY DREAM JOURNAL

_____
_____
_____
_____
_____
_____
_____
_____

SCRIPTING

_____
_____
_____
_____
_____
_____
_____
_____
_____
_____
_____
_____
_____
_____
_____

_____
_____
_____
_____

RITUAL TIME   MINDFUL MINUTES

5
10
15
20
25
30

POSITIVE THOUGHT I AM CARRYING TO SLEEP

_____
_____

1 THING I DID TO MOVE FORWARD

_____
_____

DAILY

I AM GRATEFUL FOR

_____
_____
_____

MOOD TRACKER

😠 😟 😐 🙂 😄

SELF-CARE

MY AFFIRMATION FOR THE DAY

_____
_____

MY DREAM JOURNAL

_____
_____
_____
_____
_____
_____
_____
_____

SCRIPTING

_____
_____
_____
_____
_____
_____
_____
_____
_____
_____
_____
_____
_____

_____
_____
_____
_____

RITUAL TIME   MINDFUL MINUTES

5
10
15
20
25
30

POSITIVE THOUGHT I AM CARRYING TO SLEEP

_____
_____

1 THING I DID TO MOVE FORWARD

_____
_____
_____

DAILY

I AM GRATEFUL FOR

_____
_____
_____

MOOD TRACKER

SELF-CARE

MY AFFIRMATION FOR THE DAY

_____
_____

MY DREAM JOURNAL

_____
_____
_____
_____
_____
_____
_____
_____

SCRIPTING

_____
_____
_____
_____
_____
_____
_____
_____
_____
_____
_____
_____

_____
_____
_____
_____

RITUAL TIME   MINDFUL MINUTES

5
10
15
20
25
30

POSITIVE THOUGHT I AM CARRYING TO SLEEP

_____
_____

1 THING I DID TO MOVE FORWARD

_____
_____
_____

DAILY

I AM GRATEFUL FOR

_____

_____

_____

MOOD TRACKER

SELF-CARE

MY AFFIRMATION FOR THE DAY

_____

MY DREAM JOURNAL

_____

_____

_____

_____

_____

_____

_____

_____

_____

_____

_____

_____

SCRIPTING

_____

_____

_____

_____

_____

_____

_____

_____

_____

_____

_____

_____

_____

_____

_____

_____

RITUAL TIME

5
10
15
20
25
30

MINDFUL MINUTES

POSITIVE THOUGHT I AM CARRYING TO SLEEP

_____

_____

1 THING I DID TO MOVE FORWARD

_____

_____

DAILY

I AM GRATEFUL FOR

_____
_____
_____

MOOD TRACKER

😠 😟 😐 🙂 😄

SELF-CARE

MY AFFIRMATION FOR THE DAY

_____
_____

MY DREAM JOURNAL

_____
_____
_____
_____
_____
_____
_____
_____

SCRIPTING

_____
_____
_____
_____
_____
_____
_____
_____
_____
_____
_____
_____
_____
_____
_____

_____
_____
_____
_____

RITUAL TIME   MINDFUL MINUTES

5
10
15
20
25
30

POSITIVE THOUGHT I AM CARRYING TO SLEEP

_____
_____

1 THING I DID TO MOVE FORWARD

_____
_____
_____

WEEK AHEAD

Sunday

_____
_____
_____
_____
_____
_____

Monday

_____
_____
_____
_____
_____
_____

Tuesday

_____
_____
_____
_____
_____
_____

Wednesday

_____
_____
_____
_____
_____
_____

Thursday

_____
_____
_____
_____
_____
_____

Friday

_____
_____
_____
_____
_____
_____

Saturday

_____
_____
_____
_____
_____
_____

NOTES:

DAILY

I AM GRATEFUL FOR

_____
_____
_____

MOOD TRACKER

😠 😦 😐 🙂 😄

SELF-CARE

MY AFFIRMATION FOR THE DAY

_____
_____

MY DREAM JOURNAL

_____
_____
_____
_____
_____
_____
_____
_____

SCRIPTING

_____
_____
_____
_____
_____
_____
_____
_____
_____
_____
_____
_____
_____
_____
_____
_____
_____

_____
_____
_____
_____

RITUAL TIME

MINDFUL MINUTES

5
10
15
20
25
30

POSITIVE THOUGHT I AM CARRYING TO SLEEP

_____
_____

1 THING I DID TO MOVE FORWARD

_____
_____
_____

DAILY

I AM GRATEFUL FOR

_____
_____
_____

MOOD TRACKER

SELF-CARE

MY AFFIRMATION FOR THE DAY

_____
_____

MY DREAM JOURNAL

_____
_____
_____
_____
_____
_____
_____
_____
_____
_____
_____
_____
_____

SCRIPTING

_____
_____
_____
_____
_____
_____
_____
_____
_____
_____
_____
_____
_____
_____
_____
_____
_____

RITUAL TIME   MINDFUL MINUTES

5
10
15
20
25
30

POSITIVE THOUGHT I AM CARRYING TO SLEEP

_____
_____

1 THING I DID TO MOVE FORWARD

_____
_____
_____

DAILY

I AM GRATEFUL FOR

_____

_____

_____

MOOD TRACKER

SELF-CARE

MY AFFIRMATION FOR THE DAY

_____

_____

MY DREAM JOURNAL

_____

_____

_____

_____

_____

_____

_____

SCRIPTING

_____

_____

_____

_____

_____

_____

_____

_____

_____

_____

_____

_____

_____

_____

_____

_____

_____

_____

_____

_____

RITUAL TIME   MINDFUL MINUTES

5
10
15
20
25
30

POSITIVE THOUGHT I AM CARRYING TO SLEEP

_____

_____

1 THING I DID TO MOVE FORWARD

_____

_____

_____

DAILY

I AM GRATEFUL FOR

_____
_____
_____

MOOD TRACKER

SELF-CARE

MY AFFIRMATION FOR THE DAY

_____

MY DREAM JOURNAL

_____
_____
_____
_____
_____
_____
_____
_____
_____
_____
_____

SCRIPTING

_____
_____
_____
_____
_____
_____
_____
_____
_____
_____
_____
_____
_____

RITUAL TIME   MINDFUL MINUTES

5
10
15
20
25
30

POSITIVE THOUGHT I AM CARRYING TO SLEEP

_____
_____

1 THING I DID TO MOVE FORWARD

_____
_____
_____

THIS LUNATION

☐ Full Moon   ☐ New Moon

The sign the moon is in _____ and transits the _____ house,

meaning _____

_____ for me.

Build your Moon ritual: _____

_____

_____

_____

_____

_____

_____

_____

CANDLES	CRYSTALS
HERBS	OTHER

Card 1	Card 2	Card 3
_____	_____	_____
Deck	Deck	Deck
_____	_____	_____
Card	Card	Card

Interpretation & Meaning _____

_____

_____

_____

_____

_____

Intentions for this lunation: _____

_____

_____

_____

_____

_____

_____

_____

DAILY

I AM GRATEFUL FOR

_____

_____

_____

MOOD TRACKER

SELF-CARE

MY AFFIRMATION FOR THE DAY

_____

_____

MY DREAM JOURNAL

_____

_____

_____

_____

_____

_____

_____

_____

SCRIPTING

_____

_____

_____

_____

_____

_____

_____

_____

_____

_____

_____

_____

_____

_____

_____

_____

RITUAL TIME   MINDFUL MINUTES

5
10
15
20
25
30

POSITIVE THOUGHT I AM CARRYING TO SLEEP

_____

_____

1 THING I DID TO MOVE FORWARD

_____

_____

_____

DAILY

I AM GRATEFUL FOR

_____
_____
_____

MOOD TRACKER

SELF-CARE

MY AFFIRMATION FOR THE DAY

_____
_____

MY DREAM JOURNAL

_____
_____
_____
_____
_____
_____
_____
_____

_____
_____
_____

SCRIPTING

_____
_____
_____
_____
_____
_____
_____
_____
_____
_____
_____
_____
_____
_____
_____
_____

RITUAL TIME

MINDFUL MINUTES

5
10
15
20
25
30

POSITIVE THOUGHT I AM CARRYING TO SLEEP

_____
_____

1 THING I DID TO MOVE FORWARD

_____
_____
_____

DAILY

I AM GRATEFUL FOR

_____
_____
_____

MOOD TRACKER

SELF-CARE

MY AFFIRMATION FOR THE DAY

_____
_____

MY DREAM JOURNAL

_____
_____
_____
_____
_____
_____
_____
_____
_____
_____
_____
_____

SCRIPTING

_____
_____
_____
_____
_____
_____
_____
_____
_____
_____
_____
_____
_____
_____
_____
_____

RITUAL TIME   MINDFUL MINUTES

5
10
15
20
25
30

POSITIVE THOUGHT I AM CARRYING TO SLEEP

_____
_____

1 THING I DID TO MOVE FORWARD

_____
_____
_____

WEEK AHEAD

Sunday

Thursday

Monday

Friday

Tuesday

Saturday

Wednesday

NOTES:

DAILY

I AM GRATEFUL FOR

_____
_____
_____

MOOD TRACKER

SELF-CARE

MY AFFIRMATION FOR THE DAY

_____
_____

MY DREAM JOURNAL

_____
_____
_____
_____
_____
_____
_____
_____

SCRIPTING

_____
_____
_____
_____
_____
_____
_____
_____
_____
_____
_____
_____
_____
_____
_____

_____
_____
_____

RITUAL TIME

MINDFUL MINUTES

5
10
15
20
25
30

POSITIVE THOUGHT I AM CARRYING TO SLEEP

_____
_____

1 THING I DID TO MOVE FORWARD

_____
_____
_____

DAILY

I AM GRATEFUL FOR

_____

_____

_____

MOOD TRACKER

SELF-CARE

MY AFFIRMATION FOR THE DAY

_____

_____

MY DREAM JOURNAL

_____

_____

_____

_____

_____

_____

_____

SCRIPTING

_____

_____

_____

_____

_____

_____

_____

_____

_____

_____

_____

_____

_____

_____

_____

_____

_____

_____

_____

_____

RITUAL TIME   MINDFUL MINUTES

5
10
15
20
25
30

POSITIVE THOUGHT I AM CARRYING TO SLEEP

_____

_____

1 THING I DID TO MOVE FORWARD

_____

_____

_____

DAILY

I AM GRATEFUL FOR

_____
_____
_____

MOOD TRACKER

😠 😞 😐 🙂 😄

SELF-CARE

MY AFFIRMATION FOR THE DAY

_____
_____

MY DREAM JOURNAL

_____
_____
_____
_____
_____
_____
_____

SCRIPTING

_____
_____
_____
_____
_____
_____
_____
_____
_____
_____
_____
_____
_____
_____

_____
_____
_____
_____

RITUAL TIME   MINDFUL MINUTES

5
10
15
20
25
30

POSITIVE THOUGHT I AM CARRYING TO SLEEP

_____
_____

1 THING I DID TO MOVE FORWARD

_____
_____
_____

DAILY

I AM GRATEFUL FOR

_____
_____
_____

MOOD TRACKER

SELF-CARE

MY AFFIRMATION FOR THE DAY

_____
_____

MY DREAM JOURNAL

_____
_____
_____
_____
_____
_____
_____
_____
_____
_____
_____
_____

SCRIPTING

RITUAL TIME

MINDFUL MINUTES

5
10
15
20
25
30

POSITIVE THOUGHT I AM CARRYING TO SLEEP

_____
_____

1 THING I DID TO MOVE FORWARD

_____
_____
_____

DECEMBER

SUNDAY	MONDAY	TUESDAY	WEDNESDAY
4	5	6	7 FULL MOON IN GEMINI
11	12	13	14 GEMINIDS METEOR SHOWER
18	19	20	21 URSIDS METEOR SHOWER
25	26	27	28

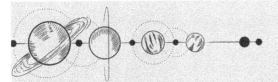

THURSDAY	FRIDAY	SATURDAY	NOTES
1	2	3 NEPTUNE RETROGRADE ENDS	
8	9	10	
15	16	17	
22 URSIDS METEOR SHOWER	23 CAPRICORN SEASON NEW MOON IN CAPRICORN	24	
29 MERCURY RETROGRADE -	30	31	

SMART Goal & Action Plan

This month I will accomplish...

_____
_____
_____
_____
_____
_____
_____

Make your goals easier by making them SMART goals. Know what you want to accomplish and then simply word it to be specific, measureable, attainable, realistic, and time-specific.

Specific → **Measurable** → **Attainable** → **Realistic** → **Time-Specific**

My SMART Goal

_____
_____
_____
_____
_____

What I need to attract to do this

_____
_____
_____
_____

My Action Plan

_____
_____
_____
_____
_____

What I need to release to do this

_____
_____
_____
_____

CREATING THE REALITY YOU WANT

Scripting
Check-in

How has your scripting been going? Take some time at the beginning of the new month to look over last month's work. Did you use enough detail? Did you honestly believe the changes were possible? Did any of your scripting come true? Use this private space to be honest with yourself. Include changes you want to make to your scripting next month.

_____

_____

_____

_____

_____

_____

_____

_____

_____

• •

Science tells us that it takes roughly 30 days to break or build habits. this wheel will help you keep track of how well you are showing up for your habits. Add up to 7 habits you want to track. whether you want to break old/unhealthy habits or build new/healthier ones.

To make it more interactive use the following key to color-code your habits. by adding the color of your choice. If there is a day you don't have a positive result simply don't color in that day. From month to month evaluate how you are doing with your goals. look for patterns where you've had success or challenges.

☐ Habit 1   ☐ Habit 2   ☐ Habit 3

☐ Habit 4   ☐ Habit 5   ☐ Habit 6

☐ Habit 7

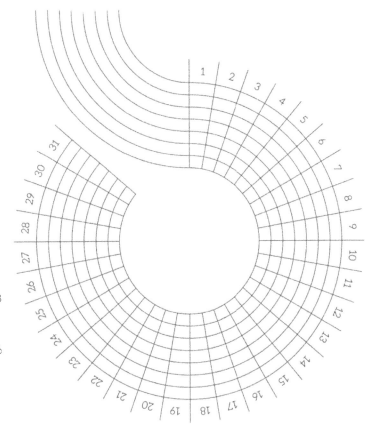

COLD MOON

ZODIAC

SAGITTARIUS CAPRICORN

ELEMENT

FIRE   WATER

HERBS

- HOLLY
- ENGLISH IVY
- FIR
- MISTLETOE
- CEDAR WOOD
- JUNIPER
- SAGE
- NARCISSUS
- DAFFODIL

CRYSTALS

- TURQUOISE
- SERPENTINE
- JACINTH
- LAPIS LAZULI
- SMOKY QUARTZ
- LAZULITE
- GARNET

COLORS

WHITE
BLACK
SILVER
GREEN

DEITIES

JUNO
HERA
ISIS
NEITH
CERRIDWEN
GREEN MAN

ENERGY

- REFLECTION
- DEVELOPMENT
- CHANGE
- PEACE
- GROWTH
- REAWAKENING

MAGIC

- TRANSITIONS
- LONG-TERM
- PROJECTS
- LIFE EVALUATIONS
- ANCESTRAL WORK
- INNER RENEWAL

DECEMBER

DIVINATION TRACKER

DATE	PULL	MESSAGE

DAILY

I AM GRATEFUL FOR

_____
_____
_____

MOOD TRACKER

SELF-CARE

MY AFFIRMATION FOR THE DAY

_____
_____

MY DREAM JOURNAL

_____
_____
_____
_____
_____
_____
_____
_____

_____
_____
_____

SCRIPTING

_____
_____
_____
_____
_____
_____
_____
_____
_____
_____
_____
_____
_____
_____
_____
_____

RITUAL TIME   MINDFUL MINUTES

5
10
15
20
25
30

POSITIVE THOUGHT I AM CARRYING TO SLEEP

_____
_____

1 THING I DID TO MOVE FORWARD

_____
_____
_____

DAILY

I AM GRATEFUL FOR

_____
_____
_____

MOOD TRACKER

😠 😟 😐 🙂 😄

SELF-CARE

MY AFFIRMATION FOR THE DAY

_____
_____

MY DREAM JOURNAL

_____
_____
_____
_____
_____
_____
_____

SCRIPTING

_____
_____
_____
_____
_____
_____
_____
_____
_____
_____
_____
_____
_____

_____
_____
_____

RITUAL TIME

MINDFUL MINUTES

5
10
15
20
25
30

POSITIVE THOUGHT I AM CARRYING TO SLEEP

_____
_____

1 THING I DID TO MOVE FORWARD

_____
_____
_____

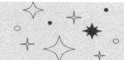

DAILY

I AM GRATEFUL FOR

_____
_____
_____

MOOD TRACKER

😠 ☹ 😐 🙂 😃

SELF-CARE

MY AFFIRMATION FOR THE DAY

_____
_____

MY DREAM JOURNAL

_____
_____
_____
_____
_____
_____
_____
_____

_____
_____
_____

SCRIPTING

_____
_____
_____
_____
_____
_____
_____
_____
_____
_____
_____
_____
_____
_____
_____
_____
_____

RITUAL TIME

MINDFUL MINUTES

5
10
15
20
25
30

POSITIVE THOUGHT I AM CARRYING TO SLEEP

_____
_____

1 THING I DID TO MOVE FORWARD

_____
_____

WEEK AHEAD

Sunday
_____
_____
_____
_____
_____

Monday
_____
_____
_____
_____
_____

Tuesday
_____
_____
_____
_____
_____

Wednesday
_____
_____
_____
_____
_____

Thursday
_____
_____
_____
_____

Friday
_____
_____
_____
_____
_____

Saturday
_____
_____
_____
_____

NOTES:

DAILY

I AM GRATEFUL FOR

_____

_____

_____

MOOD TRACKER

😠 ☹️ 😐 🙂 😄

SELF-CARE

MY AFFIRMATION FOR THE DAY

_____

_____

MY DREAM JOURNAL

_____

_____

_____

_____

_____

_____

_____

_____

SCRIPTING

_____

_____

_____

_____

_____

_____

_____

_____

_____

_____

_____

_____

_____

_____

_____

_____

_____

_____

_____

_____

RITUAL TIME   MINDFUL MINUTES

5
10
15
20
25
30

POSITIVE THOUGHT I AM CARRYING TO SLEEP

_____

_____

1 THING I DID TO MOVE FORWARD

_____

_____

_____

DAILY

I AM GRATEFUL FOR

_____
_____
_____

MOOD TRACKER

SELF-CARE

MY AFFIRMATION FOR THE DAY

_____
_____

MY DREAM JOURNAL

_____
_____
_____
_____
_____
_____
_____
_____
_____

SCRIPTING

_____
_____
_____
_____
_____
_____
_____
_____
_____
_____
_____
_____
_____
_____
_____
_____

_____
_____
_____
_____

RITUAL TIME

MINDFUL MINUTES

5
10
15
20
25
30

POSITIVE THOUGHT I AM CARRYING TO SLEEP

_____
_____

1 THING I DID TO MOVE FORWARD

_____
_____
_____

DAILY

I AM GRATEFUL FOR

_____
_____
_____

MOOD TRACKER

SELF-CARE

MY AFFIRMATION FOR THE DAY

_____
_____

MY DREAM JOURNAL

_____
_____
_____
_____
_____
_____
_____
_____

SCRIPTING

_____
_____
_____
_____
_____
_____
_____
_____
_____
_____
_____
_____
_____

_____
_____
_____

RITUAL TIME

MINDFUL MINUTES

5
10
15
20
25
30

POSITIVE THOUGHT I AM CARRYING TO SLEEP

_____
_____

1 THING I DID TO MOVE FORWARD

_____
_____

DAILY

I AM GRATEFUL FOR

_____
_____
_____

MOOD TRACKER

😠 😞 😐 🙂 😃

SELF-CARE

MY AFFIRMATION FOR THE DAY

_____
_____

MY DREAM JOURNAL

_____
_____
_____
_____
_____
_____
_____
_____

SCRIPTING

_____
_____
_____
_____
_____
_____
_____
_____
_____
_____
_____
_____
_____
_____

_____
_____
_____
_____

RITUAL TIME   MINDFUL MINUTES

5
10
15
20
25
30

POSITIVE THOUGHT I AM CARRYING TO SLEEP

_____
_____

1 THING I DID TO MOVE FORWARD

_____
_____
_____

THIS LUNATION

☐ Full Moon   ☐ New Moon

The sign the moon is in _____ and transits the _____ house,
meaning _____
_____ for me.

Build your Moon ritual: _____

_____

_____

_____

_____

_____

_____

_____

_____

CANDLES	CRYSTALS
HERBS	OTHER

Card 1	Card 2	Card 3
Deck	Deck	Deck
Card	Card	Card

Interpretation & Meaning _____

_____

_____

_____

_____

_____

_____

Intentions for this lunation: _____

_____

_____

_____

_____

_____

_____

_____

DAILY

I AM GRATEFUL FOR

_____
_____
_____

MOOD TRACKER

SELF-CARE

MY AFFIRMATION FOR THE DAY

_____
_____

MY DREAM JOURNAL

_____
_____
_____
_____
_____
_____
_____
_____
_____
_____
_____
_____

SCRIPTING

_____
_____
_____
_____
_____
_____
_____
_____
_____
_____
_____
_____
_____
_____
_____
_____

RITUAL TIME

MINDFUL MINUTES

5
10
15
20
25
30

POSITIVE THOUGHT I AM CARRYING TO SLEEP

_____
_____

1 THING I DID TO MOVE FORWARD

_____
_____
_____

DAILY

I AM GRATEFUL FOR

_____
_____
_____

MOOD TRACKER

SELF-CARE

MY AFFIRMATION FOR THE DAY

_____

MY DREAM JOURNAL

_____
_____
_____
_____
_____
_____
_____
_____
_____
_____
_____

SCRIPTING

RITUAL TIME   MINDFUL MINUTES

5
10
15
20
25
30

POSITIVE THOUGHT I AM CARRYING TO SLEEP

_____
_____

1 THING I DID TO MOVE FORWARD

_____
_____
_____

DAILY

I AM GRATEFUL FOR

_____
_____
_____

MOOD TRACKER

SELF-CARE

MY AFFIRMATION FOR THE DAY

_____
_____

MY DREAM JOURNAL

_____
_____
_____
_____
_____
_____
_____

SCRIPTING

_____
_____
_____
_____
_____
_____
_____
_____
_____
_____
_____
_____
_____
_____
_____
_____

_____
_____
_____

RITUAL TIME   MINDFUL MINUTES

5
10
15
20
25
30

POSITIVE THOUGHT I AM CARRYING TO SLEEP

_____
_____

1 THING I DID TO MOVE FORWARD

_____
_____
_____

WEEK AHEAD

Sunday

Thursday

Monday

Friday

Tuesday

Saturday

Wednesday

NOTES:

DAILY

I AM GRATEFUL FOR

_____
_____
_____

MOOD TRACKER

😠 😞 😐 🙂 😀

SELF-CARE

MY AFFIRMATION FOR THE DAY

_____
_____

MY DREAM JOURNAL

_____
_____
_____
_____
_____
_____
_____
_____
_____
_____
_____

SCRIPTING

_____
_____
_____
_____
_____
_____
_____
_____
_____
_____
_____
_____
_____
_____
_____
_____
_____

RITUAL TIME   MINDFUL MINUTES

5
10
15
20
25
30

POSITIVE THOUGHT I AM CARRYING TO SLEEP

_____
_____

1 THING I DID TO MOVE FORWARD

_____
_____
_____

DAILY

I AM GRATEFUL FOR

_____
_____
_____

SCRIPTING

_____
_____
_____
_____
_____
_____
_____
_____
_____
_____
_____
_____
_____
_____
_____
_____
_____
_____

MOOD TRACKER

SELF-CARE

MY AFFIRMATION FOR THE DAY

_____
_____

MY DREAM JOURNAL

_____
_____
_____
_____
_____
_____
_____
_____

_____
_____
_____

RITUAL TIME   MINDFUL MINUTES
5
10
15
20
25
30

POSITIVE THOUGHT I AM CARRYING TO SLEEP

_____
_____

1 THING I DID TO MOVE FORWARD

_____
_____

DAILY

I AM GRATEFUL FOR

_____
_____
_____

MOOD TRACKER

😠 😦 😐 🙂 😀

SELF-CARE

MY AFFIRMATION FOR THE DAY

_____
_____

MY DREAM JOURNAL

_____
_____
_____
_____
_____
_____
_____

SCRIPTING

_____
_____
_____
_____
_____
_____
_____
_____
_____
_____
_____
_____
_____
_____

_____
_____
_____
_____

RITUAL TIME

MINDFUL MINUTES

5
10
15
20
25
30

POSITIVE THOUGHT I AM CARRYING TO SLEEP

_____
_____

1 THING I DID TO MOVE FORWARD

_____
_____

DAILY

I AM GRATEFUL FOR

_____
_____
_____

MOOD TRACKER

SELF-CARE

MY AFFIRMATION FOR THE DAY

_____
_____

MY DREAM JOURNAL

_____
_____
_____
_____
_____
_____
_____
_____

_____
_____
_____
_____

SCRIPTING

_____
_____
_____
_____
_____
_____
_____
_____
_____
_____
_____
_____
_____
_____
_____
_____

RITUAL TIME   MINDFUL MINUTES

5
10
15
20
25
30

POSITIVE THOUGHT I AM CARRYING TO SLEEP

_____
_____

1 THING I DID TO MOVE FORWARD

_____
_____
_____

DAILY

I AM GRATEFUL FOR

_____
_____
_____

MOOD TRACKER

😠 😟 😐 🙂 😀

SELF-CARE

MY AFFIRMATION FOR THE DAY

_____
_____

MY DREAM JOURNAL

_____
_____
_____
_____
_____
_____
_____
_____
_____
_____
_____
_____
_____

SCRIPTING

_____
_____
_____
_____
_____
_____
_____
_____
_____
_____
_____
_____
_____
_____
_____

RITUAL TIME   MINDFUL MINUTES

5
10
15
20
25
30

POSITIVE THOUGHT I AM CARRYING TO SLEEP

_____
_____

1 THING I DID TO MOVE FORWARD

_____
_____
_____

DAILY

I AM GRATEFUL FOR

_____
_____
_____

MOOD TRACKER

SELF-CARE

MY AFFIRMATION FOR THE DAY

_____
_____

MY DREAM JOURNAL

_____
_____
_____
_____
_____
_____
_____
_____
_____
_____
_____
_____
_____

SCRIPTING

_____
_____
_____
_____
_____
_____
_____
_____
_____
_____
_____
_____
_____
_____
_____
_____
_____
_____
_____

RITUAL TIME   MINDFUL MINUTES

5
10
15
20
25
30

POSITIVE THOUGHT I AM CARRYING TO SLEEP

_____
_____

1 THING I DID TO MOVE FORWARD

_____
_____
_____

DAILY

I AM GRATEFUL FOR

_____

_____

_____

MOOD TRACKER

SELF-CARE

MY AFFIRMATION FOR THE DAY

_____

_____

MY DREAM JOURNAL

_____

_____

_____

_____

_____

_____

_____

_____

SCRIPTING

_____

_____

_____

_____

_____

_____

_____

_____

_____

_____

_____

_____

_____

_____

_____

_____

_____

_____

_____

_____

_____

RITUAL TIME   MINDFUL MINUTES

5

10

15

20

25

30

POSITIVE THOUGHT I AM CARRYING TO SLEEP

_____

_____

1 THING I DID TO MOVE FORWARD

_____

_____

_____

WEEK AHEAD

Sunday
_____
_____
_____
_____
_____
_____

Monday
_____
_____
_____
_____
_____
_____

Tuesday
_____
_____
_____
_____
_____
_____

Wednesday
_____
_____
_____
_____
_____
_____

Thursday
_____
_____
_____
_____
_____
_____

Friday
_____
_____
_____
_____
_____
_____

Saturday
_____
_____
_____
_____
_____

NOTES:

DAILY

I AM GRATEFUL FOR

_____
_____
_____

MOOD TRACKER

😠 🙁 😐 🙂 😄

SELF-CARE

MY AFFIRMATION FOR THE DAY

_____
_____

MY DREAM JOURNAL

_____
_____
_____
_____
_____
_____
_____
_____
_____

SCRIPTING

_____
_____
_____
_____
_____
_____
_____
_____
_____
_____
_____
_____
_____
_____

_____
_____
_____
_____

RITUAL TIME   MINDFUL MINUTES

5
10
15
20
25
30

POSITIVE THOUGHT I AM CARRYING TO SLEEP

_____
_____

1 THING I DID TO MOVE FORWARD

_____
_____
_____

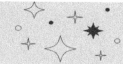

DAILY

I AM GRATEFUL FOR

_____
_____
_____

MOOD TRACKER

SELF-CARE

MY AFFIRMATION FOR THE DAY

_____
_____

MY DREAM JOURNAL

_____
_____
_____
_____
_____
_____
_____
_____

SCRIPTING

_____
_____
_____
_____
_____
_____
_____
_____
_____
_____
_____
_____
_____
_____
_____
_____
_____
_____

_____
_____
_____
_____

RITUAL TIME   MINDFUL MINUTES

5
10
15
20
25
30

POSITIVE THOUGHT I AM CARRYING TO SLEEP

_____
_____

1 THING I DID TO MOVE FORWARD

_____
_____
_____

DAILY

I AM GRATEFUL FOR

_____
_____
_____

MOOD TRACKER

SELF-CARE

MY AFFIRMATION FOR THE DAY

_____
_____

MY DREAM JOURNAL

_____
_____
_____
_____
_____
_____
_____
_____

SCRIPTING

_____
_____
_____
_____
_____
_____
_____
_____
_____
_____
_____
_____
_____
_____
_____

_____
_____
_____
_____

RITUAL TIME   MINDFUL MINUTES

5
10
15
20
25
30

POSITIVE THOUGHT I AM CARRYING TO SLEEP

_____
_____

1 THING I DID TO MOVE FORWARD

_____
_____
_____

DAILY

I AM GRATEFUL FOR

_____
_____
_____

MOOD TRACKER

😠 😟 😐 🙂 😀

SELF-CARE

MY AFFIRMATION FOR THE DAY

_____
_____

MY DREAM JOURNAL

_____
_____
_____
_____
_____
_____
_____
_____
_____
_____
_____

SCRIPTING

_____
_____
_____
_____
_____
_____
_____
_____
_____
_____
_____
_____
_____
_____
_____
_____

RITUAL TIME   MINDFUL MINUTES

← 5
← 10
← 15
← 20
← 25
← 30

POSITIVE THOUGHT I AM CARRYING TO SLEEP

_____
_____

1 THING I DID TO MOVE FORWARD

_____
_____
_____

DAILY

I AM GRATEFUL FOR

_____

_____

_____

MOOD TRACKER

SELF-CARE

MY AFFIRMATION FOR THE DAY

_____

_____

MY DREAM JOURNAL

_____

_____

_____

_____

_____

_____

_____

SCRIPTING

_____

_____

_____

_____

_____

_____

_____

_____

_____

_____

_____

_____

_____

_____

_____

_____

_____

_____

_____

RITUAL TIME   MINDFUL MINUTES

5
10
15
20
25
30

POSITIVE THOUGHT I AM CARRYING TO SLEEP

_____

_____

1 THING I DID TO MOVE FORWARD

_____

_____

_____

DAILY

I AM GRATEFUL FOR

_____
_____
_____

MOOD TRACKER

😠 😞 😐 🙂 😄

SELF-CARE

MY AFFIRMATION FOR THE DAY

_____
_____

MY DREAM JOURNAL

_____
_____
_____
_____
_____
_____
_____
_____

SCRIPTING

_____
_____
_____
_____
_____
_____
_____
_____
_____
_____
_____
_____
_____
_____
_____

_____
_____
_____
_____

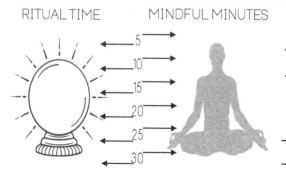

RITUAL TIME   MINDFUL MINUTES

5
10
15
20
25
30

POSITIVE THOUGHT I AM CARRYING TO SLEEP

_____
_____

1 THING I DID TO MOVE FORWARD

_____
_____
_____

THIS LUNATION

☐ Full Moon   ☐ New Moon

The sign the moon is in _____ and transits the _____ house,
meaning _____
_____ for me.

Build your Moon ritual: _____

_____

_____

_____

_____

_____

_____

_____

CANDLES	CRYSTALS
HERBS	OTHER

Card 1	Card 2	Card 3
_____	_____	_____
Deck	Deck	Deck
_____	_____	_____
Card	Card	Card

Interpretation & Meaning _____

_____

_____

_____

_____

_____

_____

Intentions for this lunation: _____

_____

_____

_____

_____

_____

_____

_____

DAILY

I AM GRATEFUL FOR

_____
_____
_____

MOOD TRACKER

SELF-CARE

MY AFFIRMATION FOR THE DAY

_____
_____

MY DREAM JOURNAL

_____
_____
_____
_____
_____
_____
_____
_____

SCRIPTING

_____
_____
_____
_____
_____
_____
_____
_____
_____
_____
_____
_____
_____

_____
_____
_____

RITUAL TIME   MINDFUL MINUTES

5
10
15
20
25
30

POSITIVE THOUGHT I AM CARRYING TO SLEEP

_____
_____

1 THING I DID TO MOVE FORWARD

_____
_____

WEEK AHEAD

Sunday

_____
_____
_____
_____
_____
_____

Monday

_____
_____
_____
_____
_____
_____

Tuesday

_____
_____
_____
_____
_____
_____

Wednesday

_____
_____
_____
_____
_____

Thursday

_____
_____
_____
_____
_____
_____

Friday

_____
_____
_____
_____
_____
_____

Saturday

_____
_____
_____
_____
_____

NOTES:

DAILY

I AM GRATEFUL FOR

_____

_____

_____

MOOD TRACKER

SELF-CARE

MY AFFIRMATION FOR THE DAY

_____

_____

MY DREAM JOURNAL

_____

_____

_____

_____

_____

_____

_____

_____

_____

_____

_____

_____

SCRIPTING

_____

_____

_____

_____

_____

_____

_____

_____

_____

_____

_____

_____

_____

_____

RITUAL TIME   MINDFUL MINUTES

5
10
15
20
25
30

POSITIVE THOUGHT I AM CARRYING TO SLEEP

_____

_____

1 THING I DID TO MOVE FORWARD

_____

_____

_____

DAILY

I AM GRATEFUL FOR

_____

_____

_____

MOOD TRACKER

SELF-CARE

MY AFFIRMATION FOR THE DAY

_____

_____

MY DREAM JOURNAL

_____

_____

_____

_____

_____

_____

_____

_____

_____

_____

_____

_____

_____

SCRIPTING

_____

_____

_____

_____

_____

_____

_____

_____

_____

_____

_____

_____

_____

_____

_____

_____

_____

RITUAL TIME   MINDFUL MINUTES

5
10
15
20
25
30

POSITIVE THOUGHT I AM CARRYING TO SLEEP

_____

_____

1 THING I DID TO MOVE FORWARD

_____

_____

_____

DAILY

I AM GRATEFUL FOR

_____

_____

_____

MOOD TRACKER

SELF-CARE

MY AFFIRMATION FOR THE DAY

_____

_____

MY DREAM JOURNAL

_____

_____

_____

_____

_____

_____

_____

SCRIPTING

_____

_____

_____

_____

_____

_____

_____

_____

_____

_____

_____

_____

_____

_____

_____

_____

_____

_____

RITUAL TIME   MINDFUL MINUTES

5
10
15
20
25
30

POSITIVE THOUGHT I AM CARRYING TO SLEEP

_____

_____

1 THING I DID TO MOVE FORWARD

_____

_____

_____

DAILY

I AM GRATEFUL FOR

_____

_____

_____

MOOD TRACKER

SELF-CARE

MY AFFIRMATION FOR THE DAY

_____

_____

MY DREAM JOURNAL

_____

_____

_____

_____

_____

_____

_____

_____

SCRIPTING

_____

_____

_____

_____

_____

_____

_____

_____

_____

_____

_____

_____

_____

_____

_____

_____

_____

_____

_____

_____

_____

RITUAL TIME

5
10
15
20
25
30

MINDFUL MINUTES

POSITIVE THOUGHT I AM CARRYING TO SLEEP

_____

_____

1 THING I DID TO MOVE FORWARD

_____

_____

_____

DAILY

I AM GRATEFUL FOR

_____
_____
_____

MOOD TRACKER

SELF-CARE

MY AFFIRMATION FOR THE DAY

_____

MY DREAM JOURNAL

_____
_____
_____
_____
_____
_____
_____
_____

SCRIPTING

_____
_____
_____
_____
_____
_____
_____
_____
_____
_____
_____
_____
_____
_____

_____
_____
_____

RITUAL TIME   MINDFUL MINUTES

5
10
15
20
25
30

POSITIVE THOUGHT I AM CARRYING TO SLEEP

_____
_____

1 THING I DID TO MOVE FORWARD

_____
_____
_____

DAILY

I AM GRATEFUL FOR

_____
_____
_____

MOOD TRACKER

SELF-CARE

MY AFFIRMATION FOR THE DAY

_____
_____

MY DREAM JOURNAL

_____
_____
_____
_____
_____
_____
_____
_____

SCRIPTING

_____
_____
_____
_____
_____
_____
_____
_____
_____
_____
_____
_____
_____
_____
_____

_____
_____
_____
_____

RITUAL TIME

MINDFUL MINUTES

5
10
15
20
25
30

POSITIVE THOUGHT I AM CARRYING TO SLEEP

_____
_____

1 THING I DID TO MOVE FORWARD

_____
_____
_____

DAILY

I AM GRATEFUL FOR

_____

_____

_____

MOOD TRACKER

SELF-CARE

MY AFFIRMATION FOR THE DAY

_____

_____

MY DREAM JOURNAL

_____

_____

_____

_____

_____

_____

_____

_____

SCRIPTING

_____

_____

_____

_____

_____

_____

_____

_____

_____

_____

_____

_____

_____

_____

_____

_____

_____

_____

_____

_____

_____

RITUAL TIME   MINDFUL MINUTES

5
10
15
20
25
30

POSITIVE THOUGHT I AM CARRYING TO SLEEP

_____

_____

1 THING I DID TO MOVE FORWARD

_____

_____

_____

NOTES

NOTES

NOTES

NOTES

2023

January

S	M	T	W	T	F	S
1	2	3	4	5	6	7
8	9	10	11	12	13	14
15	16	17	18	19	20	21
22	23	24	25	26	27	28
29	30	31				

February

S	M	T	W	T	F	S
			1	2	3	4
5	6	7	8	9	10	11
12	13	14	15	16	17	18
19	20	21	22	23	24	25
26	27	28				

March

S	M	T	W	T	F	S
			1	2	3	4
5	6	7	8	9	10	11
12	13	14	15	16	17	18
19	20	21	22	23	24	25
26	27	28	29	30	31	

April

S	M	T	W	T	F	S
						1
2	3	4	5	6	7	8
9	10	11	12	13	14	15
16	17	18	19	20	21	22
23	24	25	26	27	28	29
30						

May

S	M	T	W	T	F	S
	1	2	3	4	5	6
7	8	9	10	11	12	13
14	15	16	17	18	19	20
21	22	23	24	25	26	27
28	29	30	31			

June

S	M	T	W	T	F	S
				1	2	3
4	5	6	7	8	9	10
11	12	13	14	15	16	17
18	19	20	21	22	23	24
25	26	27	28	29	30	

July

S	M	T	W	T	F	S
						1
2	3	4	5	6	7	8
9	10	11	12	13	14	15
16	17	18	19	20	21	22
23	24	25	26	27	28	29
30	31					

August

S	M	T	W	T	F	S
		1	2	3	4	5
6	7	8	9	10	11	12
13	14	15	16	17	18	19
20	21	22	23	24	25	26
27	28	29	30	31		

September

S	M	T	W	T	F	S
					1	2
3	4	5	6	7	8	9
10	11	12	13	14	15	16
17	18	19	20	21	22	23
24	25	26	27	28	29	30

October

S	M	T	W	T	F	S
1	2	3	4	5	6	7
8	9	10	11	12	13	14
15	16	17	18	19	20	21
22	23	24	25	26	27	28
29	30	31				

November

S	M	T	W	T	F	S
			1	2	3	4
5	6	7	8	9	10	11
12	13	14	15	16	17	18
19	20	21	22	23	24	25
26	27	28	29	30		

December

S	M	T	W	T	F	S
					1	2
3	4	5	6	7	8	9
10	11	12	13	14	15	16
17	18	19	20	21	22	23
24	25	26	27	28	29	30
31						

GLOSSARY

Affirmation - The act of affirming one's own worthiness and value as an individual for beneficial effect (such as increasing one's confidence or raising self-esteem).

Astrology - The study of the movements and relative position of celestial bodies interpreted as having an influence on human affairs and the natural world.

Bibliomancy - Foretelling the future by interpreting a randomly chosen passage from a book, especially the Bible.

Bone Reading - A divinatory method of throwing bones and reading them based on how they land.

Crystal Ball Reading - A common ball/sphere made of glass or crystal to tell fortunes.

Dice Divination - A method to use dice for fortune telling.

Full Moon - A phase of the moon when the moon is in full view and closest to the earth. This moon phase is representative of when things reach a pinnacle and it's time to release what doesn't serve you.

Intention - An aim, plan or declarative statement. Used to set your eyes upon a goal.

Limiting Belief - A constraint or belief which self-imposes limits on what we say, do, or believe about ourselves.

Lunar Eclipse - An event in which the moon is hidden by the sun to reveal itself hours later.

Lunation - A lunar month. The period of time from one new moon to the next new moon. Approximately 29.5 days.

Oracle Cards - A tool for divination that relies on intuition.

Osteomancy - The divinatory term for bone reading.

Manifest - To create the life you want.

Mantra - (originally in Hinduism and Buddhism) a word or sound repeated to aid concentration in meditation. A statement or slogan repeated frequently.

Meditation - Meditation can be defined as a set of techniques that are intended to encourage a heightened state of awareness and focused attention. Meditation is also a consciousness-changing technique that has been shown to have a wide number of benefits on psychological well-being.

Mirror Scrying - Divination using a mirror.

GLOSSARY CONT.

Natal Chart - A map showing the positions of the planets at the time of someone's birth, from which astrologers are able to deduce character traits or potential.

New Moon - A phase of the moon in which the moon is not visible in the sky, which is representative of a time of new beginnings.

Retrograde - When the planets appear to be moving backwards from our viewpoint here on earth.

Rising Sign - An aspect in your natal chart. The time when the sun was passing over the horizon the minute you were born.

Ritual - A religious or solemn ceremony consisting of a series of actions performed according to a prescribed order.

Runes - A mark or letter of mysterious or magic significance. Small stones, pieces of bone, etc., bearing marks, and used as divinatory symbols.

Scripting - To journal as if the future has happened so that you are able to bring in your manifestation.

Shadow Work - Working on the "shadow" part of yourself. Things you hide from yourself that may include but are not limited to trauma, limiting beliefs, and the way you grew up.

Solar Eclipse - An event in which the sun is covered by the moon.

Star Sign - Interchangeable term to describe sun sign, the time of day you were born during the 30 day constellation.

Super Moon - The phenomenon whereby the moon appears particularly large in the sky owing to the coincidence of its closest approach to the earth with a full moon.

Tarot Cards - A divinatory method of 78 cards with its own rules for readings.

Tasseomancy - Tea leaf reading. A divinatory method to see images and times.

Transit - A term in which is used by astrologers to refer to the movement of planetary bodies relative to where they were previously.

Whole Sign - A method of house division that uses the rising sign as the first house, and then the rest of the houses are assigned to each of the signs in zodiacal order, each zodiac getting 30 degrees.

Waxing Moon - A phase of the moon which follows the new moon but precedes the full moon.

Waning Moon - A phase of the moon which follows the full moon but precedes the new moon.